THE BETRAYER

How A Top Secret Undercover Unit Infiltrated The Global Drug Trade

GUY STANTON

with PETER WALSH

MILO BOOKS LTD

Published in July 2022 by Milo Books

ISBN 978-1-908479-96-9

Typeset by e-type

Printed in Great Britain by CPI Group (UK) Ltd,
Croydon, CRO 4YY

www.milobooks.com

Suspect: Guy Stanton

Suspected of being engaged in arranging the transportation and financing of large shipments of cannabis from Morocco to Spain and the UK.

Stanton is known to own or have part ownership in several vessels. He has been the subject of departmental interest for the past year-and-a-half. Known to be ostentatious and aggressive, shows obvious signs of wealth and is surveillance aware. Warning, he will deliberately confront any suspected surveillance.

Suspect movement report issued by
HM Customs and Excise

CONTENTS

PROLOGUE

Curaçao, the southern Caribbean, 10.30 a.m.

Lightning crackled through the heavy air under dark, looming clouds, but no rain came, only waves of heat. I made my way over the swing bridge across Saint Anna Bay towards Otrobanda. It was too humid to take more than a slow walk. Otrobanda means 'the other side', presumably of the bay. Not an imaginative name but at least you know where you are.

Curaçao is the largest of the three 'ABC' islands of the Lesser Antilles, the others being Aruba and Bonaire, and is within speedboat reach of Venezuela's north coast. It has been part of the Kingdom of the Netherlands for centuries and rows of quaint Dutch colonial buildings hem the streets. But these homes are Caribbean at heart, painted in dazzling mango yellows and melon reds and built with the essentials for a hot climate: verandas, porches and shutters.

The ABCs share a dark history. In the eighteenth century, Curaçao became a transfer centre for slaves. That terrible trade was abolished in 1863, only to be replaced by a modern form of serfdom in which poor tenant famers had to surrender most of their produce to rich landowners. In the early twentieth century the discovery of oil in Venezuela turned the island into a refining centre. The resulting economic boom brought with it the usual pros and cons: overnight wealth, corruption and ruthless men on the make. From the nineteen-seventies onwards, another dark trade flourished. The islands became one of the main transfer points for Colombian cocaine bound for Europe.

The gang I was about to meet wanted someone to ship high-grade marching powder into Curaçao and then on to Holland, via a circuitous route. I had been working hard to ensure I was that someone. As an illicit transport specialist, one of the best in the business, I had convinced them that I could ship their coke by sea under a legitimate cover load of fruit pulp.

I had known this outfit, a mixed bunch of Venezuelans and Dutch-Surinamese wideboys, for some time. We had first met as bit-part players in a couple of other people's deals. They liked the way I did business and we got along. However they insisted on checking me out and visited me in London and again in Rotterdam to give me the once-over. Now we were meeting in their backyard to flesh out the details of our deal.

As with many of these jobs, their talk had been of multi-tonnes. A more likely outcome would be a first run of 500 to 750 kilos – still a hell of a lot of cocaine. At the birth of a deal, the traffickers like to boast how much they can move. But the nearer they get to handing over their valuable cargo to a moody transporter like me, they suddenly become reluctant to risk a mega quantity. I understood this. I don't exactly look user-friendly and an element of distrust keeps everyone on their toes.

I turned up early at our appointed meeting place, a patch of wasteland used for car parking at the end of a deserted, boarded-up street in the shadow of the swing bridge. A first twinge of anxiety hit me. *Why did they want to meet here instead of my air-conditioned hotel suite?* We weren't trading today: no money, no gear, no guns, no minders, just some guys shooting the breeze to finalise what, to anyone watching or listening, would sound like a standard business deal. Having agreed to the meet, I now felt a little vulnerable.

A black sedan swung into view and a horn toot let me know it was them. They never ceased to amuse, these lads. They loved the Hollywood image of the narco, all big watches, gold chains, vintage champagne, fast cars. Most of the real top players shun that nonsense. As the sedan pulled up I smiled. *They think I'm one of them.*

Five of us talked out in the open, like men with nothing to hide. They were calm and businesslike. We confirmed the size of the load, the pick-up point by boat, security for both sides, contact numbers, coordinates and timings, and how to safely exchange the money and the product without starting World War Three. Despite the amicable chat, nobody trusted anybody, which was just fine.

As we talked, I saw a beaten-up, beige Oldsmobile bear into view, its body more primer than paint. It slowed and cruised towards us, its exhaust pipe growling. I noted it was four-up and the front passenger was staring hard at us. He had a large, jowly, unshaven face, topped by corkscrew-curled black hair matted into a solid mass, and he glistened with sweat. His eyes bored through me. I can feel them to this day.

The car moseyed past, turned and moved off. Then it turned again and began another circuit of the waste ground. It had my full attention now, but I said nothing to the others, who had not noticed.

Who are these guys? What do they want? We haven't got any gear or money. I was not armed and nor were the others, so far as I could tell.

The Olds crept back towards us. Suddenly its engine gunned. It leapt forward, hurtled directly at us and ploughed into the side of the sedan. The jowly man flung open his door and sprang out. In that instant I saw his Uzi submachine gun. He raised it and let rip.

We scattered. I dived down and my face hit the ground as my brain raced in several directions, all of them bad. *Was it a set-up? Were they local cops? Were they a rival gang?*

Bullets punched the tarmac and slammed into cars. I heard the shouts and groans of injured men. Crawling around to the better-protected front side of the sedan, I heard the wail of a siren and saw the flash of lights. A police car flew into view and, without stopping, rear-ended the Olds with a crunch. The Uzi man stopped firing and turned with a look of shock. Then his head exploded in a haze of red.

People lay wounded around me. My great fear had been that it would end like this, far from my home and family, the truth of my parallel life dying with me.

I don't get paid enough for this, I thought, as petrol began to drip onto my head.

The Betrayer is the story of my service in Beta Projects, the secret undercover unit of the Investigation Division of HM Customs and Excise. You won't find references to it in newspaper archives or on the internet, because almost no-one knew we existed. Throughout my decade undercover, even my mum, dad and siblings thought I worked in a quiet customs policy office.

In fact my colleagues and I were travelling the world, clandestinely and incognito. We jetted many thousands of miles, braved stormy seas in small boats, drove into jungles and deserts, and spent long days and even longer nights cultivating some of the most dangerous criminals on the planet. We sipped champagne in the finest hotels and weak black tea in unspeakable fleapits. We cut deals with master deal-makers, faced down psychopaths, and sometimes only emerged unscathed by the skin of our teeth. And we did it all in the shadows.

None of that is a boast. It was simply our job.

Beta Projects was formed early in the early nineteen-nineties to target the biggest illicit drug smugglers in the world.

The idea was simple: train a small, handpicked cadre of men and women to enter the underworld and bring back intelligence, for as long as it took. We would undertake this most stressful and arduous of taskings on a full-time basis, often away from our friends and loved ones, for years if need be. Those selected received fake identities, offices, homes, vehicles and documents, and were, for the first time, properly trained, equipped and supported in the field.

To set our initiative in context, my co-author, Peter Walsh, has endeavoured to tell the background history of covert infiltration as practised by my organisation (his contribution throughout is italicised to distinguish it from my own). Beta Projects was a new and ground-breaking endeavour but it did not spring, fully formed, from nothing. It was adapted from an existing, fledgling team, and even before that, various brave and enterprising officers had ventured out into the underworld, equipped with only their native wits, their nerve, and a flimsy cover story. 'Detection by deception is as old as a constable in plain clothes,' a judge once said. He was right, but it was only towards the end of the twentieth century that HM Customs, and British law enforcement generally, began to think deeply about how it should best be done and how to resource it properly.

I was in HM Customs for more than thirty years, twenty-three as an investigator and ten as a deep undercover operative, known as a UCO or UC. I achieved some spectacular results and faced some sticky situations. But what I recall most vividly is the black humour the Beta team shared and how life and circumstance will conspire to blindside the most careful planning and create chaos. As I was told when I used to box: 'Everybody has a plan until they get hit.'

The book is dedicated to all my old Beta colleagues. They will recognise themselves in the story even though names have been changed or truncated to protect their identities. The operations in the book are all true and the events happened as written. I hope no confidences have been betrayed and no classified information disclosed. Those who worked with me know who they are and how it went down.

They were brave and dedicated people. It is a given that all UCs need courage and resourcefulness. But in the final analysis, all such operatives are betrayers. They build up relationships only to reveal them as false, leading to a mortal sense of treachery among those they have tricked. That's too bad. I have little sympathy for the criminals I deceived. They were all adults, they all knew what they were doing, and they almost all had the same prosaic motivations – money and power, by any means necessary.

The team I was proud to serve in no longer exists. But there are still police and other undercover operators out there doing this dangerous and sometimes dirty work, at great personal risk. I also dedicate this tale to them.

Guy Stanton

1

THE ART OF BETRAYAL

*T*o *catch a crook, think like a crook.*

That was the enduring insight of Eugene Vidocq, the Rabelaisian Frenchman said to be the father of undercover investigation. By repute Vidocq was the first person to use the techniques of espionage, such as false identities, disguises and cover stories, to fight crime. As a former crook himself he could play the part to a tee, and laid the foundations for what would become a pillar of detective work around the world.

The art of deception is as old as humanity. Certainly spies and informants have been deployed for as long as peoples have come into conflict, or at least distrusted one another. Sun Tzu, the Chinese master of warfare theory, believed that subterfuge was the key to military victory. In neighbouring Japan, the ninja were deployed by feudal lords to inveigle their way into the camps of their rivals. Spies were prevalent in the Greek and Roman empires, while the Aztecs sent agents among their enemies dressed in local costume and speaking the local language.

It was inevitable that when the first modern, uniformed police force was created, in 1667 under King Louis XIV of France – 'police' is a Middle French word – it would eventually employ similar methods. It was not until the early nineteenth century, however, that a team of clandestine agents was mobilised specifically to penetrate the underworld and trap the most prolific and incorrigible criminals. The man responsible was Vidocq.

Born in 1775 into a rich family, Eugene Vidocq was drawn to mischief from an early age. He developed a penchant for stealing – silver plates were a particular favourite – and at the age of fourteen ran away from home to escape parental disapproval, surviving for a time as an itinerant street entertainer. After a series of outlandish scrapes, he joined a cavalry unit and saw action in battle but also deserted several times, once after striking a senior officer, which potentially carried the death penalty. He seduced numerous women, fought numerous duels, survived the terror of the French Revolution, and went to gaol for various petty crimes, only to escape repeatedly. At the age of thirty-four, tired of his peripatetic life, he approached the police and offered to inform against his fellow criminals. He was allowed to fake yet another prison escape and became a professional snitch, at the zenith of Napoleon Bonaparte's First Empire.

Surviving sketch portraits of Vidocq show a worldly-wise rogue with runaway eyebrows over knowing eyes, a hard mouth flanked by mutton-chop whiskers, and an unruly shock of curly hair. He had the look of a man who could spot human weakness and use it to advantage. He was also very persuasive. In 1811 he prevailed on the authorities to let him create an informal plainclothes unit, the Brigade de la Sûreté (Security Brigade), to continue his subterranean work. By 1824 it had more than thirty agents.

The French police had occasionally employed freelance snoops but Vidocq put them on an organised footing. Many of his recruits were themselves old lags and knew how to act the part. He trained them further to lie and dissemble and created disguises for each job. He also continued to go out himself on the hunt and his memoirs brim with tales of him outwitting villains while posing as a beggar, a fugitive or a robber. In one case he even simulated his own death.

Vidocq and his crew were allowed to rove across the whole of Paris at a time when most police forces were confined to specific areas. It was this freedom and not their covert origins that came to define the Sûreté and eventually it became La Sûreté Nationale, with authority over the whole country. Vidocq is also credited with innovations in forensics, ballistics and fingerprinting. Doubts about his men's reliability as witnesses, however, dogged his progress and he eventually left under a cloud – only to then create the first private detective agency.

Across the English Channel, the fledgling British police were also using covert methods to fight crime. The Metropolitan Police of London, established by Sir Robert Peel as England's first modern constabulary, occasionally employed undercover detectives from its inception in 1829. One of its first commissioners, Charles Rowan, had held an intelligence role as an officer in the Duke of Wellington's army and well understood the value of subterfuge.

But 'the Met', as it came to be known, faced recurring public anxiety that undercovers were being misused for political repression rather than legitimate criminal investigation. In 1833 a House of Commons committee examined the case of a policeman who had spent a year infiltrating the National Political Union of the Working Class. In part due to such concerns, from 1845 official orders required all undercover operations to be authorised by a superintendent.

In 1869 the Met's commissioner established a plainclothes detective division, with officers sometimes adopting the garb of the working man. The Special Irish Branch, a new section of the Criminal Investigation Department, or CID, followed in 1883. Initially created to thwart the bombing campaign of the Irish Republican Brotherhood, within five years it had also turned its attention to immigrant European anarchists. The 'Irish' was dropped from its name as its remit expanded to countering general terrorism, foreign subversion and organised crime.

Law enforcement bodies elsewhere established similar branches, notably the Italian Squad in New York City. Various US federal agencies began undercover programmes and in 1908 the Federal Bureau of Investigation was founded. Under its famously paranoid director J. Edgar Hoover, the FBI would use its covert capabilities against prominent celebrities, politicians and campaigners as well as criminals and subversives.

Disquiet about the use of such underhand tactics persisted. In England and Wales, courts accepted the need to sometimes conceal the involvement or identity of informants, whose role was similar to that of undercover officers, in order to protect them from reprisals, but the practice was controversial, and a Royal Commission on policing in 1929 advised that such activities should be used sparingly, as the public might deplore them.

Nevertheless in 1945 the Met created the Special Duty Squad, quickly nicknamed the 'Ghost Squad'. Formed partly in response to rising crime and a police staffing crisis after Word War Two, it was the first unit to be tasked solely with collecting and disseminating criminal intelligence, which it passed to the Flying Squad or the CID for action. Led by Detective Inspector Jack Capstick, the Ghost Squad targeted serious, rather than petty, crime, though its four officers received no formal training and had to learn on the job. Its operations tended to be of three types: infiltrations, 'stings', and befriending missions known as 'honey traps'. In one year it claimed responsibility for 186 arrests, most of them for burglary or handling stolen goods; its most famous investigation, the 'Case of the Green Taxi', targeted black-marketers forging clothing coupons. The Ghost Squad influenced other constabularies to set up similar units, but was disbanded in 1949 and recombined with the Flying Squad.

It was Special Branch that continued to make most use of covert spies. In 1954 the Met commissioner used its remit, defined as 'to keep watch on any body of people, of whatever political complexion, whose activities seem likely to result sooner or later in open acts of sedition or disorder', to justify far-reaching actions to contain new social movements that were deplored by the state. As radical politics mobilised across Europe, authorities in London sought novel ways to gather intelligence that could undermine its advocates.

In response to escalating protests against the Vietnam War in 1968, a chief inspector, Conrad Hepworth Dixon, conceived the idea of the Special Demonstration Squad, originally called the Special Operations Squad. The SDS was to be a unit of officers within Special Branch who would infiltrate suspected subversives, in strictest secrecy so as not to compromise the government. Rather than returning to uniformed duties after conducting a quick operation, its officers lived long-term within the cultures of the groups they targeted. To create false identities, they sometimes used the real details of children who had died at birth or in infancy, apparently inspired by a scenario in Frederick Forsyth's best-selling thriller The Day of the Jackal. Over the next forty years the SDS would penetrate over 400 activist groups, from left-wing and far-right extremists to animal rights campaigners and Irish nationalists. Their targets were sometimes known by the derogatory term 'wearies' because they were regarded as hard work and tiresome.

The counter-culture and re-emergent Irish terrorism were not the only causes of concern to the British establishment. Drugs had appeared, almost from nowhere. The police were responsible for the pursuit of dealers and distributors, and constabularies began to form their own anti-drug units. It was a milieu ripe for so-called bust-buy operations, to trap dealers in the act of selling. Detectives from the Met's Central Drug Squad, the biggest, began to pose as willing buyers to ensnare pushers, sometimes in partnership with the US Drug Enforcement Administration, whose agents carried 'flash rolls' of money for just such a purpose.

At the importation level, it was Her Majesty's Customs and Excise (HMCE), in particular its small, elite Investigation Branch, that pursued the most serious drug offenders. In 1968 HMCE's top investigator, a former bomb disposal officer called Sam Charles, learned that a group of Indian immigrants were planning to import cannabis resin, or hashish, inside cases of mango pickles sailing from Pakistan on a merchant ship. When the cases landed at a warehouse at Tilbury Docks for collection, Charles and his team opened them and found 113 kilos of hash, a huge amount for the time. They replaced it with sawdust and sand, then accompanied a delivery driver hired to take the cases to a house in east London, where the Indian gang was waiting. Charles posed convincingly as the driver's mate, and one of the gang even offered him a £1 tip. The traffickers were all arrested, leading to a string of further seizures in what was the biggest case of its day.

This was undercover work at its simplest. Drugs often arrived in the UK in the parcel post and it was a relatively easy matter, once they had been discovered at a sorting office, for an officer to pose as a postman or delivery driver and take them to the onward address in order to catch the recipients. As the trade surged and narcotics took over the bulk of the Investigation Branch's workload, it was enlarged into the Investigation Division (ID) and organised into small teams, each named alphabetically (Drugs A, Drugs B, etc) and led by a senior investigation officer, or SIO.

Yet despite the growth in its use, undercover work was still not regulated by statute. The closest it came was a 1969 Home Office circular, laying down instructions that such officers – often referred to UCs – could not engage in planning or committing crime and could play only minor roles, while their participation had to be 'essential' to frustrate the criminals before they could harm or damage person or property. An Appeal Court judge in the same year ruled, 'It is vitally important to ensure, so far as possible, that the informer does not create an offence, that is to say, incite others to commit an offence which those others would not otherwise have committed.'

This injunction, that an officer or an informant could not act as an agent provocateur, became a key legal principle. Even though the defence of entrapment, available in the USA, had no place in British law (although it could count towards mitigating any sentence), officers could not create a crime that otherwise would not have taken place. In a case in 1973, three men were charged with possessing controlled drugs. It emerged at trial that an undercover policeman had approached one of them and persistently requested the drugs; when they eventually supplied some, they were arrested. The defence argued successfully that the officer had overly encouraged the offence and the three men were acquitted.

It was a fine line. In November 1973 an undercover Met sergeant met two criminals at a London hotel and was offered cases of stolen spirits. He agreed to take a thousand assorted bottles of whisky, Bacardi, brandy and vodka, and was told to await a phone call to arrange delivery. A few days later, the criminals broke into the Seagram distillery and stole £25,000-worth of booze. Both men were subsequently tried, convicted and sent to jail, but appealed on the imaginative grounds that they had only executed the crime because the sergeant had said he wanted the booze and therefore had *entrapped them. On this occasion the Appeal Court rejected their claim, accepting that the pair had already planned to commit the crime and therefore the offence had been 'laid on'.*

Another appeal case dealt with the thorny issue of 'infiltration'. A police informer, Kenneth Lennon, had penetrated an Irish Republican group in Luton and collaborated in a robbery conspiracy to obtain funds. Three men were subsequently jailed for ten years for the offence. Two of them, Mealey and Sheriden, appealed, largely on the basis that Lennon had instigated the whole thing. Their case failed when the court said that common sense indicated that anyone infiltrating a suspect group on behalf of the police must show a certain enthusiasm for its activities in order to maintain his or her cover. (The Lennon affair ended mysteriously: he made a statement to a lawyer from the National Council for Civil Liberties, claiming he had been forced by blackmail to work for Special Branch, and three days later was found shot dead in a ditch in Surrey. His killers have never been caught.) These two principles, of a 'laid-on' offence and of 'due enthusiasm', became twin pillars of UC guidance.

The murky conflict in Northern Ireland proved to be an important, if high-risk, training ground for covert techniques. Its inherent dangers were brutally exposed in May 1977 when a dedicated but reckless British army captain, Robert Nairac, was attacked by republicans while drinking in a rural Ulster pub, posing as a member of the Official IRA. After a scuffle, Nairac was kidnapped, beaten and shot dead. He was posthumously awarded the George Cross for his undoubted bravery, but appeared to have been acting with little control from above.

Such lax supervision was not confined to the military. As the growth of drug markets continued to prove fertile territory for UC work, in the mid-seventies several police officers adopted false 'hippy' identities in a landmark probe,

Operation Julie, into the production and distribution of LSD. Growing their hair long and living out of the back of a van to ingratiate themselves with a community of dropouts in Wales, the officers were left largely to their own devices. They drank heavily and smoked cannabis with their targets. Although the job was successful, it raised unease about the supervision of UCs in the field and the lengths to which they should be allowed to go. While undercover work became increasingly prevalent throughout the eighties for both the police and HMCE, it remained troublesome, unstructured and overly secretive, with no training and numerous shortcomings.

By 1990 there was still no legal foundation specifically dealing with bust-buys and similar work. Instead there was a patchwork of caselaw on officers and informants being deployed in fields such as theft, robbery and illegal political organisation. The message from these cases remained that while due participation was acceptable, targets must never be incited to commit offences which otherwise they would not have.

The courts accepted, as a 1991 judgment set out, that some crimes were almost impossible to prosecute without covert methods: 'It is notoriously difficult to apprehend those at the centre of the drug trade: it is only their couriers who are usually caught. If the courts were to regard the penetration of a drug-dealing organisation by the agents of a law enforcement agency ... as an abuse of process, it would indeed be a red-letter day for the drug barons.' Yet even as such work became increasingly ubiquitous, the authorities failed to put it on a truly professional footing.

There is something inherently absurd about pretending to be someone else in the line of work, an absurdity made only more acute when the stakes are high. Actors know that what they do is fake, as do their audiences. The deception of a spy is to be both fake and real at the same time. How to tell which is which can become deeply problematic, not least for the officers themselves. It requires rules, guidance and continual psychological assessments that, for most of the twentieth century, did not exist.

At the same time, it could be spectacularly effective, putting law enforcement right at the heart of a criminal enterprise as it conducted its illicit business in real time. The most famous example was that of 'Donnie Brasco', a pioneering FBI agent (real name Joe Pistone) who infiltrated the Bonnano crime family of New York in the late seventies. Pistone rose higher in that organisation that any cop ever had and his revelations shattered the air of impregnability that surrounded La Cosa Nostra, destroying its mystique for ever.

In the year 1990, a west London lad of working-class parents began a similar journey. He would go on to be Britain's own Donnie Brasco, living as a high-level gangster for almost a decade, and has been called one of the country's most successful undercover investigators. He has never spoken publicly about his work and his real name is still closely protected. To the underworld, he was Guy Stanton.

2

LEARNING THE ROPES

The average price of a house in Fulham today is well over a million quid. Well it wasn't like that in 1957, when I was born there. Before gentrification, most of the area's terraced streets were solidly working class. My grandad was a painter and decorator, my dad a car mechanic. My mum was a cleaner, one of a family of twelve kids out of Battersea. The people we knew struggled for money.

Everyone did what they could to get by. We had a fair few tearaways in our neighbourhood, like John Bindon, whose family lived nearby and whose sister used to babysit me. A notorious hardcase, he combined an acting career with running protection rackets. He was later sensationally cleared of stabbing to death fellow gangster Johnny Darke, claiming self-defence.

I wasn't averse to the odd tear-up myself, being of stocky build and handy with my fists. I boxed as a youth and got caught up in the odd fracas while standing on the Shed end at Chelsea FC during the bootboy era of the early seventies. I learned to spot trouble brewing, to smell the danger of an impending row and tell a bluffer from a headcase. But I was never a full-on hooligan and never instigated a fight. Perhaps that's why I dodged the hand of the law.

I contrived to leave school in the summer of 1975 with six mediocre 'O' levels, a Saturday job and no idea what to do with my life. My careers master had scotched my wish to be an air steward on account of the fact that I was 'built like a brick shithouse' and wouldn't suit the uniform. 'And besides,' he said, 'it's not all hostesses and travel.' They were my two reasons for wanting the job. On the advice of my dad, I instead applied to join the civil service because, as he put it, 'Son, you'll always need a good pension.' It turned out he was dead right. I joined Her Majesty's Customs and Excise.

I was pretty happy to land the job, figuring that I would wear a brand new uniform and work at a shiny new airport, as the docks, the traditional home of customs officers, were in decline. But when I pitched up at Kings Beam House, the grey headquarters building in Mark Lane, not far from the Bloody Tower, it reminded me depressingly of school: long, granite-floored corridors, radiators as big as submarines, doors and walls of drab green and drab blue. My instinct was to run along the corridor yelling and letting off the fire extinguishers. I resisted the urge.

My first six months were spent in the Central Registry, a large, dreary filing office with a loud ticking clock and an assortment of eccentric staff. They included Mr Thorp, who was always asking people if they would like to come and see his dog, and Jules, a studious-looking chap who walked around the building telling people it was morning in America (even if it wasn't). Officers would come in and hand over small slips of paper requesting files, everything from customs duty enquiries to parliamentary questions. I would mark the movement of each file, in pencil if it was a temporary loan or red ink if it was permanent, and woe betide me if I got it the wrong way round. I knew things would get worse when I was promised I might get to actually handle the files after a year or so – the expectation was electrifying. To stay sane, I linked up with a couple of like-minded lads, Graham and Jack. Graham's dad ran a fish-and-chip shop and Jack's dad was a tailor, so I wasn't short of fish suppers and trousers for some time.

Six more months of shuffling letters in the post room left me bored brainless, so one lunchtime I decided to start digging an escape tunnel. Picking up a copy of the internal *Headquarters Directory* and flicking through the vacancies, I came across the words 'Investigation Division' and read 'DRUGS B selected operations, targets'. Whatever this meant, it sounded far more exciting than what I was doing.

The Investigation Division, or ID, was an elite group of officers within HMCE who carried out clandestine operations against criminals smuggling drugs, guns, tobacco, spirits and pornography, and committing tax and excise fraud. This was for me. I immediately sought a transfer, not realising that I was too low in rank to qualify for the ID and would not be eligible for vetting and selection for another six years.

Instead I was put in the Central Reference Unit, or CRU, another filing office at New Fetter Lane, in the commercial district of the City of London. This building was, however, the spiritual home of the ID, so I was getting warmer. The ID was then a small outfit, served by a close-knit band of experienced officers, many of whom would later become legends in my eyes. And although I was again in a registry, not a ledger was to be seen. The CRU held all of the ID's operational records and background material on criminal targets, past, present and potential. It also held a live terminal for checking car registrations, linked to the Police National Computer.

My new workmates were no less eclectic than those I had left. Tom, the nominal head of the room, seemed to be in charge for no other reason than that he said so. He was only one rank above me, as an executive officer, but thought he was chairman of the board. Despite that, he was a good chap who did his best to make me feel at home. He kept a smallholding and a pig called Justine. Richard, who really was in charge, was one of a number of Poles working for the ID. He had remarkable, mauve-coloured sideburns and smoked a cigarette in the manner of a B-movie villain, holding it between thumb and all four fingers while quietly purring, 'Verrry interestink,' in a strong Polish accent.

Paul was the same rank as me, an assistant officer. He insisted on coming to work in a Cavalier outfit, as he was a member of the Sealed Knot and was forever getting into mock sword fights on the Underground. Then there was Doug, who became a firm friend. A Cockney-Italian, Doug ate a lot of pasta and smoked a lot of dope. His love of a reefer meant that he was destined for a short career in HM Customs. With him was Graham, a bespectacled Harry Potter lookalike who somehow believed he was cool. Finally were the elder statesmen, Steve and Neil, a full three years older than the rest of us and regarded as the 'South London Crew'. I sensed that neither of them would be around for long, as both felt the lure of more adventurous and lucrative opportunities elsewhere.

There were also lots of women, including an entire typing pool. This was more like it. However my lowly rank still precluded my selection as an operational officer, so I wound up shuffling more papers for a year. After much haranguing on my part, the ID finally let me act as a support officer, or 'bag-carrier', on some of their less risky probes. In time I was allowed to work with an operational team, which gave me the opportunity to carry the bags for one particular group.

My first teams were Customs Intelligence and Customs Targets, who shared rooms. They were staffed with veterans, many from the old Waterguard, the formal name for the uniformed branch that covered the docks and airports. I had two bosses in that period. Les, the first, was intellectually brilliant, wrote superbly and was destined for high rank, and thus frightened everyone around him. Tony, the second, was a suave ladies' man who drove an MG sports car but unfortunately based his look on the character Jason King, a hirsute, metrosexual crime investigator popular on TV.

Of the other officers, Frankie was a Chinese lad brought in to crush the Triads, which was rather a tall order as he was raw and quite timid. Then there was a relatively new duo, known as Len the Lad and Dangerous Don. Len was renowned for his time-keeping: come hell or high water, he would be on the 3.15 train home to Chelmsford every afternoon. He was also one of the most cunning, streetwise men I have ever met, and remains my closest friend. Dangerous Don was named for his propensity to get into scrapes. My fellow administrative officer, or AO, Charlie, was from Lebanon and got arrested each time he went home to visit, as he would insist on taking holiday snaps near secret airbases.

My appetite for frontline action was whetted on a small operation to track down a pornographer in rural East Anglia. The team picked for the job, under the leadership of Ron, a hard ex-Navy boxer, was deployed to Norfolk to track down the originator of a spate of postal deliveries of hardcore 8mm porn films and magazines, marketed under the title 'Colour Climax'. This material was prohibited, containing as it did bestiality, paedophilia and bizarre sex. I was invited along.

We arrived mob-handed in the pretty village of Hunstanton and parked in the high street to discuss where best to plot up. By chance, a battered estate car pulled up in front of us. The driver, a thin, long-haired lad who looked like he hadn't washed or eaten properly for weeks, went to his boot, removed two large, bulging sacks and dragged them across the pavement. He then began posting packages from the sacks into the outside post-box of Hunstanton Post Office, where by pure chance we had parked. It seemed we had solved our case before it had begun.

Tony, a sanguine Scouser, was the case officer for the job, which meant he was responsible for its progress. He slipped out of the car and approached the lad.

'Alright, son?' he said, as if concerned for his health.

'What?' said the long-haired lad.

'I said, are you alright?'

'Err, yeah.'

'Good,' said Tony, smiling. 'What's in the parcels then?'

'Err,' stammered the lad, realising that he was in trouble. Within seconds, he was surrounded and separated from his sacks. A peek inside revealed numerous copies of *Colour Climax Sex Bizarre* and *Colour Climax Animal Lover*. It took no imagination to guess the contents.

Jobs pan out in strange ways. This one had taken a few hours to plan, a couple of hours to reach Norfolk and five minutes to 'knock'. For some of the team, a celebration drink was in order; for others, paperwork, formal charging of the suspect and court preparation. It was my first real taste of the ID in action. If only every job was so easy.

It was the outcome of one that went tragically wrong that cemented my desire to join the ID. In late 1979, Operation Wrecker targeted a serious criminal gang importing large amounts of cannabis. The chief suspects were well known to us and the police: 'Duke' Osborne, a former associate of the Krays; George Francis, a major gangland fixer; and Lenny Watkins, a wildcard nutter who had met Osborne in prison. This mob, backed with funding from heavies in the London underworld, had been bringing in tonnes of 'Pakistani black' hashish. The ID and the police launched a joint operation to catch them red-handed.

Watkins was followed as he drove a container lorry to Limehouse in east London, but spotted the surveillance and panicked. When a team moved in to arrest him, he produced a handgun and started shooting. One bullet killed ID investigator Peter Bennett before Watkins was brought down and handcuffed by two unarmed cops and a customs officer in an act of great bravery. Peter left a widow and a young child.

For us, this was a game-changer. Peter's death in the line of duty brutally drove home the fact that some would stop at nothing to preserve their goods and their liberty. Later, as an undercover operative, I would witness the drugs world become ever more violent.

Lenny Watkins was convicted, jailed for life and died in prison. Duke Osborne briefly disappeared, only for his body to turn up on Hackney Marshes in east London; some say he died of natural causes; others that he expired while being 'interviewed' by his colleagues. Whatever the cause, the coroner noted that his body had at some stage been stored in a deep freeze. Francis denied everything and escaped conviction but was later jailed for cocaine-running, then murdered by rivals in 2003. The press called his killing part of 'the curse of Brinks-Mat', a reference to a £26 million gold bullion robbery at Heathrow Airport in which Francis had been a suspect.

I told my boss, Ron, that my long-term plan was to join the ID. Agreeing to help, he said that I would need more experience and should first apply to be an anti-smuggling officer at an airport. To me, this meant 'proper' work – and a uniform at last.

When my transfer finally came through, Ron called me into his office, where I saw him studying a map of the UK. He asked me to guess which airport I was going to. Naturally I tried the big ones: Heathrow, Gatwick, Manchester, Glasgow Prestwick – all negative. After Leeds Bradford, Luton, Newcastle and Liverpool, I was struggling. 'Birmingham,' he said. I didn't even know there was an airport there.

I moved to Birmingham International in December 1979 and it turned out to be much busier than I expected. A year later, Concorde made its first visit, so the place was, literally, looking up.

As at all airports, smuggled drugs had moved to the top of the customs agenda. Heroin, cocaine and cannabis were the 'big three' and received the most attention, but the only way we could begin to estimate how much was being trafficked was by the crude method of extrapolating from how much we seized.

Marijuana and cannabis resin seizures had been rising year-on-year all around the world. I was in my early twenties and some of my close friends enjoyed the occasional joint. They considered it innocent and harmless. After all, some of them argued, cannabis has been used for thousands of years for therapeutic purposes, from relieving the pain of childbirth in Roman Palestine to cheering up Greek philosophers. The same arguments exist today.

I'm not a judgemental person but I knew that, as with most things that are too good to be true, there was a downside. Career criminals had realised they could make more money selling cannabis than robbing banks, and with less risk. As a result, smuggling and peddling bush and resin progressed from a relatively harmless, hippified cottage industry to a cash cow for brutal thugs. Some of the profits were then funnelled into other criminal enterprises. Many of these cannabis gangs would progress to smuggling Class A drugs, though in my time at Birmingham Airport there was little sign of the impending explosion in cocaine and heroin.

Cocaine was still expensive and a tad exotic, while heroin was largely the indulgence of wasted rock stars. In the US, 'smack' had held some inner-city areas in its grip for years, but their agencies seemed to be stamping on it hard. Turkey, which once supplied eighty per cent of US heroin, had virtually stopped growing illicit opium under American pressure. Mexico to some extent took up the slack, but was now eradicating its own crop with the help of millions of dollars in US aid. The world's biggest source of opium had become South-eastern

Asia's 'Golden Triangle' of Burma, Thailand and Laos, but these countries suffered successive years of drought in the late seventies. Heroin, and the crop of poppies that supplied it, was dying out – or so international law enforcement thought.

No one foresaw that, within five years, Class A drugs would trigger one of the UK's biggest social crises since World War Two. Not that I would see much of this unfold at Birmingham.

The two years I spent there did give me an insight into the day-to-day life of what was at the time a dated and somewhat peripheral airport. The officers were old-school, prim and almost oblivious to drugs. They invested their energies in what they knew best: nabbing holidaymakers bringing back too many cigarettes and bottles of booze.

Yet even in this comparatively quiet outpost, I began to see how inventive and prolific the traffickers were becoming. During an evening watch in high summer in the green channel, my preventive officer, Al, stopped an elderly lady coming off a flight from Tenerife with a suitcase almost as big as her.

'Officer,' said Al, pointing at me, 'help the lady with her bags and put them up here.' He indicated one of the benches that lined the arrivals hall. 'Now, madam,' he continued, turning on the charm, 'have you had a nice holiday?' He could sense a seizure: maybe a couple of bottles of gin or a carton of fags, perhaps both if he was lucky.

I flicked up the suitcase lid. The sickly-sweet scent of hash hit me.

'Al,' I said.

'Not now, officer. I'm talking to the lady.'

'I know. But you'd better have a quick look.'

He did. 'Bloody hell! Where did that come from?'

'A nice couple on the flight asked me to carry it for them,' explained the old lady.

We tore outside and arrested the pair just as they were climbing into their car for a getaway. It turned out they were a professional couple who, while holidaying, had spotted a commercial opportunity.

Days later, a colleague of mine stopped a West African lady with a pile of tan briefcases neatly stacked on a sack barrow. This and the lady's appearance – she was dressed from head to toe in leopard-skin print – aroused his suspicions. Coming down the stairs into the green channel, I could smell the gear long before I saw it: each briefcase had high-grade cannabis resin concealed in its sides. I was sympathetic, sensing that some sort of debt or blackmail had forced her into making what we called a 'suicide run' though our controls, but she refused to talk and wound up going to prison. I was wrong about her and our paths crossed again later in my career.

In 1984, after a brief spell as a VAT control officer – some villains were turning to tax fraud as a less risky way to make money – I finally joined the local collection investigation unit on promotion to the rank of executive officer. The collection units carried out a similar role to the ID's teams but at a strictly local or regional level, and were often a stepping stone to the national ID itself. They were much derided by the elitist ID officers, but I was proud to be a so-called 'unit tosser' and gained valuable experience.

My first target was not a drugs baron but a tandoori restaurant chain believed to be cooking more than curries; we suspected they were failing to record many transactions and thereby avoided VAT payments. The potential proof lay in the restaurant's rubbish bags. For a week I pored through pungent waste sacks in search of ripped-up credit card receipts, piecing together the soggy yellowed remnants to secure a prosecution. Many years passed before I could face my next vindaloo, but it taught me patience, a skill every good investigator needs. It also kept my feet on the floor: no fast chases and Mr Bigs for me.

One of my first drug cases involved keeping watch on a residential address. I was told a big consignment of cannabis was expected to arrive in the area and the suspects would use this house to store it. Our observation point was in the shell of a large detached home nearby. In its day this pile had been magnificent but time had overtaken it. The surrounding area had declined and seen minor street riots in which the house had been burned out, leaving it gutted but still standing.

The officer showing me the ropes was a Welsh lad. He was okay but had a high opinion of his abilities. Our routine was to park on the edge of the area, walk to the house under cover of darkness and remain in post until we could sneak out the following night. To get to our obs point, in what had been the front master bedroom, we had to cross a first floor with no floorboards, only crossbeams. This was obviously dangerous. It was also mid-winter and freezing.

Several nights in, I was on duty with the Welshman when I felt the need to pee. I got up and with great care balanced my way back across the beams, over to what had been an old closet. As I began to urinate, steam rose from the depths of the closet. So did a voice.

'Fucking 'ell, where's that coming from? I'm soaking.'

I leapt back, missing a fall through the crossbeams by inches.

We had somehow failed to spot that the local tramp, Roger, had been using this closet as a bedroom. There was little we could do, apart from replace the clothes I had ruined. Roger subsequently became a fixture of the obs point. We bought him food, drink and bedcovers, and during the entire time we ran the job he did not once get in the way. He seemed happy to watch our coming and goings, munching on his government-funded cheese sandwiches. The operation was a success and, as far as I know, Roger never told anyone about his new friends.

On the last night, my Welsh mentor and I walked back to his car in the bitter cold and he took a final opportunity to wax lyrical about his time in the job. He had, in fact, not been in customs as long as I had but had joined Investigation some three months before me, which apparently qualified him as an expert. He explained how you needed your wits about you, how dangerous the job was and how sharp he was.

'You have to get up early to catch me out, boyo,' he boasted.

I said nothing but looked at the spot where he had parked his car.

'You see, I got street cred,' he continued. 'I blend in, no one would guess what I was. I bring in my motor, park wherever I like and bond with the locals. It's a Rover, so it looks the part.'

'It looks like you've over-bonded,' I said.

'What?'

He peered into the gloom and let out a wail of despair. 'Oh fuckin' hell, my car.'

His Rover, its wheels removed, was neatly balanced on four piles of bricks and had been firebombed into a burnt-out husk. So much for street cred.

3

GOING UNDERGROUND

The first ID investigator to distinguish himself working undercover was a cocksure, headstrong Londoner called Mike Stephenson. 'Stevo', as colleagues knew him, had the attitude and self-confidence to carry off the role. Yet he made his mark more by chance than design.

From an informant, the ID learned that a gang of heavies known for strongarm work and robbery had acquired a large quantity of Turkish heroin and were looking for a buyer. Stevo, it was decided, could be introduced to them as a dealer wanting a wholesale amount, with a view to trapping the men as they handed over the drugs. The informant arranged for him to meet them at a house in South London.

It turned out that the heavies, more used to pointing shotguns at terrified bank tellers than selling 'smack', did not really know what they were doing. Stevo was also flying by the seat of his pants, trying to imagine how a regular dealer of heroin would behave in such a scenario.

He walked into the house to find the gang in a darkened front room behind drawn curtains – on a weekday morning at half past ten. Overcoming his nerves, Stevo had the presence of mind to exclaim, 'What are you doing with the curtains closed? Anyone going past will think there's either a funeral or something dodgy going on.' The gang leader, realizing his error, quickly said, 'Oh yeah, you're right, pull those curtains back.' It broke the ice and assured the gang that Stevo knew his business.

After further discussion, during which Stevo was able to confirm that the heroin was actually in the house, he agreed a deal and left to 'get the money'. He walked out to his car, lit a cigarette and took off a shoe as if it had a stone in it, his signal that the drugs were there. His colleagues burst into the house, backed up by armed police, and arrested the whole crew.

The operation, known in the parlance as a bust-buy, had been a success. But the gang members were furious with Stevo, who they suspected of being a criminal 'grass', and let it be known they planned to find and kill him. It was decided to reveal Stevo's true background, for his own safety. At their first remand hearing, the gang saw him walk into court to give evidence as a customs officer, realised who he really was, and immediately changed their pleas to guilty.

Stephenson became the ID's go-to infiltrator. He was larger than life, could play a part and had the patter of a Cockney wideboy. He proved that the ID could successfully conduct regular covert operations, but such work remained an under-used weapon in their armoury.

Other officers were called upon to play similar roles from time to time, usually posing as a delivery driver or postman after the discovery of a parcel of drugs in the mail, which required little forethought or aptitude. One officer masqueraded for a while as a baggage handler at Heathrow Airport, where smuggling was rife. But the idea of building proper 'legends', the plausible fake biographies that operatives needed in case they were challenged, had not yet been developed. Most UC jobs happened on the spur of the moment. Long-term infiltration was an untried concept in the ID – until Operation Quest.

In 1984, an ID team and the Essex-based No. 5 Regional Crime Squad (RCS) undertook a joint inquiry into Edwin 'Eddie' Cook, a prolific and well-connected trafficker. Aged in his mid-fifties, Cook supplied a large chunk of the London cannabis market. He had previously been jailed for five years for importing through Dover in a caravanette, but had absconded while on home leave and disappeared. Four years later, the RCS found him living under an assumed name in north London. Rather than rearrest him, they put him under surveillance, as they suspected he was still smuggling and wanted to catch him in the act.

With the ID's help, they learned that Cook had agreed to buy four tonnes of cannabis from Nigeria and was sending a freighter to collect it. The freighter would return and 'cooper', or transfer, the cannabis to a fishing boat on the open sea, probably somewhere in the English Channel. The fishing boat would then land the illicit cargo on the coast of Kent, where a waiting shore team would drive it away.

Operation Quest stalled, however, when Cook went to Africa to sort out a problem with the load and was held in custody by the Nigerians for 'cargo irregularities'. When he was finally allowed back to the UK – suffering from malaria, which briefly put him in hospital – the Home Office insisted he be arrested to finish his original sentence.

The investigation team continued to monitor him in prison. Sure enough, they learned that he was trying to set up a new plot, this time hiding drugs in shipping containers, and was looking for someone who could 'rip off' the arriving containers at a British port before they came under customs scrutiny. Such corrupt dockers were much prized by smugglers, as they could circumvent the control system at the border points of entry.

The ID and the RCS saw their chance. They would introduce two UCs into Cook's organisation to assist his smuggle.

This would give them the inside track on his plans and hope-fully lead to the arrest of his entire network.

A thirty-year-old Liverpudlian ID officer called Eddie was working on some Quest paperwork when the investigator in charge of the case came to his desk and asked, 'Are you busy?'

'No.'

'Good. You're from Liverpool, you don't look like a police-man, you'll do.'

That was the extent of his selection and training for an undercover assignment. 'Don't worry,' the case officer told him, 'it'll all be wrapped up in three weeks.'

It took fourteen months.

Eddie constructed the basic fake identity of a Scouse crimi-nal with extensive contacts among corrupt dockworkers, but kept his real first name, so he would not have to think about it. The fact that both he and the target, Cook, were called Eddie did not seem significant, but would later help to avert a disastrous blunder. Eddie was partnered with an RCS detec-tive called Dick, another Liverpudlian who had the benefit of being a trained lorry driver.

Eddie and Dick contrived to meet one of Cook's lieuten-ants in a pub in London's theatre district. Posing as 'a couple of bad lads from Liverpool', they said that Eddie's links with dockers meant he could smuggle a consignment through any port in the country, while Dick could drive any vehicle they wanted. They were in.

Released from prison on licence soon after, Cook met the pair himself to size them up. He came across as a bumbling older man, but was in fact an experienced crook and very shrewd. He was suspected of having major financial backers in South London and at one meet flashed a pistol to show he meant business. Eddie and Dick, true to their jack-the-lad legends, affected to be unimpressed.

Over more than thirty meetings they got to know Cook

and his circle of underlings well, in particular a Scotsman called 'Haggis' who had recently come out of Barlinnie Prison for murder. The men talked about football, women and life, sometimes drank too much – it was hard to sip lemonade and stay in legend – and built a rapport. The UCs used a hidden Nagra tape recorder about the size of a large paperback to record conversations. It was usually worn by Dick, whose stocky build was less likely to reveal its outline under his clothes.

Cook preferred meeting in the same regular haunts, where he felt secure. One day he took them to a pub in Shepherd's Bush which, he said, no 'cops or cuzzies' could enter without him knowing. At the moment he said it, he was talking to a cop and cuzzie and the only other customers were members of their covert back-up team.

But the team's inexperience almost proved costly. Cook had only ever been introduced to the two UCs as 'Eddie' but their intelligence team told them that he was sometimes known as 'Ted' to family and friends. Shortly afterwards, Eddie met Cook alone for a critical discussion. They began to argue over which boat the gear would arrive on, and the exasperated Eddie exclaimed, 'Oh for fuck's sake, Ted.'

Cook stopped him dead. 'Why did you call me Ted?'

Eddie's blood ran cold; he realised that Cook only used that name with his nearest and dearest, which Eddie could not possibly have known. But he had a sudden brainwave.

'Well my name is Eddie, same as yours,' he said, 'and I get called Ted, Ed, Edward, you name it. All the time.'

'Strange, though, that you would call me that.'

If Cook's suspicions had been triggered, the moment passed. But the ID had learned the hard way never to give their UCs sensitive information that they could not have gleaned from their own contact with the targets.

Another mistake was in expecting Eddie to fulfil his

normal duties while also working undercover Quest. ID officers worked in small teams and operated what was called the 'squad' system, in which each team took a turn to be on call for a week for any random jobs that came in out-of-hours.

One Sunday, Eddie was sent to Heathrow's Terminal 3 to watch and confirm the arrival of a target on a job unrelated to Quest. Normally on such occasions he would wear a covert radio and might pop in to see colleagues on the airport's own investigation unit for a chat. This time, by chance, he didn't.

He was standing in the arrivals hall, looking for his target, when a hand grabbed his shoulder. It was Cook. He laughed at the look of horror on Eddie's face.

'Ah, ha,' he exclaimed triumphantly, 'you thought you were being nicked!'

Once again Eddie had to think on his feet. At any time, one of the airport staff might come over to say hello. He had to get away from Cook, but also to explain why he was there.

'Look,' he said, 'we shouldn't be seen together. I'm up to no good.'

Not to be outdone, Cook replied, 'No sweat, I don't want to be seen with you either. The feller organising our job from Nigeria is flying in today. That's why I'm here.'

They agreed to meet in a few days and parted. Eddie sought the nearest toilet cubicle and vomited with fright. Had Cook stood back and watched his movements, rather than approaching him, he would almost certainly have been sussed.

The next time they met, Cook asked what Eddie had been up to. 'Meeting a diamond smuggler,' he replied. Cook was impressed, but cautioned that he did not want Eddie 'doing another piece of work' while working for him.

Cook then confirmed that he had a container due into the docks at Immingham, Lincolnshire, from Ghana, and a *second into Tilbury from Nigeria. Dick and Eddie would take them both away before customs inspections and deliver them to a 'slaughter' in Essex, from where the drugs would be removed and distributed. If successful, Cook planned to import one container every month for a year, then retire on the proceeds.*

The undercover duo duly collected the first container from Immingham dock, loaded it onto a flatbed truck, took it to a bungalow in Basildon and dropped off 465 kg of cannabis. The second container arrived two days later, carrying 670 kg. All of the drugs were seized and the gang arrested.

Cook was told during his subsequent interrogation that his group had been infiltrated, but not by whom. It was only when Dick and Eddie walked into the interview room that he understood. Turning to his solicitor, he said, 'I'm going to have to have another word with you. I've got serious problems here.' Haggis, Cook's sidekick, burst into tears when confronted with their betrayal, sobbing, 'Not the boys, the boys wouldn't do this to me.'

The ID learned invaluable lessons from Quest. In terms of best practice, Eddie should not have worked on the operation before being deployed as a UC, as this gave him prior knowledge that could have compromised him. He also should not have been sent on unrelated jobs that took him out into public spaces.

Eddie also discovered that ennui set in after the operation was over. 'While you are the UC, you are the main man,' he later recalled. 'You are special – until it's all over, and then you are not.' For those who would go on to undertake even longer covert deployments, this feeling would be even more marked.

Eddie and Dick were the main prosecution witnesses at trial at Chelmsford Crown Court. Cook, aged fifty-nine, was jailed for fourteen years for conspiring to import cannabis and possessing cocaine with intent to supply. 'Execution would be simpler and cheaper, your honour,' he grimly told the judge. Haggis received ten years. The judge commended Dick and Eddie for their exceptional work.

Another ID officer, Brian, worked with, and learned from, Mike Stephenson. The son of an Indian mother, Brian could pass for West Asian, which was particularly useful in investigating the heroin trade from that region. So when a Pakistani confidential informant, working for the American DEA, reported that heroin was for sale from a ship, the Sibi, docked at Liverpool, Brian was called in to help.

Suppliers in Pakistan were known to approach departing seamen and offer them quantities of heroin on a sale-or-return basis. This they could sell to customers in different parts of the world. Many worked for the Pakistan National Shipping Corporation (PNSC), which became notorious among law enforcement. The Sibi was a PNSC vessel.

Brian did not speak Urdu, so was paired with a Yorkshire policeman of Pakistani descent who did. They met the corrupt seaman through the informant and arranged to visit his ship to buy the heroin. Brian was given £5,000 in cash and was wired for sound, while surveillance officers spread around the docks. Brian and the policeman were taken to a cabin on the ship and shown 1.5 kg of heroin hidden in a gallon tin of cooking oil. So convincing was their cover that when they revealed who they were and told the sailor he was under arrest, he didn't believe them and started laughing.

Brian went on, like Stevo, to become a go-to UC for the ID. He even managed one of the first successes against the burgeoning Colombian cocaine trade, arranging a bust-buy for a kilo of coke outside a London pub. Given the ruthless reputation of Colombian cartels, Brian was allowed to enter Southwark Crown Court through the judges' entrance so he could not be targeted in the public concourse.

Brian, like Eddie and others before him, received no formal training for his roles but was left to his own devices to develop the persona of a wealthy young trafficker. 'I was in my late twenties, single, had plenty of money, would dress well in Yves St Laurent suits and Gucci shirts, a man about town,' he said. 'I wore seized Rolex watches, often fake, and drove a Mercedes Benz or BMWs.'

His bosses refused to stump up more than half the cost of his expensive suits but did eventually provide him with a bank account, credit card and fake passport and driver's licence. 'They begrudgingly put me in touch with someone in our financial branch who liaised with bank officials, and I got one to agree to set me up with a false account and made-up statements showing large sums of money coming in and out. But you would think I was asking for the crown jewels.'

Nevertheless Brian 'adored' the work. 'It was so much fun,' he recalled.

In the summer of 1985, Prime Minister Margaret Thatcher publicly declared war on drug dealers during a visit to customs officers at Heathrow Airport. 'We're after you,' she warned. 'Pursuit will be relentless. We shall make your life not worth living.' Stopping hard drugs in particular from hitting the streets became the number one priority for HMCE.

Not long afterwards, a significant heroin job came into our Collection Investigation Unit in Birmingham. These jobs were rotated among the troops and it was my turn to run one as the case officer. It was an importation in the parcel post.

We had discovered a package of brown heroin, weighing about one-third of a kilo, addressed to someone in the suburb of Stirchley. Officers watched the house while I contacted the police drug squad at Bournville. These cops knew the local scene and were always happy to accompany us on raids, as they could gain intel for their own daily work. They had some cracking operators with an encyclopaedic knowledge of who was doing what on their patch.

The squad assigned two experienced detectives, Phil and Kirk. Phil was able to identify the target to me, a man called Khan, right down to a description of his distinctly pockmarked face. The drug squad boys knew him and were keen to accompany us on the parcel delivery. We first removed the heroin and carefully replaced it with a substitute powder. We also inserted a light-sensitive device that would transmit a signal when the package was opened.

On a bright morning our own postman, known as 'Mad Dog', was sent to deliver the parcel while we waited. A man signed for it at the house door and Mad Dog re-joined our team. After twenty long minutes, the device indicated that the parcel had been opened. Cue the cavalry.

I thumped on the front door, flanked by a couple of my team and the drug squad lads. Hearing no answer, I flicked up the letterbox, just in time to see the pockmarked Khan legging up the staircase with the parcel. Kirk, who was a big lad, put the front door in with one kick and we raced after him.

We caught Khan in the loo, trying to flush the parcel contents away. I hauled him across the landing to a bedroom and arrested him. His shocked girlfriend was arrested too. The raid was over in minutes.

We had left a team outside in a car to watch for anything suspicious. Some thirty minutes into the raid, a thin, studious-looking Asian man carrying a light briefcase walked along the street and stopped at the house. The door by then was back in place, and he knocked on it. When it was opened by the towering Kirk, the man's face fell.

'Yes?' said Kirk.

'Oh,' said the thin man. 'Wrong house.'

'Really?' said Kirk, then picked up the man and whisked

him through the door, to the amusement of the car team watching from down the street.

I was still upstairs with the target, and heard the subsequent interrogation.

'Sit down,' said Kirk.

The thin man did so, clutching his briefcase and nervously looking around the room.

Kirk took out a small device with a lanyard and clip on it, and attached the clip to the thin man's shirt collar. He was too cowed to protest.

'Now,' said Kirk, 'What's your name?'

'Sultan,' stammered the thin man.

Kirk stared at the device, which bleeped. 'That's right,' he declared. 'Now then, Sultan, how old are you?'

'Erm, twenty-five,' said Sultan, who was looking distinctly pale by this time.

Kirk looked hard at the device. *Bleep*, it chirped.

'Correct,' he said. 'Where are you from, Sultan?'

'Stirchley,' said Sultan weakly

Bleep! 'Correct again,' said Kirk. 'Now for the big one. What's in the briefcase?'

'I don't know.'

Bleep! Bleep! Bleep!

'Ah ha!' said Kirk dramatically. 'The lie detector says otherwise.'

'Oh my God, a lie detector,' said Sultan. 'Okay, okay, I tell you, there's ten thousand pounds in the case to pay for the delivery.'

I went down the stairs just in time to see Kirk reattach his pager to his belt with the lanyard. I said nothing. Kirk just smiled.

The house was searched but nothing more was found. Weeks later, an informant told me we had missed three kilos under the floorboards. I never knew if this was true, and hope it wasn't – three kilos is a lot of gear. Sultan and Khan got ten years' jail apiece. Khan died in prison two years later, of a coronary brought on by an enlarged heart from heroin addiction.

In 1987 I ran a job that was the only time in my career I came across white heroin, the most highly refined form of the narcotic. It began when we intercepted a Pose Restante air mail envelope sent from India. It was handwritten, stuck down on four sides and contained two ounces of heroin, with a very high purity of eighty-seven per cent. It had been sent by an English lad living in Delhi and addressed to his brothers in a small terraced house in Moseley. I did background checks on the family and had a stop put on any mail to the address. My checks threw up another brother living five miles away, so his mail was stopped too.

We next intercepted a letter from the same sibling in India containing instructions on where to sell the gear, where to send payment and what the consequences would be if they were discovered: in India, a one-lakh fine, twenty lashes and imprisonment. Over the next fortnight we intercepted other letters with small amounts of white.

When we knocked the job, we found not hardened criminals but a close family trying to deal with their brother's heroin addiction. Among the items removed in the search of premises was a photograph of the boy in India, dressed in an *achkan*, a knee-length jacket worn with loose trousers. He looked contented enough and I wondered what had led him down this path.

These lads were not villains and the job had quite an effect on me, as I saw the human cost of drug-trading. When the lad who received the letters admitted involvement, and went to jail for importing a controlled drug, it was the one time in my career that I was saddened by the result. I often looked at the photo and wondered what became of the brother in India.

I later heard a rumour that he overdosed and died but never had it confirmed.

Towards the end of my time in Birmingham, I led on a peculiar case far removed from the world of narcotics. The phone rang one morning and a customs officer based at the Mount Pleasant postal office in London explained that a sorting boy had just inspected a partially opened parcel and been bitten by its disgruntled occupant – a pit viper. Luckily for the postie he was treated immediately and suffered no lasting harm.

Later that day five similar parcels, all from the West Coast of the USA, were intercepted at Mount Pleasant. Three contained live Gila monsters, while the other two contained a pit viper and a Gabon viper. Gila monsters are particularly nasty. They sometimes lock their teeth onto a victim and can only be removed by great force. Their mildly venomous bite does not kill humans but is by all accounts very painful. Someone clearly had a penchant for hard-ass lizards and snakes. I was detailed to find out who.

The parcels were addressed to a house in Kenilworth, Warwickshire, where we approached the homeowners, an elderly couple. They admitted that their son had an interest in reptiles but said he currently lived near Portsmouth. Satisfied that the parents were not involved, we set off for the south coast, arriving as evening fell. We gathered outside a small suburban semi, keen to go straight in to secure any evidence. Our boss demurred.

I carried a writ of assistance but was careful about using it. The writ was available to officers in hot pursuit of uncustomed, smuggled or prohibited goods, allowing entry to property without a search warrant. Its justification was that the goods could be destroyed or disposed of while officers waited for a warrant to be sworn out. This was particularly useful when chasing drugs and was a powerful tool – perhaps too powerful. After the Police and Criminal Evidence Act of 1984, its use was restricted.

As darkness settled at around eight o'clock, light shone from every room in the house, a muted white glow that seemed to rise from the floor. We decided to go in. The first thing to hit us was the tropical heat. The second was the source of the light: fluorescent tubes covering hundreds of reptile tanks. The house was packed with them, and it was eerily disconcerting to enter the half-light and hear the scrape and rustle of exotic creatures.

The owner arrived after an hour and was arrested for trafficking in endangered and rare animals. He immediately apologised and seemed mortified that a postal worker was hurt because of his obsession. He had over 150 vivarium tanks, holding some of the most toxic creatures on earth: rattlesnakes, vipers, a tiger snake, a taipan and a krait, as well as more Gilas and venomous lizards. The collection was rounded off with a number of deadly spiders.

We needed to clear the house and remove the lad under arrest. First, however, we waited for a snake expert to arrive. He turned out to be a pompous chap who insisted that we call him a 'reptile wrangler', something I refused to do. He had a small van and wore a belt with numerous torches on it. I suspected what he really wanted was a gun. He carried a long pole, hinged at the top with a noose.

'Make way, let me through, snake wrangler here, stand back,' he barked as he headed up the stairs, followed by three curious officers. There was a scrape, a crash and a scream. Down the stairs at a furious lick came the three officers, followed by Snake Man, white-faced and wild-eyed. The whole ensemble was pursued by what I later learned was a Gabon viper. Apparently they are dangerous, as Snake Man's actions confirmed. The group burst through the front door and into the street. Fortunately the snake stopped and lay on the stairs, seemingly content.

Snake Man regained his composure and returned to the stairs, where he used his noose stick to capture the viper and pop it into a box. After this he didn't say much but continued to box up the inhabitants of the upstairs tanks. By the time he had finished, and we prepared to secure the premises and leave, Snake Man had recovered his swagger. Jumping into his van, he told us how risky his job was and how skilled he was at handling deadly reptiles.

I learnt later that on his journey home, the Gabon viper, which we dubbed 'Houdini', made another break for freedom while Snake Man was driving. Luckily there was no major crash but I would have paid to witness the carnage.

Some days later, I found myself with six Gila monsters at Chester Zoo, which is renowned for herpetology. The chief scientist was examining the Gilas, the only venomous lizard native to North America, while I explained that our smuggler was mounting the defence that he had been conducting a captive breeding programme because of their comparative rarity in the wild.

The scientist looked hard at me. 'Do you know how we sex Gilas?' he asked.

'No.'

'Well, my advice is stand back and be prepared to run.'

I watched, fascinated, as two scientists advanced on the first Gila. Nearly two feet long, black-and-orange in colour with a warty skin, it hissed loudly, as though it knew what was coming. Each scientist wore what looked like the chain-mail gloves of mediaeval knights. One grasped the Gila's head while the other took a small glass rod and proceeded to apply it in the vicinity of the Gila's tail.

The Gila reacted instantly: it hissed, squirmed, and tried to bite the arm off the head-holding scientist. I led the retreat to the lab door and remained there while the other five were subjected to the same procedure, under extreme protest.

The job had an unusually satisfying ending. The smuggler was ordered to pay a fine, but it was obvious that he had a passion for his subject. He owned a herpetological library that the zoo-keepers called one of the most complete they had seen, and his misguided smuggling was due to an eagerness to collect the animals. After deliberations with the court and the zoo, he was offered a job and as far as I know still works in the reptile field.

During my time in Birmingham I had also married and separated. I then met my future, second wife, Jo, who also worked for HMCE. An eight-and-a-half-stone ex-gymnast, she was physically my opposite, but we clicked. I had found my lifetime soulmate.

My performance in Birmingham also led to further promotion, which meant a return to London. I would be going back to the ID with the rank of higher executive officer, or HEO. A friend, Dave, the head of one of the ID's cocaine teams, phoned and asked if I knew where I would be assigned.

'Well, I don't mean to boast,' I told Dave, 'but I thinks it's your elite cocaine target team.'

'Think again,' said Dave, trying to suppress a laugh. He had moved to a team investigating VAT fraud in nightclubs, and I would be joining him there. I was to be part of a squad targeting Soho's seedier clip joints and the wealthy but elusive men who ran them.

Soho then was full of these 'near-beer' bars, underground dives which used pretty girls to lure in passers-by. The punter would agree to buy the girl a glass of 'champagne' – actually cheap plonk – only to receive a bill for hundreds of pounds. This was presented by a broken-nosed heavy who brooked no argument. These operations were not illegal as such, but were highly unethical and we were keen to clean them up. We also wanted the VAT due from their doubtless substantial profits.

'Tony' was one of the main Soho bosses on our radar. No matter how secretive his clip joints were, we knew that somewhere he had to keep accurate paperwork. He would need to know what money was coming in and what his expenses were, if only to ensure that his managers and staff weren't ripping him off.

We placed him under surveillance. He drove the obligatory sports car, had a distinctive bouffant hairstyle and wore the sharpest suits, so he should have been easy to follow. Yet day after day our teams would lose him in the same place, an underground car park near The Strand. It took us weeks to figure out his trick: he would park his car, remove his jacket and, crucially, his *wig*, and stroll baldly out of the car park, a different man. It was only when we finally caught up with him, and his errant paperwork, that we learned his nickname was 'Tony the Wig'.

The case officer on this job was Mike. He was fastidious in dress and in particular about his hair – if things had been different, he and The Wig would have got along well. Whenever the team worked away, we had to check our hotel had working hairdryers in the bedrooms; only then would Mike join us.

After the Soho job, we were assigned to follow the owner of some mobile burger outlets, who was suspected of not declaring his full take. In fact he wasn't declaring anything, avoiding tax on an industrial scale. We holed up in a forest outside Shrewsbury to keep watch on him. It was mid-summer and the weather was lovely. I parked off a country lane in a black Peugeot with Ged, a Mancunian with a dry sense of humour. Just over the way from us was Mike in a Vauxhall Belmont.

By and by, a young lady on horseback came trotting down the lane. The horse must have caught something ominous out of the corner of its eye – probably Ged and me in the black car – because within seconds it went berserk. The girl did her best to hold on as it galloped up to Mike's Belmont and began to rear up and kick out wildly. For a few seconds Ged and I were in hysterics as Mike was thrown around in the car.

We managed to get across to the girl and calm the horse down. She climbed from the saddle and thanked us, but we could see she was shaken up. Mike, meanwhile, was lying in the wreckage of the Belmont. The horse, in its moment of madness, had done a number on the car, which looked like it had been assailed with a sledgehammer. Amazingly, it could still be driven. The sole damage that Mike had sustained was to his coiffure, which was decidedly askew. Trying to hold back our laughter, Ged and I got him out.

We asked the girl where she lived and, out of concern, offered to escort her home. Mike trailed us, lurching along in what was left of his car. When we arrived, a hard-looking geezer came out of the house. He took one look at the visibly upset girl, who it turned out was his daughter, one look at me and Ged, then his eyes fell upon the hapless Mike, who was trying to re-hang one of the car doors. He then put two and two together and came up with five. Ged and I spent the next few minutes trying to keep him off Mike's throat as he sought to strangle him for driving around country lanes like a maniac.

Once the situation was under control and the man realised it was his horse that was at fault, he invited us in for tea. Ged and I were all for it but Mike would not be seen in public with his hair in such a mess, so it was back to our hotel to find a hairdryer.

Not long afterwards, I was made the case officer in a large gold fraud. A bent jeweller in Southall, west London, was relieving the taxpayer of the VAT on each export sale he made. After a while he decided that he could claim back more if he just invented the sales, and he was right – he made over £500,000 more.

The job led to wide-ranging enquiries in India, for which I selflessly volunteered. My boss, Dave, decided he should accompany me to handle the difficult political cocktail parties and embassy soirées. Dave was an expert on soirées. He was also a laugh and an ideal travelling companion.

While Dave frolicked in New Delhi, I headed off on a grand tour of the Indian legal system. The fraud involved forging the signatures of advocates and public notaries. Over an eight-week period I visited Delhi, Bombay, Madras, Jaipur and Calcutta. Bombay was the highlight, starting at the Central Criminal Court, where a sign above the judge's head read: 'No spitting and no animals allowed in court.'

I was accompanied by Chief Inspector Malik of the Bombay police, a lean, middle-aged man with greying hair, a thin, military-style moustache and a devious mind. One day while driving to interview a witness, I inadvertently opened my briefcase, revealing a cache of stationery. Inspector Malik's eyes lit up.

'What are those?' he said, pointing at a stack of shorthand pads and pens.

'Oh,' I said without thinking, 'go on, take some.' I handed him a bunch of coloured pens, a ruler and a few pads.

The following day at the police station, I waited with the local team. The door flew open and in came Inspector Malik. He wore a crisp white shirt and in the top pocket carried, with pride, every pen I had given him. Under his arm he held four of the shorthand pads and from his trouser pocket protruded the ruler. He lined his men up and flicked open one of the pads. Pen at the ready, he approached the first officer.

'What is your name?'

'You know what it is, Dad,' said the exasperated constable.

'What is your name?' shouted Malik

Inspector Malik clearly saw the pens and pads as affirmation of his power. All day the scene was repeated in various offices. Malik would take out pen and pad, line everyone up and proceed to ask obvious questions, noting the answers with a flourish. The cops had no choice but to go along with it, as none of them had pens or pads and no one had ever seen a ruler.

This procedure, repeated for several days, was only upstaged when I bought an *A to Z* of Bombay into the office. The reaction could not have been more startling had I brought a Shakespeare first folio. The whole team, led by Malik, laid out the map on the table and began to search for their own addresses, which was not what I'd had in mind.

The next day we travelled to the police HQ in our official car, a fifties Morris Oxford known in India as an 'Ambassador'. I asked Malik who I should give gifts to as thanks for their help.

'Gifts?' he said suspiciously. 'What have you got?'

'Well, I have an enamel plaque from HM Customs Investigation Division, a few ties, a set of glasses engraved with the ID emblem of a portcullis, and a silver tray.'

I neglected to mention that I also had two bottles of Johnnie Walker Black Label whisky. I wanted to see the reaction when these entered the equation.

'Hmm,' he said, as if giving the matter deep thought. 'The plaque should go to the team, so I will have it in my office.' He paused, as if still thinking. 'Of course, with my rank I should have a tie. Better still, give them all to me and I'll hand them out.'

Laughing inside at his unashamed venality, I said, 'I thought of giving the glasses to your boss.'

'Yes, yes,' he said, 'that's a good idea. But he wouldn't appreciate it, he's teetotal.'

'He wouldn't have to drink alcohol but he could drink lemonade.'

'Yes, but I know him better than you. Best to give the glasses to me and I'll hold on to them.'

'What about the tray?'

'Well, obviously that should go with glasses, so I'll look

after that as well.' A logical argument which conveniently served his purpose.

As we pulled into the police compound, I produced my ace in the hole. 'Oh,' I said, as if just remembering, 'I've got a couple of bottles for the boys.'

'Bottles? Bottles of what?'

'Johnnie Walker Black Label. I didn't know if they would like it.'

At this point our driver's ears pricked up. A big man of few words, he stared hard at Malik in the rear-view mirror.

'Oh dear, oh dear,' mumbled Malik. 'It's best that I take those, you see it could be misconstrued as a bribe.'

'Of course,' I said. 'What will you do with them, as I wouldn't like people to think I had bribed you?'

'Don't you worry about that, I'll think of something,' said the inspector, with a glint in his eye.

A few days later, on a hot, humid day in downtown Bombay, I interviewed the head of the city's postal system. His ramshackle office had little furniture: an old table, with one leg balanced up on a pile of old books; two chairs, a big one for him and a small one for guests; a book cabinet (empty); and a clattering ceiling fan. The room was dusty and dingy, and the fan gave little relief from the stifling heat. We were on the third floor and two large windows, each with a set of broken shutters hanging off at the hinges, opened onto a bustling road below.

I was shown to where Mr Memon sat behind the table. On it sat an antique Bakelite box.

'Please do come in,' he said. From outside came a constant din of people and traffic. 'I was just about to have tea, would you like some?'

'Black tea, please.' I had learned that the fastest way to tummy trouble was to drink milk or eat dairy.

He leaned towards the Bakelite box and pressed a buzzer.

'Allo?' came a voice from the box.

'Chai liana (Get the tea),' my host shouted self-importantly. He was clearly proud of his intercom. He turned back to me.

'Now tell me, sir, where are you from?'

'London,' I replied

'Ah, London. Did you grow up there?'

'Yes I did, but now I live in Surrey.'

'Surrey? Is that anywhere near Oxford?'

'It's not too far.'

Much to my surprise, a pigeon flew in through the open window as we talked. It collided full-on with the fan, and the clanking noise was accompanied by a desperate cooing, which rotated with the bird caught on the fast-moving fan blade.

Mr Memon didn't blink. 'Ah, Oxford. The dreaming spires. I went there, do you know? Yes, Oxford. Phuut! Phuut!'

He blew air from the side of his mouth to expel a small cloud of white and grey feathers. At this point the pigeon was slung off the fan and smashed into the wall, where it lay dazed, giving out the occasional weak coo.

Mr. Memon forced a smile, rolled his eyes, leaned towards the box again and buzzed.

'Allo?' came the same ghostly voice.

'Pigeon ko le ke jaana (Come and take the pigeon),' said my host through gritted teeth, trying to keep his composure. 'Now where were we? Ah yes, Oxford. I remember once ...'

The door behind me crashed open and in came a small, thin man in the minimum of clothing, carrying an enormous butterfly net. Man looked at pigeon, pigeon at man. The bird must have guessed it was for the pot and bestirred itself.

'Yes, Oxford is a lovely city,' continued Mr Memon dreamily as the pigeon-wallah set off in pursuit. He thrashed around the room while Mr Memon reminisced.

'Mr Memon,' I said, trying to set our meeting back on track, 'as you know it's about a fraud that has occurred ...'

The pigeon and the man passed me in a swirl of swish-
ing nets and flying feathers. 'Coo!' the pigeon called one last
time, before careering out of the window into the hot air. The
pigeon-wallah made a final effort, swung the net with all his
might – and flew out of the window himself, following the
bird down into the fruit market below.

For a moment all was calm in the room. A few sad feathers
floated down from the ceiling fan amid dust motes lit by the
sunlight, a window shutter squeaked and the fan whirred on.
My host forced a smile and once again pressed the buzzer on
his beloved Bakelite box.

'Allo?'

'Bunde ko le kar aana (Go and get the bloke),' he said,
almost in tears.

My scarcely believable Indian experiences with the venal
inspector and the exploding pigeon taught me two memorable
and valuable lessons: corruption makes the world go round, and
be prepared for anything. They were lessons that would serve
me well when, a short time later, I was asked to go undercover.

4

INFILTRATORS

On 18 September 1988, a bearded Italian-American in dark, double-breasted Armani strode through Heathrow Airport off the transatlantic Concorde flight. Bob Musella was an East Coast financial manager who oozed wealth and success. He had also, by his own account, committed 'more crime than many people serving a life prison sentence'. He was, in fact, one of the best money launderers on earth. Yet he was also unknown to law enforcement. He had no criminal convictions, no record of arrest, and never went near a drug shipment. On paper, he was as clean as his polished cotton shirt, and expected to breeze through UK immigration without a hitch.

When he showed his passport at the booth, however, one of the date stamps looked phoney. A polite but sceptical officer was unconvinced by his explanation. The next thing he knew, Musella was in a private room in the bowels of the terminal building, being asked to strip for a body search. Only when officers found a recording device hidden in his Renwick briefcase did he admit who he really was, and ask them to stop.

'Bob Musella' was really Robert Mazur, US Customs special agent and audacious undercover officer. He was travelling to London in legend to conclude one of the biggest and most ambitious sting operations ever attempted. And he wanted very few people to know.

Mazur was the point man in Operation C-Chase, a deep probe into the crooked Bank of Credit and Commerce International (BCCI), which had over 400 branches in seventy-eight countries. For two years he had convincingly posed as the Mob-connected owner of several investment and mortgage firms, cash-churning businesses ideal for washing funny money. His forte was shifting large sums to banking-secrecy havens such as Panama, where big cash deposits were welcome, no questions asked. His cover included director-ship of an air charter service, with the use of a private Cessna Citation jet (seized by the US government in another case).

Mazur managed to woo not only major Colombian narcos wanting to wash the proceeds of their drug sales but also the corrupt banking officials prepared to facilitate the flow of this illicit money without reporting it. He was in the UK to meet some of his targets based in London, and to give a confiden-tial briefing to the ID. His trip and his identity were secrets known only to a handful.

A phone call from Heathrow to the US embassy confirmed Mazur's extraordinary story, and when the ID also vouched for him, he was released and his passport returned. The next day, he and the officer running the British end of the case talked through their moves over a late breakfast. At American instigation, the Brits had been watching the offices of Capcom Financial Services, a BCCI-linked firm in London. Capcom made a huge number of foreign currency transactions, moving billions of dollars through the futures markets. This included Medellin Cartel money, some of it bribes to General Manuel Noriega, the corrupt dictator of Panama. Capcom also appeared to be siphoning off assets from BCCI to a safe haven outside the bank's official structures.

Mazur's meetings with the Capcom people were a success. When he told them he could wash $10 million of dubious money through their firm every month, they were delighted.

His elaborate sting came to its climax a month later in spectacular fashion. To gather as many of the conspirators as possible into one place for their arrest, Mazur staged his own wedding to a business associate – a female undercover officer – and invited them all. For two days, dodgy bankers, financiers and narcos were to be pampered at a country club near Tampa, Florida, prior to the nuptials. They rolled up in a fleet of Lincolns, anticipating a bachelor party to remember. Instead they were greeted by armed US Customs agents. 'Welcome to Tampa,' said one. 'You're under arrest.' (They were not arrested at the wedding itself, as the film The Infiltrator, *based on Mazur's autobiography, suggests.)*

At the same time, coordinated raids took place in London and Paris, ultimately resulting in what the New York Times *called the biggest money laundering conviction in American history. BCCI collapsed into insolvency and infamy.*

Mazur later returned to England to testify at the Old Bailey. He also gave a lecture to selected ID officers, warning the Brits that Colombians had begun targeting Europe in earnest, as higher street prices meant they could double their cocaine profits there compared to the USA.

One of the keenest observers was a talented financial investigator known as Keef. A fit, lean West Londoner with a sharp mind, Keef had worked on the British side of the case. He had joined HMCE at sixteen to work in the cargo sheds at Heathrow Airport. After four years he was elevated to a four-man team that searched for drugs passing through the airport's freight village. He also did a stint in VAT fraud investigation before joining the ID as an officer in 1982. Despite having contrived to leave school with only a grade-four CSE in arithmetic, Keef was comfortable with figures and learned how to sniff out fraud just by looking at a balance sheet. 'Establish the norm, then look at the abnormal,' was his rule of thumb.

Keef had been on the raid of Capcom's London headquarters

and had trawled through piles of seized material and records revealing numerous curious transactions. He was impressed by Mazur, and also by a lecture given to ID staff by a visiting Canadian police officer, Garry Clement, who had implemented a proceeds-of-crime and money laundering programme within the Royal Canadian Mounted Police. 'Our drugs teams used to arrest bodies, seize gear and that was it,' recalled Keef. 'Then someone decided there must be more to this, and it was the money. So we followed the lead of the Americans and, more particularly, the Canadians.' Parliament had just passed the first Drug Trafficking Offences Act, and the identification and confiscation of illegally obtained assets was to become a key component of the ID's work. 'They wanted officers to apply for this type of work, running alongside the operational teams and looking at the finances of individuals. What car does he drive, what is his business, how does he pay for travel? When the operational team did the knock, we would be there to sift all the paperwork and trace any assets.'

Mazur's lecture gave Keef his first insight into undercover work. 'But at that stage it wasn't on the cards for us,' he said. 'We didn't have the capability. There was also a lot of resistance from the police, who didn't think Customs should do it. Well, if you are professional about it and cooperate properly, you should not get blue-on-blue incidents. It happened a lot in the US, because the DEA and the FBI didn't cooperate with each other, but there was no reason it had to happen in the UK.'

Like the ID's previous Operation Quest, however, C-Chase had flaws. Mazur's true identity was supposed to stay secret but his name was inadvertently leaked to an American defence attorney in the case. He had to move home, reduce contact with family and friends, and change his name. Despite such precautions, the DEA received intelligence that a Colombian hit squad was being sent to find and kill him. Mazur had a lawyer draw up his will, just in case.

Nevertheless, C-Chase showed the ID how a convincing, dedicated and well-supported UC could infiltrate a top-level, multi-national organisation for a prolonged period. Until then, UC ops tended to be short-term and impromptu. Anyone with 'the gift of the gab and the bottle' might be asked to go into a pub to buy drugs, recalled one senior investigator. 'You would walk in and front it out. Next morning, you'd be out as a surveillance officer doing another job. You could bump into anybody. It was amateurish.'

If they were going to continue to do it, they had to do it properly. They would also need to pick the right people.

At around the time that Robert Mazur was concluding Operation C-Chase, a senior British customs investigator was attending a training course at Templer Barracks, near Ashford in Kent. Named after Sir Gerald Templer, who fought in both world wars and defeated the insurgency in Malaya, the barracks was home to the Joint Services School of Intelligence, the repository of some of the military's dirtiest tricks. Senior ID officers were sometimes invited there for instruction in dark arts and cutting-edge tradecraft.

The investigator was there not just to learn but to make contacts that might serve the ID in the future. Among his fellow students was a brash young army intelligence officer called Stephen Watson, and the two fell into conversation. Watson had been commended for clandestine work in Eastern Europe. He had also served in a secret unit that tested for weaknesses in domestic security, on one occasion successfully planting a fake car-bomb at the Earls Court exhibition centre in London during the Royal Tournament military tattoo.

The customs man sensed a possibility and invited Watson to a barbecue at his home at the end of the course. Over burgers and salad, Watson was introduced to some of the ID's senior managers, including Terry Byrne, the powerful deputy chief in *charge of drugs. They discussed undercover work and Byrne mentioned Harry's Game, a television mini-series based on a novel by former journalist Gerald Seymour. Its plot involved an army officer, Harry Brown, going incognito into Catholic Belfast to track down the IRA killer of a cabinet minister. Given that it ended with Brown being shot in the head, it was not perhaps the best example of covert infiltration, but Byrne said they wanted to deploy selected officers in a similar way against smugglers and other criminals, and thought Watson could help. 'If you ever got bored, come over to us,' he said.*

By then the ID had grown to almost 1,000 staff and its bosses were looking at ways to better deploy their officers. They had long mastered one particular art, that of telephone tapping, conducted from a secret London base by a mysterious team called Alpha. The division was weaker, however, in other areas: tailing moving suspects, recruiting and handling informants, planting listening devices in cars, rooms and offices, and infiltrating criminal organisations. Byrne and his colleagues wanted to do something about it.

Watson subsequently helped to arrange a training contest between the army and the ID. A customs surveillance team was challenged to track a soldier posing as a smuggler as he drove from London to the port of Dover, while army intelligence officers versed in counter-surveillance tried to spot and photograph the customs team, some by hiding in roadside foliage. In the event, according to Watson, the army squad not only identified all of the ID cars involved but also intercepted their radio calls with a frequency scanner.

Watson was invited to join the ID. He was felt to be an ideal recruit: a fresh, unknown face with experience in military intelligence who could spearhead their new approach. He accepted.

Watson was first deployed against so-called rip-off teams active at Heathrow Airport. He was given a false past as an itinerant labourer back from a spell in Spain, and was taken on as a cargo-shed handler by Air Canada, unloading freight from various countries. His secret role was to observe work crews believed to be removing uncleared consignments from the airport.

It did not go well. His furtive role lasted for nine months, with little visible success, after which he was reassigned to normal duties. He resigned shortly afterwards.

Watson then did something that shocked the close-knit ID to its core: he collaborated with a television documentary that exposed their work in a highly critical way. He complained on camera that he had been given inadequate protection and poorly prepared identity documents – the home address on his fake driving licence was actually an empty office block, which would have put him at risk if discovered – and called his assignment 'frankly Mickey Mouse'. 'They are not able to mount covert, undercover operations against serious major drugs targets,' he said. Even worse, he claimed to have uncovered internal corruption that went unpunished.

The exposé, aired on Channel 4's Dispatches strand, was a minor disaster. Watson not only revealed some of the ID's methods but also disclosed their undercover initiative. The opposition Labour Party called for an immediate inquiry and the affair was raised before the House of Commons public accounts committee.

One of Watson's key claims, however, was based on a misapprehension. A freight handler he suggested was corrupt, and whom he met and secretly recorded for the programme, was actually working for the ID as an informant and had been pretending to be bent to gather information. Watson never knew this. The broadcast blew the informant's cover and caused him and his family to be rehoused to avoid reprisals, something later condemned by a judge as 'the height of irresponsibility'.

Nevertheless some of Watson's complaints struck a nerve, a cautionary tale of an outsider with no investigatory experience being placed in an unfamiliar situation and feeling bereft of support. It sent ID bosses back to the drawing board.

John Hector, the SIO of an intelligence-gathering team, had already been tasked with putting the covert deployments on a firmer footing and with trying to build more durable legends, the plausible biographies that such officers might need in case they were challenged. This included creating footprints that could be checked by anyone consulting official sources.

A practice of using the identities of dead children had begun in the Met in the Sixties. Names and birth dates were lifted from gravestones or public records and used to anchor a legend, sometimes even using the original birth certificates. The bereaved families were not told. Hector rejected this method even though it made his task more difficult, as it was almost impossible to create a fake birth certificate and slip it into the system. Instead he visited the National Insurance Contributions Office at Newcastle upon Tyne and made a successful pitch to senior managers there. Fake NI numbers became the bedrock of the ID's legend system, supplemented by bogus passports, driving licences and other documentation.

New opportunities for infiltration continued to arise. In the summer of 1990, French customs told the ID that one of their informants, an errant yachtsman living in southern Spain, had been approached by a British gang to sail hash from Morocco to the UK. Excitement stirred in the ID's offices when they learned that the gang was directed by Bobby Mills. A south London criminal from early adulthood, Mills had risen to become a major cannabis smuggler – bigger even than Eddie 'Ted' Cook – until brought down by a joint police-customs operation in the late seventies. Jailed for ten years, he had subsequently absconded from prison and disappeared. Now he was back in their sights.

Rather than seek his extradition from Spain, they decided to let the plot play out to see who else they could catch. Given that Mills was looking for boatmen to transport his load, a plan was hatched for the French informant to introduce a willing crew to him. They would in fact be three British customs officers. Operation Bacardi was born.

It was another first for the ID. A number of its investigators could sail, but none had ever been trained for such a visible covert role: they would have to play their part for weeks, possibly months, in full view of their criminal targets. There would be no going home each night after a day in the field; they would stay in legend around the clock until the job was done. And there would be risk, not just from the gangsters but from the sea and the weather.

John Hector approached a colleague, Dave, who had served as a captain in the customs cutter fleet and been trained on RAF air-sea rescue boats. Dave, without quite realising what he was getting into, agreed to skipper the yacht. Like his predecessors, he received no special training. He was simply told to play the part of a professional yachtsman who was not fussy about how he made money. The ID created a veneer of cover by setting him up with a bogus company called Yachtmasters, with a mailing address and business and credit cards, and obtained false passports for him and his two crew, one a qualified yachtsman, the other a trained ship's engineer.

They flew to Spain, where the informant introduced Dave to Mills in the swanky resort area of Sotogrande, near Cadiz. Dave was to sail a motor yacht provided by the informant, with a tracking beacon hidden aboard. He berthed on the boat and would hang out a Liverpool FC beach towel if he had vital news to pass on, the signal for a discreet meeting with his operational boss, who kept watch from a hotel overlooking the harbour.

The plan was for Dave and his men to sail to the coast of Morocco, where a boat would bring out the hashish to transfer to their vessel. On their first trip, however, the suppliers failed to appear. After sailing around all night looking for them, Dave moored at Ceuta, the autonomous Spanish city on the African coast. He was approached that evening by suspicious port officers, taken to a police station and quizzed for several hours, while his two colleagues slept on the boat, blissfully oblivious. He stuck to his story of engine trouble and was eventually released. Mills later told him that the delivery had been aborted because of enhanced security in the area for a surprise visit by the king of Morocco.

They tried again and this time collected 600 kilos of hashish without a hitch before turning for home. But off the coast of Portugal the weather worsened and a gale whipped up to Force 9. They lowered the sails but the mainsail ripped along the reefing line and was rendered unusable. Soon after, the engine packed up; the boat had previously been moored for so long that algae had grown in the fuel tank and blocked the filter. A filter change was only effective for half an hour before the engine stopped again. They were unable to steer the right course. Then the hydraulic steering gave up altogether.

As they drifted west, monstrous waves crashed over them. In some troughs, the tops of the crests were as high as their forty-foot mast. The anchor, stowed in blocks on the foredeck, cut loose, fell over the side and banged repeatedly against the bow, threatening to punch a hole every time a wave hit. Dave had to crawl out on a safety line to winch it back and dislocated a finger.

They rode out the storm for three days and nights, too far out to make radio contact. Eventually the engineer devised a way of filtering the contaminated fuel through a J-cloth and got the engine going, and they were able to turn and motor to Lisbon, the nearest port, for repairs. Dave called London and spent a night recovering in a luxury hotel while the boat was patched up, ready to set out again.

His crewmen had other ideas. One jumped ship to deal with a domestic issue and the other threw in the towel. Two other officers were hurriedly sent out to replace them for the final leg. One had never sailed before.

After several further adventures, they reached the English Channel and a rendezvous with the British gang's own fishing boat, which had come out from Devon. The sacks of hash were again transferred, and the fishing boat returned to Brixham. There, surveillance teams watched the shore party unload and tailed them to a motorway service station, where they were arrested.

Meanwhile Dave and his crew headed to France, prior to returning their yacht to Spain. In Cherbourg, French customs came aboard, smelt the lingering odour of cannabis and began to dismantle the boat. Dave and his fellow UCs were kept below, where they maintained their cover; one of them even stuffed the logbook down his trousers so the French wouldn't find it. 'They hounded us until I spoke to our liaison in London and someone in Paris called them off,' recalled Dave.

Dave, by now exhausted, flew back to London – where his wife was horrified to see the state of him – while another officer sailed the yacht to Portugal. Dave then took it on the final leg to Spain.

Remarkably, Mills never suspected the men of betrayal. About a year later, he contacted Dave again and asked him to do another run. But when he said he wanted him to sail into a Moroccan port to make the pick-up, HMCE management quashed it, as they had no authority to enter territorial waters and did not trust the Moroccans enough to ask their permission. (Mills was eventually caught in another sting, which involved the Special Boat Service fast-roping from a helicopter onto a merchant ship at sea and the seizure of 2.7 tonnes of cannabis, and was jailed for eleven-and-a-half years.)

The outcome was a resounding success for the new ID

approach to undercover work. Yet curiously the experienced John Hector would remain unconvinced about the value of his UCs compared to other means of intelligence gathering, such as telephone interception and informant handling. He preferred the inside-track of an informant.

'I think a live informant is the best, because you are actually getting what is happening,' he said years later. 'Second is intercept and third is undercover. The danger with undercover was that you could always be accused of creating the crime, and there's no way you can deny that. There is no way you can record meetings every time, therefore there is no way that you can stand up in court and guarantee that you never suggested the venture.' Providing transport with a boat or lorry was generally acceptable, he felt, because the undercovers were merely offering a service to people already planning a smuggle, and so could not be accused of instigating the crime.

Law enforcement had been wrestling with this dilemma for decades, and in the mid-eighties the Association of Chief Police Officers issued guidelines for any officer assigned to work on a bust-buy. The first two paragraphs read:

1. *A Police Officer must not act as an `agent provocateur'. This means he/she must not incite or procure ... a person, nor through that person anybody else ... to commit an offence, nor an offence of a more serious character, which that person would not otherwise have committed.*
2. *However, a Police Officer is entitled to join a conspiracy which is already in being, or an offence which is already 'laid on', for example, where a person had made an offer to supply goods, including drugs, which involve the commission of a criminal offence.*

The HMCE view was that a successful UC or informant was likely to be involved in the evidential chain and therefore would usually be expected to testify or at least have their role raised in court. They felt that the act of transporting drugs was a crucial part of a trafficking offence and so it was right to disclose if a UC or informant had been involved, otherwise the court might be misled. They could still be protected by giving evidence under a pseudonym and from behind a screen. If it was unlikely that their anonymity could be maintained, HMCE would sometimes decline to prosecute, instead contenting themselves with seizing the smuggled drugs.

The Metropolitan Police and the Regional Crime Squads disagreed. The Met in particular had beefed up its own commitment to such operations under a new commissioner, Sir Kenneth Newman, who had previously served as chief constable of the Royal Ulster Constabulary and who applied some of the lessons learned from covert work in Northern Ireland. The Met claimed there was ample precedent for starting the prosecution evidence from a later point in the sequence of events, thus hiding the existence of an initial covert source.

However, the courts had determined while there was a public interest in protecting an informant, there was an even stronger interest in allowing defendants to have a fair trial. That might mean being allowed to know who the informant or UC was, or at least being allowed to cross-examine them vigorously. In drug-running cases, operational bosses sought a compromise between the polarized views of police and customs, namely the introduction of at least two undercover officers, one of whom would be disclosed. This remained unsatisfactory, however.

It was in this ambiguous, changing environment that a new team was born. At its heart was 'Guy Stanton'.

5

TRANSFORMATION

I never knew why my bosses chose me.

I was approached to go undercover shortly after returning from my trip to India. Senior management probably had me down as a loud and irreverent guy, a bit of a raconteur. I had a lot of front and was known for being part of a team that wrote comedy scripts for our annual ID dinner, a raucous, boozy affair in which we lampooned each other and our managers in sketches and song. They must have felt I was the type of character that would not buckle under social pressure or shy away from confrontation.

They told me they were launching a special covert unit to target the major criminals flooding the UK with drugs. Like everyone in the firm, I had heard about the debacle of the guy we had picked from the military to pose as an airport baggage handler. It was a mistake. Some of my relatives worked at airports and I knew how tight-knit the crews were. It was like trying to plant a stranger into a family business and I am sure he was sussed straight away.

In consequence, we decided to use our own people rather than outsiders, and I was one of a handful asked to apply. I thought it couldn't be any worse than trying to do interviews in Bombay. In truth, it sounded like everything I wanted from the job.

By then, Jo and I knew we wanted to spend our lives together. Fortunately she knew the demands of the job, felt that under-cover work would come naturally to me, and urged me to go for it. Selflessly she agreed to move down to London to start this new life. We bought a house and planned to get married. But my new career path would test our relationship to the limit.

I was still on the nightclub team but my SIO, Dave Parker, a great mate, released me to start building a legend. We had no undercover training course of our own, so I had to pick up tips from colleagues who had done it in the past. Mike Stephenson, who had worked on numerous clandestine assign-ments, was a big help. Eddie, who had broken new ground on Operation Quest five years before, also came to see me and talked through the lessons he had learned. In particular, he recounted how he had attended an operational briefing and heard that his target was sometimes called 'Ted', which he would not otherwise have known. When he later let this slip in a meet with the target, it nearly brought disaster. I took this on board and made sure that I was kept away from our teams so as not to be contaminated by their knowledge.

Otherwise I had to suck it and see. My early deployments were what we called bust-buy. The first notable one was a potential heroin deal in Glasgow, in an operation run by our regional office there. This Asian gang claimed to have a large amount of smack for sale. We finagled an introduction and told them we had £1 million in cash ready to go, and were prepared to let them see it. We then persuaded a bank to lend us the cash, in freshly printed twenties and fifties, which we piled into four holdalls as flash money. Our plan was to show it to them in a secure vault, usefully covered by CCTV. They would come into the bank, see me flash the cash and be caught on camera, which would be invaluable evidence.

Like all big deals, it took some setting up. One slight hitch was that it coincided with the date of my wedding to

Jo back in London. I should have been at home to help with the arrangements but found myself in Scotland for weeks on end. Jo had to buy both our rings, enduring the humiliation of watching another loving couple choosing theirs together in the same jeweller's while I was absent. She organised the caterers, tidied the garden, scrubbed the house and dealt with a thousand details.

Our big day was set for a Saturday. I was due home the Thursday before, but the job was at a critical juncture. On the Friday morning, I phoned her with bad news.

'I'm still in Scotland,' I said meekly.

For once on our life together, Jo snapped. 'Do I ever cause you any grief?' she said.

'No dear.'

'Have I ever been stroppy about your work?'

'No dear.'

'Then get your arse down here. Now!' She slammed down the phone.

My bosses relented and I flew home on the next plane. Jo handed me an overnight case and my suit, and I went to my mum and dad's for the night. The wedding went off perfectly, just a small family affair – and I was banned from taking any calls for the day.

In the end the Glasgow job fell down when the Asians' top man could not deliver. He turned out to be more of a talker than a doer, as would often be the case. I banked what I had learned, chalked it down to experience, and moved on to the next one.

In 1990, John Hector shifted to a cocaine team and another SIO, Keith Bowen, took over the task of organising the fledgling UCs. It remained a part-time role, as Bowen also had his own team to run, specialising in drugs intelligence. He inherited three or four officers who already had crude legends and asked a number of others if they would like to join his new covert unit.

Bowen looked at the training methods of others to see what he could learn. His first port of call was the Metropolitan Police, which in 1988 had created SO10, a formalised branch deploying undercover officers against serious crime. Prior to this, police UCs were deployed on a localised basis with no central policy or guidance – sometimes with disastrous results.

In the mid-eighties, the Met had sent plain-clothes detectives to mingle among the football hooligan 'firms' that were causing havoc around the capital. Gangs from West Ham, Millwall, Chelsea and Arsenal were prosecuted with evidence gathered by the officers. But all of the trials subsequently collapsed or were lost on appeal when it emerged that some of the officers had lied about making contemporaneous notes or claimed to have witnessed fights when they had not. In all, nearly 150 convicted men were acquitted.

Determined to avoid such fiascos, SO10 designed a 'specialist operations' training course to professionalise the role. Every police UC was issued with a small report book to record the times, dates and details of their contacts, as well as six short instructions on conduct. An officer could not act as an agent provocateur, but was entitled to join a conspiracy which was already in effect; could participate in an offence if it was suggested by others; and could use 'the weapon of infiltration of groups or organisations'. The instructions concluded: 'Invariably this means you enter a criminal conspiracy or become part of a pre-arranged criminal offence.' Under Section 78 of the Police and Criminal Evidence Act (PACE), a judge would take into account how evidence was obtained when considering the fairness of any court proceedings.

Like their customs counterparts, most SO10-trained UCs were still not deployed full-time, and long-term infiltrations were infrequent. Many simultaneously worked on specialist crime squads, such as the famous Flying Squad, or in busy CID offices. If called on for covert deployment, they had to obtain permission from their immediate boss, which was not always given. Sometimes they maintained their normal day jobs while working covertly in the evening or at weekends. While this could be exciting, juggling two distinct roles was stressful and problematic.

Bowen found other things about the Met system that he did not like. SO10 focused on buying drugs, weapons and stolen goods, to the extent that UCs were referred to as 'buyers' in their written guidance. Customs investigations, targeted as they were at cross-border smuggling, often required a different covert role, perhaps in transport or logistics. The police also let their UCs interact with their operational teams, which Bowen disliked. Nor did they have a single designated handler for each UC; sometimes one sergeant might be handling up to half a dozen at the same time, which was too many.

Bowen cast his net further afield, looking at the methods used by both MI5 and MI6 and by foreign police forces, but was not convinced they would work for the ID either. Then came a chance meeting that would have a profound impact on British law enforcement. In late 1990 a colleague of Bowen's attended a national police conference and heard a talk on undercover operations by a detective from Greater Manchester Police. Henri Exton led the Omega Squad, which had enjoyed great success infiltrating football hooligan gangs in the Manchester area. He had also devised his own training course, using psychological methods and a handler system for each UC.

It was, for the ID, a light-bulb moment. 'He had the keys to the door,' recalled Bowen. 'His method was just what we wanted. The difference between his training and the Met's was the thought process that the trainees had to go through. They were taken to the lowest of low points and their reactions gauged. He would leave them alone with a lot of uncertainties about what was going to happen next, whereas SO10 was more of a classroom situation.'

Bowen met Exton in January 1991. The next day, the two of them gave a presentation to senior ID managers in a closed office. The audience included the chief investigation officer, Doug Tweddle, his deputy, Terry Byrne, and Nick Baker, the assistant chief in charge of Branch Ten, which ran intelligence-gathering. Bowen's pitch for greater professionalism was well received. 'Exton was very impressive,' recalled one of those present. 'He was easy to like, that was one of his skills, he could ingratiate himself with anybody.' The chiefs decided to commit more resources to Bowen's Intel H team and to move it into Baker's branch. Bowen was also told to write some operational guidelines for undercover work, as the ID had none.

At that time the ID had around a thousand investigators, from among whom Bowen was to build his small volunteer unit. He met various prospects over the next few weeks, some from the regional offices in Birmingham, Bristol, Glasgow and Manchester. Next, he began to prepare fake CVs for those chosen, contacting the Inland Revenue, the Department of Social Security and other official bodies to create back-up records. He consulted the Driver and Vehicle Licensing Agency about obtaining driving licences in pseudonyms, the Passport Office about creating fake passports, and the Health and Safety Executive about the risks inherent in tasks such as long-haul lorry-driving and deep-sea diving. There were business fronts to set up at Companies House and heavy-goods-vehicle tests to arrange. He met with the Royal Yacht Association and travelled to the Registry of Shipping and Seamen, in Cardiff, to acquire sailing qualifications and build legends of boat ownership.

Bowen wanted to put his UCs into the areas where they could have the most impact on the drug trade, including logistics and the movement of money. He knew it would not succeed overnight and that he needed 'thinkers, not gung ho types'. His team began to take shape.

That February, two ID officers became the first to attend Exton's GMP training course in Manchester. Three more followed over the next two months. Bowen also spoke to SO10 about sending his tyros on their course in north London. But when the Met heard what he was planning, they were distinctly unhappy. They protested that the ID's move into regular UC work could lead to blue-on-blue incidents, where both police and customs officers worked on the same case without knowing it. HMCE thought their fears were overblown, if not deliberately exaggerated, an attempt by the police to protect their turf from incursion by another agency. Ultimately the cops could not stop them, and agreed to take them on their course.

Having evaluated both the London and Manchester police courses, Bowen drafted guidelines for his unit and submitted them for approval. None of his recruits had distinct alter egos at that stage. 'My intention was to make sure they had the proper handler and were in the right scenario,' said Bowen. Their intelligence would go directly to operational teams, to support seizures and arrests. He then started sending his best prospects to the SO10 course at Hendon in north London. They included the man who would become 'Guy Stanton'.

There were initially just five of us working to Keith, a talented SIO and a cerebral bloke. I knew the other four, all good lads, though one of them left the team quite early.

Although I had already been working undercover, I had to get through the training process, a system with more failures than passes. I took the SO10 course in the autumn of 1991. The instructors – Peter H, Larry C, Dick H, Graham C, Jason

S – were all experienced detectives who had been there and done it on the street. They tried to pass on all they knew and I owe them a debt for their patience and dedication. Having themselves been deployed against some of the most dangerous gangs in the UK, they knew how to deal with criminals in their own world. They also gave me a grounding in the creation of a fake persona.

Much of the course was classroom-based but we also engaged with 'criminals' in various scenarios. One was a mock kidnap. Another test was to go to Hendon Underground station to buy a stick of dynamite. At a prearranged meet with some guys, one of them started to get heavy with me, to test my reaction. I have always boxed, and I told him bluntly, 'I'm a good fighter and a very good dirty fighter. Now go and stand over there.' And he did.

The most impressive instructor, Peter H, was a superb UC in his own right, and in a long career had featured in a number of trials that had helped to establish legal precedents. It was he who, nearly twenty years earlier, had testified in a celebrated case in which he had agreed to buy a large amount of booze from a gang, only to find they had not yet stolen it. Questions were raised about whether he had encouraged a crime that would not otherwise have taken place, but the Appeal Court found he had not. This helped encapsulate the notion of a laid-on offence, where a crime is already in the minds of the criminals and the UC merely goes along with it.

We went through examples which tested the boundaries of this notion. Contrary to popular belief, there is no defence of entrapment in English law, although it may be considered in mitigation of sentence after conviction. What a UC or informant cannot do is act as an *agent provocateur* to persuade someone to commit a crime. An example would be if a drug dealer said, 'I can give you half a kilo of blow,' and you said, 'That's no good, I want five kilos of heroin.'

Generally the judiciary took a realistic view. In 1992 the Court of Appeal upheld the convictions of two men who had sold stolen goods to Stardust Jewellers, a secondhand store set up by the police to trap thieves. Despite pleading guilty at trial, the men appealed, claiming they had been tricked. In another judgment, the Appeal Court found against two men who had separately approached undercover officers to murder their wives. They argued the officers had been *agents provocateurs* and that by posing as contract killers had obtained covert recordings by entrapment. These pleas of unfairness fell on stony judicial ground.

An important phrase for UCs was 'due enthusiasm'. During his stolen booze case, Peter H had been asked by the gang if he could get them some bolt-cutters to raid the warehouse. Given that they were already planning the crime, he was okay to go along with it. This was more problematic in areas like football hooliganism, where it is hard for a UC to appear authentic without actually having a fight at some stage – which would itself be a criminal act and also might harm another person.

Training was the easy part. Heading off into the real world was entirely different. I spent a year building up a skeleton legend: where I was from, who I knew, where I lived, what I did, getting seen and getting known. I needed a deep, unassailable character – someone who really existed.

I would eventually have three legends. My first fake name was 'Gary Stevens', which served me well on my early deployments. My main one, with the deepest and most foolproof background, would be 'Guy Stanton'. The third, 'Mike Standring', was what we called an 'escape' legend, which I rarely used but was there when needed. Each of these characters had slightly different personality traits, depending on what I thought was most suitable for that particular deployment.

I continued to dip in and out of operations but only in walk-on parts. The ID always had dozens of cases on the go and a request might come at short notice for someone to pose as a buyer, a driver or a minder. This gave me experience and helped to burnish my legend among the criminal fraternity. What my bosses wanted, however, was something deeper than the crash-bang-wallop of a bust-buy or a controlled delivery. They wanted long-term intelligence-gathering that could take us to the dark heart of the narcotics trade. This would require a different mental toolkit.

And so I was sent to covert offices in Manchester for training with a deeper psychological bent. It was less about acting the wideboy and more about coping with the stress and hidden fear of working incognito. Intensive, indeed mind-blowing, the training was run by Henri Exton. I regard him as one of the best UCs ever, having operated all over the world in different environments against many targets. He had no precursor; so far as I know, he devised the course himself. I nicknamed him 'the Raven' for his dark, foreboding looks.

Anyone, Henri argued, can go out and buy illegal contraband: drugs, stolen cars, blank MOTs, prescriptions, passports, guns. The real challenge of undercover work is handling pressure, isolation and paranoia. His course was designed to test if you had the mental strength for the job. To find out, Henri and his team would subject you to maximum duress. You were never told how long the course would last or what lay ahead each day. Instead you were bounced into real-time situations in the real world, day after day, to see how you coped.

One morning, one of his trainers told me the name of a pub in a particularly rough area of a large industrial town. I was to go there and find a man called Paulie, a low-level street dealer who sold small wraps of cannabis and coke. Apart from a vague physical description, I had nothing to go on. My task was to pose as a buyer and convince Paulie to take me to a bigger supplier, who I then had to 'get into' – win his confidence and negotiate a substantial buy.

'They don't sell anything. You go in there as a man to be turned into a woman.'

'What?'

'I don't have time to explain. We're pulling up now. You've got your brief. Go on, off you go.'

He pointed me to a shop. Judging by the window, it appeared to sell clothing and other products for transvestites and people of fluid gender. The sign above the door said *Transformation*.

Degsy dropped it right on my toes. I stood outside, looked at the display mannequins in flimsy dresses, thigh-length boots and man-sized stilettos, and took a deep breath. A big, burly geezer with a stubble beard, I doubt I was anyone's idea of a typical cross-dresser. But I have never been homophobic, sexist or racist. Be who you want, is my outlook. In I went.

'Hello,' I said to a girl behind the counter. 'I wonder if you can help me. I've taken to wearing the wife's underwear and clothes but they are a bit small.'

'Yes?' said the girl, with an understanding look.

'I wonder, is there some advice you can give me and any clothes I can look at?'

'We can sort this out, no problem, love. If you wait there.' She indicated a small waiting lounge with seating. 'Tea or coffee?'

I sat down. The wall facing me was covered with Polaroids of blokes posing in dresses.

Another man came in and sat down. A thin chap in middle age, he was wearing red latex thigh boots, the full kit.

'Hello,' he said, 'who are you?'

I spun him some yarn, then told him how natty his outfit was.

'I'm a civil servant,' he said. 'My name is Richard, but for two weeks of every year I become Loretta. I dress like this and drive around the country having adventures.'

Another man came in. He picked up some magazines, took them to the counter to pay and joked with the staff, who seemed to know him. Obviously a regular. Only later did I find out he was one of Henri's team and had dropped in to see how I was doing. He said the funniest sight was me trying to drink my coffee without touching the cup. Well, maybe I was a bit cautious.

I was in there for a good hour, trying on clothes, chatting and learning as much as I could about the place. The girls behind the counter were helpful and obviously trained to deal with shy or embarrassed customers. They gave me notes on what to do and I bought one of their magazines. It helpfully had a plan of the shop, which I could show to my trainer.

When I left, I noticed what appeared to be a utility crew working on a public telephone kiosk nearby. As I walked away, they started shouting and calling me names: 'Gayboy! Go on, fuck off, go to another town, take your dirty habits with you!' This, of course was another part of the test, to gauge my reaction. I ignored them and walked up the road, where Degsy picked me up.

I wrote all of my notes and handed them in. I had passed with flying colours.

Big Pete went after me. Pete had been recruited into the ID after many years serving in the Special Air Service. He was a killing machine, afraid of no man. But the examiners saw him eye the window display with evident distaste, and he walked past the shop two or three times before entering. He was obviously struggling with the task.

In he went like a bulldozer, straight up to the counter and said, 'Do you want to buy some porn videos?' They threw him out.

As poor old Pete stood in the street, the lads in the kiosk started calling, 'Whoo-oo, gayboy.' He gave them his thousand-yard stare and for a moment, they later recalled, it looked like he was going to rampage over and dismember the lot of them. Fortunately he didn't.

To be fair to Pete, it was something that, as a long-serving soldier, he had never been exposed to. I had grown in inner-city schools surrounded by females, and had no qualms about going in.

When we finished the course, I asked Henri about the purpose of the visit to *Transformation*, which was a genuine, well-established store with no links to illegality of any kind.

'What do you think the test is?' he asked back.

'Obviously to see if you can get the intelligence. But is it an attack on your sexuality?'

'Exactly. To see how you cope with that. What happens, there are two checks. One is the threat to your sexuality, can you handle it? The other is a test of integrity, because we have had subjects leave the shop with items or literature and not hand them over. They might have a personal preference that we didn't know about. Now if they are prepared to do that in a test, what might they do on a real job? If they left a meet with some gear or cash, could you be sure they would declare it to their handler?' Henri said it was one of the hardest tests.

Another trial was an interview scenario, in which the student pretended to be a hardcore criminal resisting a police interrogation across a table. During the course of the questioning, the interviewer suddenly reached out and put his hands on yours, in a gentle way, and said, 'I don't know how to say this but ...' The student would often tense and pull away. The interrogator has won then, he is suddenly in charge, having disconcerted and wrongfooted the interviewee. Another interesting lesson.

Henri and his team kept on us at all times, akin to elite military selection. The most physically arduous test was nicknamed 'Long Day'. Towards the end of the course, the instructors told us how well we were all doing and took us for a slap-up curry, washed down with copious amounts of

lager. Everyone was ready to decompress and we all got out-
rageously drunk, until finally crashing out in the small hours.

Two hours later, at around 5 a.m., we were rousted from
out beds and told to muster. Four of us were ushered into the
back of a transit van and driven for nearly an hour, our heads
pounding, some of us vomiting. When the doors opened, we
appeared to be on the bleak Pennine moors between Lancashire
and Yorkshire. I was dropped in a valley by a small tarn and a
sheep pen. The only route in and out was a farm track. I was
handed a twenty pence piece and a card with a number on it.
and was told to get back to central Manchester and ring the
number at 6 p.m. I would be watched and was not allowed to
call anyone else or to steal anything that might assist me. They
drove off to drop the others elsewhere, leaving me alone.

Wearing just jeans, a jumper and a top-grade hangover, I
set off up the track to try to find a road. I ended up walking
twenty miles back to Manchester. It rained most of the way.

Big Pete did much better, managing to cadge a couple of
lifts despite his forbidding appearance. At one stage he passed
me in a lorry while I trudged along in the drizzle. Of course he
didn't stop, and quite right too. He was also picked up in a car
by a lady with two kids. When she dropped him off he scolded
her never to do that again, because of the risk.

I finally got back into town, made my call, and was simply
told, 'Go to the Railway Tavern.' I quickly managed to locate
the pub but still had no money. That was no obstacle because I
was back in my comfort zone. I spotted an old bloke at a table,
looking at the horses in his newspaper, and sat down near him.

'Can I borrow your paper, mate?' I asked. 'I just want to
look at the form.'

'Sure,' he said. 'Do you like the horses?'

'Oh yeah.'

We started talking and before long he said, 'Do you want
a pint?'

'That's good of you, I'll have a Guinness.'

Now I had a drink and a reason to be in the pub. You don't want to be sitting there potless and alone and have the barman ask what are you doing.

Some of the other lads began to appear and sit in different spots around the pub, all studiously pretending not to know each other. Then Henri arrived. He summoned us all together and told us to stand down. Then he went mad.

'Well done, all of you. You're all in the wrong fucking pub. You were supposed to observe a major incident and you have all missed it. Congratulations. What a bunch of clowns.'

All being so tired and hungover, none of us had questioned if there were two Railway Taverns in Manchester. Of course, there were. It showed the need to pass the information clearly and correctly, and not to jump to premature conclusions. Information has to be right. You can't be saying to an operational team, 'Well I think this smuggle is going to happen on Monday at Dover. Or it could be Tuesday at Folkestone. Maybe Wednesday at Tilbury.' The team needs to know. They have plans to make and manpower to organise, brief and equip.

The ID later adopted this test for its own training course in London: there is a historic pub on Fleet Street called Ye Olde Cheshire Cheese and another called the Cheshire Cheese nearby at Temple. You always get a leader in group activity, someone who takes over by force of personality, and they would invariably lead people to the famous pub without thinking there might be another one.

As a southerner, training in Manchester was doubly hard because I had no sense of place. They could run scenarios in locations that were unfamiliar to me. On one excursion I was taken by a big, hard-looking Liverpudlian called Scouse to an old, deserted cinema on a buy. The street was dark and deserted and it all felt a bit lairy, especially when Scouse turned to me and said, 'Give us your money.' I had £50 on me and was not sure I should part with it so easily.

'No, I'll make the buy,' I said.

'I ain't going to sit here and row with you pal,' he growled. 'You give me the wedge, I get the stuff, bring it out and give it to you. That's it.'

Wanting to pass the test, I gave him the money and off he went. Five minutes later it dawned on me that he was not coming back. Scouse had gone into the cinema and out the back, where a car picked him up. I had been royally turned over

I later found out that I had been chosen for this humiliation deliberately, because that day Nick Baker and Terry Byrne had come up for the day to see me operating. I was ripped off in front of my own masters. I was told I had failed the test and was sent home for the weekend. I drove back that night, a Friday, feeling utterly defeated, convinced I had blown the course. Jo calls it the worst night of our marriage.

Henri had told me to phone him the next evening, a Saturday, at the ridiculously precise time of three minutes past seven. I watched the clock all day, grumpy and monosyllabic, sure that I was about to be canned. At the allotted time I called Henri, expecting the worst.

He told me it was just one test and I was still on the course. Suddenly I was all smiles again. I found out later that Terry and Nick were told in advance that I was going to fail; my failure was built-in. They wanted to see how I reacted.

The last test saw each student taken into a room and told to imagine a scenario. Mine was that I had infiltrated a gang and was with them inside a motor garage. My assessor said, 'Someone suddenly comes in and confronts you and says he knows that you're an undercover officer. What would you do?'

'I would deny it,' I said.

'Right, he has picked up a wrench and has hit and incapacitated you, you are now on the floor.'

'I would still deny it.'

'They have picked you up and tied you to a chair, your head is bleeding and you're groggy and in great pain. They tell you they will really hurt you if you don't confess. What do you do?'

'Deny it completely.'

Basically I kept denying it until they killed me. Which was not the ideal outcome.

Big Pete, on the other hand, knew how to react because of his army training. Once his life was under imminent threat, he started to make admissions. What happens, apparently, is that the torturers dial down the punishment because they want to know more. It pushes away the immediate risk of death and increases the possibility that help will arrive or some other event will intervene. The military call it 'slow release under torture' and Pete did it to perfection. I did not.

Nevertheless, Henri told me I had passed the course. In fact, he confided, his lads said I had 'eaten up' most of the tests, high praise from such a savvy bunch. I had certainly found it fascinating, if brutal. I learned that I could endure setbacks and remain focused and positive. Two of Henri's expressions in particular stayed with me: 'Anxiety causes deafness' and 'Never get caught in a lie'. They would prove invaluable over the next few years.

Henri then challenged me to one of the most satisfying tasks of my career: creating my legend. This would be my alter ego when in deep cover, perhaps for many years. As such, it had to be real to me and to everyone I encountered in my new, secret life.

I had to create Guy Stanton from scratch. He would become a real person, down to the smallest detail. And he would not be alone.

6

THE BETRAYERS

Beta Projects was born in 1992 when Ray Pettit took over an empty room in the ID headquarters at Harmsworth House, an art deco office block in the historic City of London. Named after Alfred Harmsworth, the legendary magnate who spread popular journalism in Britain by founding both the Daily Mail and the Daily Mirror, the building stood at the traditional heart of the newspaper industry, on the corner of Bouverie Street, which had housed the area's first printworks and been home to the News of the World and the News Chronicle (first editor: Charles Dickens). Fleet Street itself was just yards away.

As the newspapers gradually moved out to newer, bigger offices elsewhere, the customs investigators moved in, having outgrown their own home in nearby New Fetter Lane. The legal profession was also prominent in the area: just a few yards to the west were the Tudor Gates, leading to Inner Temple and the Inns of Court. Facing the gates was the Witness Box pub, a drinking den well used by lawyers, investigators and hacks. Long a den of cynicism and intrigue, where reputations were made overnight and just as quickly destroyed, Harmsworth House was a fitting place to launch the Betrayers.

Ray Pettit was well chosen to run a team that would often

face setbacks, having lived with his own disappointment. As a young Yorkshire footballer, he made fifty-one league appearances for Barnsley FC – during which he scored his one and only professional goal – and seventy-nine for Hull City before injury cut short his career. Somehow he ended up processing VAT claims in an office in Southend.

Then a news story caught his eye. Pettit read how an ID investigator, Terry Byrne, had jumped onto the wing of a small aircraft to stop it taking off during a dramatic drug bust. The daring tale inspired him to apply to the ID. 'It was an exclusive club,' he recalled. 'You had to be a certain kind of character to join, and certainly to stay. The most important thing was that it was all for one and one for all.' The team ethic was strong in Pettit.

He passed selection and eventually joined a team investigating cannabis smuggling, mainly through the ports and airports of southern England. He learned the basics of surveillance and interviewing and how to improvise on fast-moving jobs. He graduated to Drugs B and C, two of the ID's so-called target teams, which worked on the juiciest cases. Pettit was made the case officer on Operation Quest, the long-running probe that saw his colleague Eddie infiltrate a major smuggling gang. It was his first exposure to the value, and risks, of undercover work.

Pettit was tailing someone in tandem with Eddie one day when his colleague was stopped by a man in the street. Pettit kept walking and crossed the road. After a short conversation, the two men parted and Eddie caught up with Pettit. He said the man was a villain he had met a few days before while undercover, and Eddie had had to invent a story on the spot to explain what he was doing. The experience stayed with Pettit, and formed the germ of an idea that UCs needed to be kept apart from their day-to-day workmates as much as possible.

After a stint on an intelligence team, Pettit had impressed his bosses enough to be asked to take over the role of SIO of Intel H from Keith Bowen, who moved to a senior post at Heathrow Airport. He inherited fewer than a dozen part-time UCs. Just a handful had any relevant experience and even they still did regular work for their own teams, while the tactics for penetrating crime groups were still crude. Pettit was told the undercover unit would be beefed up, better resourced and properly trained. Renamed Beta Projects, it would also become full-time.

The new SIO post was much coveted within the division, and two more experienced colleagues took Pettit to the pub to try to talk him out of it, as both wanted the job themselves. They failed, and in April 1992 he took over managing the team. He began with just one other officer to assist him.

After meeting the UCs and explaining how things were going to change, Pettit saw some drop out, deterred by the prospect of long hours and stress. The best and keenest were removed from their operational teams permanently and would no longer have to conduct surveillance, arrests or interviews on other jobs. Knowing they could no longer be seen entering Harmsworth House, he found a remote office for them to meet in or work from when necessary.

Providing the right training was essential for a full-time team and in that regard Pettit became another disciple of the enigmatic Manchester cop Henri Exton. 'He frightened me at the start,' recalled Pettit. 'He unsettled you and was always testing. For example, he would get in your car and slip the handbrake on when you were distracted, to see how you would react.' Pettit was soon a convert and Exton's advice continued to be invaluable in the expansion of Beta Projects and the tutelage of its officers.

Pettit's duties also included overseeing a tiny unit that planted listening devices and cameras in buildings and vehicles. Some years before, Nick Baker had attended an army surveillance course and met a number of Intelligence Corps officers. With those contacts, he and Pettit recruited a small method-of-entry team of ex-soldiers, some of whom had honed their skills in Northern Ireland. It included two expert locksmiths who could open any gate, door or window and could put tracking beacons on motor vehicles and boats. They were quickly nicknamed 'the Burglars', much to their dislike, as they argued that burglary victims know when their house has been entered, whereas the point of their job was total stealth. The repository of their 'product' was a secure room in Custom House, on the north bank of the Thames, known only to a handful of people and christened 'Stonehouse' after a Tory MP who had vanished after faking his own death.

Pettit was keen to get cracking, but his first big task was to handle the fallout from a job that went wrong. Operation Zulu Cricket had been a joint venture with the Metropolitan Police, arising after a tip from a DEA informant, 'Miguel', that a British-based organisation was willing to supply up to twenty kilos of heroin a week to the USA. The group had possible terrorist links and access to guns, and one of them was a former RUC officer from Ulster.

Miguel flew from Boston, Massachusetts, to London to meet the gang and then briefed three British UCs: two SO10 detectives and 'Carlos', a swarthy ID investigator of Gibraltarian extraction. The plan was to introduce them as interested local buyers. Carlos took the lead role as the financier and flashed £750,000 to the gang in a safety deposit room at the Selfridges store in west London. A large heroin deal was agreed. A police UC, 'Bleks', would collect the drugs from a gang member at the Hilton Hotel at Gatwick Airport while Carlos simultaneously paid the money to the former RUC officer at the Selfridges store.

In June 1992, armed police stood ready to make arrests

after the handovers. One of the gang duly arrived at the Hilton with a heavy holdall and was given a room set up with secret video and audio. There he met Bleks and weighed and tested the drugs. He was arrested leaving the room. In the meantime, Carlos met the other trafficker near Selfridges. They waited to hear confirmation from the Hilton that the drugs had been delivered, but when no phone call came, they split up without exchanging the money.

Other gang members were subsequently taped discussing whether Bleks was a cop and deciding to put a hit on him. The informant, Miguel, tried to maintain the pretence that all was well and set up another meet with the gang, but they were suspicious and kept cancelling. Then Miguel was paged to call a telephone in an Irish bar in Boston. 'You're fucking dead,' he was told. The case went cold.

Given the threat to life, Pettit moved Carlos and his family from their home and arranged new housing and schooling for his children. The experience proved useful when Pettit later became responsible within the ID for the protection and, if necessary, relocation of any such witnesses deemed to be under threat, but it was another addition to his heavy workload.

Most crime groups accepted arrest as an occupational hazard, but some of the more capricious vowed revenge. Having to testify in court could blow an officer's legend, potentially exposing them to retribution while also revealing any secret assets, such as boats, lorries, a warehouse or a yard, that Beta had used. The UC concerned might have to relocate for an extended period or even leave Beta altogether. Branch Ten had to devise clever ways to maintain the integrity of its investigations while also protecting its staff and informants.

'The main difficulty was trying to hide the infiltration,' said Pettit. 'We might have an informant tell his handler that an organisation was running drugs in from the Continent and

was looking for a lorry driver. One of the operational officers would ring me and we would discuss if an infiltration was feasible. Under our direction, the informant would then tell the organisation that he knew a driver who needed money, and would introduce Officer A to them. Officer A would meet them and spin a story that he couldn't do the delivery but he knew someone who could, and would then introduce them to Officer B. Sometimes B would also pull out, he might suddenly "fall ill" or be "sent abroad", but would introduce them to Officer C. By that time, you had moved several steps away from the original informant.

'So Officer C would meet them. They might quiz him, ask who he worked for and how long he had been driving. He might take them to one of our warehouses, show them his lorry, all his paperwork. All our men were self-employed owner-drivers. With our Dutch, Belgian and French friends it became a European collaboration, we could show that the guy had been driving to Europe regularly.

'When it all went tits up for them, hopefully the opposition were left baffled as to how a customs officer had got into their organisation. They would not know at which step things had gone wrong, and the idea was that they would never be able to apportion blame to the original informant.'

Pettit also fostered a strong relationship with the military. Drug investigations were becoming both more complex and more international in scope, and HMCE was starting to work regularly with Special Forces on major operations requiring, for example, interdiction at sea. Pettit met senior officers of both the SAS and the Royal Navy's Special Boat Service, whose elite commandos were experts at fast, stealthy action against dangerous threats. The different teams became close and Beta began to send officers to their military bases to train.

Branch Ten, in which Pettit's team resided, was a complete covert branch, housing the Alpha phone-tapping unit as well as liaising with the security and intelligence services, something that was to become even more important after the Security Service Act of 1996. The huge flow of intel Branch Ten provided was the foundation on which the operational teams, housed in other branches, were built, and their capabilities became known by the informal label 'Black Box'.

In November 1992 the ID produced its first ever Guidelines for Handling Informants, *an amalgamation of previous policy and advice. Managing UCs would prove to be one of the trickiest jobs in the division. 'The hardest work I ever did,' said Pettit. Fortunately he was an inspired choice.*

Ray turned out to be a great boss. He was keen and enthusiastic, supported his troops and did his best to ensure that we had proper training and equipment. Above all, he watched out for our safety. In return, we ribbed him mercilessly and drove him mad with our demands.

In his younger days, Ray had been a pro footballer. He had the build and the seventies haircut but lacked pace. He would tell of playing against the great Rodney Marsh, who swerved and nutmegged him so often that the crowd took to chanting 'Olé!' each time. It was, said Ray, the worst day of his life.

Years later, when our UC team was established, we entertained a delegation of Japanese police. Ray was chatting to some dignitaries in a crowded room when, to his horror, he saw the whole Japanese delegation perform a human wave and shout, 'Olé!' He bounded over, to be greeted by the leader of the visiting party, who spoke decent English.

'You, Ray, I remember you against Rodney Marsh many year ago. Olé!'

'Fuck off,' said Ray, forgetting where he was. He then stared hard at me. 'What have you been telling them?'

'Nothing.'

'Bleeding liar,' said Ray as he stalked off. It was one of the best tenners I ever spent. To this day Ray still isn't sure if his fame really did reach as far as Japan.

We all felt Ray had our welfare at heart. One of the first Beta jobs involved a violent thug who had escaped from prison while serving a term for attempted murder. Through an informant who knew him, we found out that he was in the London area and was trying to import drugs to raise money. One of my UC colleagues, Harvey, was able to arrange a meet with him on a train platform at Canary Wharf, ostensibly to help with his smuggling plan.

It was a brief meet, with Harvey palming him a piece of paper with his contact details after a short chat. Afterwards, I collected him and we drove back to Custom House on the River Thames, where we had offices. I made sure to park well away from the building, but we still had to walk down Sugar Quay to go in. As we did so, two river buses motored past each other and one of them loudly sounded its hooter, making everybody look round.

'Bloody hell,' said Harvey, 'suppose the target was on that boat? He might have just seen me walking to Custom House.'

We went straight up to see Ray. 'We are not doing this right,' complained Harvey. 'We can't be coming in here where people can see us.' To his credit, Ray took us in to see Nick Baker and he agreed. It was decided the UCs would no longer openly enter customs buildings, and soon afterwards we secretly rented some unobtrusive premises on the edge of London to meet when necessary.

The coda to that job was that our target never managed to import any drugs, as the closer it got to the date of his importation, the more erratic and dangerous his behaviour became. In the end it was decided to arrest him as an abscondee, for the safety of the public. These were decisions we sometimes had to make.

Running the team was like wrangling cats. Ray had to cope with a bunch of super-egos, mine included. We all thought we were the best. Like screaming chicks in a nest, we would climb over one another to get the tastiest jobs, and each of us always thought his was the most important. But when the chips were down, you couldn't meet a better team.

Above Ray was Assistant Chief Nick Baker, an urbane wine connoisseur, golfer and scourge of my expenses claims. He also had a wealth of experience as an investigator and numerous contacts in other agencies. He and Ray built up Beta Projects by careful selection. The odd maniac did seep through but did not last long. They wanted people with experience, and the team they chose had a lot. It grew and changed over the years, but the main players, with Ray as ringmaster and shoulder to cry on, remained fairly constant.

Transport is a core element of drug trafficking and it was decided that the assembly of a convincing pool of sailors was crucial for Beta to succeed. Here our senior man was Big Pete, ex-Special Forces, an experienced skipper and utterly fearless. He was joined by Eccles, a gangly south Londoner, who was also a skilled sailor; Chameleon, a Royal Marines reservist and general crew member with a lethal sense of humour; Pigpen, a trained yachtsman; Mungo, a Geordie crewman and handy fighter in a tight spot; and Chelsea, a deckhand and fixer.

Lorry transport was another key service and Charlton, another strong character, was our best HGV driver. Keef was our main money launderer and financial guru, while Little Tony, a Mackem or native of Sunderland, also dabbled as a money man. Sheen and Elvis were two excellent general UCs and even better handlers; Big Fella, an Irish giant, was a good all-round hand; Badger, a Plumstead boy, was an expert in gypsy slang; and Frankie and Steff were two streetwise Glaswegians, very useful for any jobs with a Scottish link. Laid-back Harvey was our only black UC, Big Arab was a posh red-wine-drinker with the dark, swarthy mien of a camel salesman, and Little

Scouse was sharp, streetwise and, as his nickname suggested, Liverpudlian.

It was with this bunch of reprobates that Ray began his assault on the drug underworld.

Once trained, people tended to gravitate either to handling or to working undercover. We ran a buddy system in which each UC was assigned a unique handler for each job. You would go in with a specific aim and they would run you through your tasking and the rules of engagement, reminding you to gather intelligence only and show no more than 'due enthusiasm'. At no stage would I talk to the operational team, intelligence officers or anybody else. The handler was your conduit. He was also the link to your private life, keeping your family informed about your welfare when you were out in the field.

By the early nineties, the UK's drug market was vast and chaotic. Cannabis was largely in the hands of well-established British criminals, many living in southern Spain or the Netherlands. Heroin importation had largely been taken over by organised crime groups from Turkey, who controlled the pipeline from the growing fields of the Golden Crescent to the markets of Western Europe, although Pakistani, Indian and Nigerian smugglers were also highly active. Ecstasy, an emergent problem that was underestimated for several years, was often imported from labs in Holland, Belgium and eastern Europe. Finally there was cocaine – flake, blow, marching powder, beak – which was grown exclusively in South America and would in time sweep through the UK.

At the distribution level every city and major town had its established crime groups. London, by far the biggest and wealthiest market, had any number of serious players, or what the police called 'core nominals'. East London, and the overspill towns of Essex and Kent beyond it, harboured well-established gangs into everything from hijacking to fraud to running illegal raves. In the north-east of the capital, the Adams and Reilly families held sway, protected by fear and, so it was rumoured, corrupt police officers. The vast, built-up sprawl of south London had numerous clannish, fractious tribes, many of them family based. Southall, out to the west, was a nexus of the West Asian heroin trade, facilitated by nearby Heathrow, one of the busiest airports in the world. Green Lanes to the north was recognised as a base for the distribution of imported Turkish heroin around the country. The 'yardies' of Brixton, Peckham, Tottenham and numerous other estates specialised in crack cocaine and weed. And the great financial powerhouse of the City had no end of unscrupulous opportunists prepared to wash all this illicit money through the global banking system.

In the provinces, Liverpool was recognised as a centre of excellence for trafficking, partly due to its long history as a seaport. In Manchester, warring over drug sales between gangs from Moss Side, Cheetham Hill and Salford had spawned the epithet 'Gunchester'. The Midlands had its own gangbangers as well as major importers and distributors. The southern and western coasts of England and Wales boasted some expert smugglers. In Scotland, the major urban centres of Glasgow, Edinburgh and Aberdeen were plagued by heroin. In Northern Ireland, terrorist groups were believed to control the recreational drug trade.

Customs looked outward: our targets needed foreign sources in order to import. This meant that our covert needs were somewhat different from those of the police.

There were three basic routes for our UCs to infiltrate the trade. One was through its money systems. A second was via the transport. The third was as facilitators or fixers, what in straight life would be called service providers. It was the second and third of these areas that were largely to be my role.

Others were different. Scouse Phil, a kind of odd-job man, had great success just by hanging around and running errands, often as the gofer for another UC. Hierarchy runs through all human interaction, and sometimes the best place for confidential gossip is on the bottom rung of the ladder: the Wall Street shoeshine boy who picks up stock tips; the company chauffeur who overhears back-seat deals; the barber who notes his customers' indiscreet boasts. The lower you are in the pecking order, the more invisible you are. Phil was small and slight and seemed so insignificant that nobody ever suspected him, but all the time he hoovered up intel.

The great challenge for Beta Projects was to see how far up the supply chain we could go.

In February 1992, a cool, angular blonde in a business suit descended the steps of a flight from California onto the tarmac at Heathrow Airport, accompanied by her personal minder. Heidi Herrera had been working with Colombian drug barons for more than two years, helping to repatriate the proceeds of their international cocaine sales while avoiding the attention of the authorities. She had even facilitated an historic linkup with the Italian Mafia. Her arrival signalled that the conspiracy was coming to the UK.

Herrera was really Heidi Landgraf, a special agent of the DEA working undercover. The daughter of an LA fireman and a police officer, she had studied in Mexico, had a degree in psychology and spoke Spanish, which she used to create a brazen front as the high-powered daughter of a money launderer for the Mexican cartels. Set up with a bogus financial consultancy in a California office suite with ocean views, a clifftop villa, a soft-top Mercedes, a yacht and the use of a private plane, she successfully wooed leading coke suppliers, who were taken in completely by her competence.

Operation Green Ice would become one of the best undercover investigations ever staged. From its birth in January 1990 in the Los Angeles and San Diego offices of the DEA, it would spread outwards to ensnare leading figures in the Cali Cartel, the Mafia and the Dutch underworld. The British angle opened up when some of Landgraf's clients smuggled cocaine into the UK and wanted the proceeds laundered and sent back. After discussion between the DEA and the ID, she was able to recommend a London money mover.

He was really the Beta Projects officer called Keef, assigned to his first undercover role. Having investigated VAT frauds for years and worked on the aftermath of another successful American operation, C-Chase, Keef had an intimate knowledge of dubious accounting practices, coupled with an aptitude for finance. It was he who greeted Landgraf on her arrival at Heathrow Airport.

'The Cali people were very business-like and were looking for money people in Europe,' he recalled. 'They wanted to bring their product into Europe and decided to form a relationship with the Mafia to bring shipments via Italy. Heidi went across to pick up the money from those first shipments. That money came to me in London, through my companies, and I transferred it to the USA. Heidi then asked if I could set up a mirror image of her laundering system that would work in Europe. That's how it started. Originally she brought money to me, I transferred it. Then she went back to the States and I did the pickups.'

One of the cartel, an American, was staying in London and wanted to see Keef face-to-face. They met in the public park at Berkeley Square, Mayfair, while surveillance officers snapped photos from nearby buildings. Keef said he was an investment expert who looked after wealthy private clients, opening accounts and placing their money wherever they wanted under the cover of companies trading gems and property. The stocky, moustachioed American did not really want to know. All he cared about was whether Keef could get money safely back to the Americas. Keef said he could.

They agreed to start with a transfer of £300,000, which was handed over in the lounge of a Mayfair hotel. It was allowed to go through and a second handover followed, for twice that amount. The sting was on.

The American was identified as David Lemieux, a name on the DEA's most-wanted list for moving tonnes of cocaine into Florida. He had earlier sailed a coke-laden yacht to the Isle of Wight, docking under the cover of the Cowes Week regatta, and had been selling to British gangsters. Over the next two months, he brought regular bags of cash to Keef. They even became friendly, although Keef tried to keep him at arm's length. 'He liked a beer and going out, but I played a different type of person, business was business and I didn't want to get involved with anyone in the drug side of things. In my legend I could explain away large sums of money, but being stopped with a large amount of cocaine would have been a different matter. He understood.'

Eventually Lemieux confided that he wanted to take his yacht back to the States before the weather deteriorated, but still had forty-three kilos of primo coke left unsold. He asked if Keef knew any customers. Keef refused to take it himself but said he might know someone who would.

Another Beta UC was called into service. Keef introduced his colleague Charlton, again at Berkeley Square, and Lemieux handed over a kilo of coke in a carrier bag for testing. It proved to be nearly ninety per cent pure, worth about £100,000 retail. Charlton, posing as a major distributor, agreed to take all forty-three kilos for £840,000, or £19,534 per kilo. Lemieux told Keef to put the money in with the next cash transfer.

Lemieux would never receive his money. In September 1992 officers made scores of arrests in seven countries and seized huge amounts of money and drugs. Lemieux and a sidekick were arrested in London and quickly learned that they had been duped.

The repercussions were spectacular. Keef later learned that at least five people had been executed, suspected of informing to the authorities. A $4 million bounty was reportedly put on Heidi Landgraf's head. When it came to his trial testimony, Keef was brought into the court by armed police along a secure corridor, entered the witness box via the judge's chamber and gave evidence from behind a screen. He also underwent cosmetic nose surgery, by his own choice, to alter his appearance. 'It was a distinctive feature of mine and, given that I was expecting to be continually doing operations against the cartels, I didn't want it to identify me,' he said.

Lemieux and O'Donnell were jailed for sixteen years apiece.

Keef was suddenly in demand from a variety of foreign agencies whose criminal targets used London as a conduit for their money. Beta Projects provided him with a luxury apartment in Hays Galleria, on the south bank of the River Thames, with panoramic views of the City skyline. He kept a convertible Rolls-Royce in the garage (seized from a convicted VAT fraudster) and was often accompanied by other UCs as chauffeurs or minders. He always wore a suit and tie, favoured Gucci, Armani and Hugo Boss, and flew business class as a minimum. He tried to keep his legend as close to his own personality as possible, and worked off stress by regularly hitting the gym.

Keef came to hold the view that money was the heart of the matter. 'I could get more information just sitting and talking to a boss about moving his cash than whole teams using conventional methods. Also, if I could control the money but then make a few deliberate mistakes and cause delays, the bad guys would start communicating with each other to discuss it.' By intercepting these communications, law enforcement could steal a march on the traffickers.

For more traditional narco-warriors, however, this fixation on money rather than 'powder on the table' was heresy. 'What some people never got, they could nick someone and get the drugs but never get the guys at the top,' said Keef. 'The money flows upwards. If you control their money, you can identify those at the top.'

Guy Stanton would similarly seek to aim for the top, but would use other methods. He would be one of 'them': a top gangster himself. To thrive in that world, his character needed an aura of menace. He knew just who to base him on.

7

GUY STANTON

As children, me and my nearest brother, who is two years younger than me to the day, sometimes did odd jobs for our father. Dad had a small repair garage on a trading estate near our home. He was an outstanding motor mechanic but a terrible businessman. He was too kind-hearted and often let people skip payment after hearing some sob story.

Next to our yard was a large steel stockholding company and scrapyard. Lots of interesting characters visited that yard but the most interesting was the boss. Peter was thin and wiry, with short blond hair, and always had a cigarette on. He wore a big sheepskin coat, even in the summer, and usually had several heavies around him. His most striking feature was a pronounced lisp, which gave him an almost feminine speech. But there was nothing effeminate about Peter. He oozed quiet menace. As I was only ten years old, he fascinated me.

One day my brother and I were cleaning up the yard, imbued with the twin smells of Rozalex Barrier Cream and Swarfega anti-grease cleaner, while Dad had gone off to buy some spare parts. On a concrete ramp over the inspection pit was a four-ton Bedford lorry, ex-army. Some gypsy blokes had brought it in for a general service and it was just awaiting the addition of fresh oil and payment before collection.

A small van pulled up with four travellers inside. All in their early twenties, they towered over my brother and me. The leader said he had come to collect the lorry and would pay my dad later.

Maybe it was the dismissive way he said it, or their shifty look, but I knew instinctively that if I let them take the truck they would never come back with the money. So I bundled my brother into the tyre bay and told him to lock it from the inside. Then I made a dash for the lorry. Beside it was fresh oil and the sump plug, ready to complete the service. I grabbed the plug and hurled it over the fence into the scrapyard next door. I was then chased around the yard by the furious gang of four.

In the midst of this altercation came a loud shout. 'Oi!'

At the entrance to our yard stood Peter in his sheepskin, the ever-present fag at his lips. It was not just me who sensed his latent homicidal streak. The gypsy boys stopped in their tracks while Peter walked slowly into the yard, with the steel of a man who had seen and done it all.

'What the fuck's going on 'ere?' he spat.

I blurted out that they were going to take the lorry and 'bump' my dad.

Peter produced the sump plug. 'Son, this fuckin' thing nearly took my head off,' he said. I thought he was going to clout me. Instead he handed it back and said, 'Put it back in the truck and oil it up.' I didn't question him but was distraught that my dad would lose out once again.

I was wrong. Peter summoned over the largest of the men and demanded an explanation. He listened carefully while the man stammered out some excuse for the chase. He asked if the lad knew who he was. He nodded.

Peter then asked me how much the job was. I said it was £20.

'That will be a hundred quid,' he lisped coldly to the gypsy. I was gobsmacked, but the lad visibly turned white and meekly took out a wad of notes. Pointing to me, Peter said, 'Give it to him, and don't you ever show your fuckin' face on my manor again.'

After handing over the hundred, three of the men got into the van and left without another word. The fourth drove the Bedford out of the yard.

'Give the money to your dad and tell him not to be so soft,' said Peter, with a thin smile. 'And don't throw sump plugs into my yard again.' He walked off.

When my dad came back, I told him the whole tale. He just smiled. I never found out more about Peter or who he really was, but I have never forgotten his menacing air and quiet tone.

I decided to channel the iron spirit of my dad's old neighbour to create Guy Stanton: speak quietly but carry a big stick. Stanton was nasty, rude and arrogant, with a vexed air that hinted he could explode at any moment.

By occupation, I made Stanton a middleman, a man-who-can. Someone who could get you a car or a boat, source some gear if you were desperate or take a parcel if you were selling, find you a bent passport, some burner phones or a shooter. I would claim I was the son of a London drug dealer who had died some years before in Holland. My school, if it ever came up, was an old one in south-west London that I knew had been knocked down, so there would be no records to check.

I developed several business fronts. One was Saber Investments, a gold and commodity merchants operating out of an office accommodation address in Perivale, west London. Another was a trading company called Egerton Antiques. My criminal contacts would accept these as legitimate-looking fronts for illegitimate business dealings. In fact they were fronts for my legend.

I bought an old, dark-blue Jaguar XJ6 for cash from a bloke in Tooting. I never knew whether it was going to start or not but it fitted the image I wanted to portray. Later, as Stanton became established, I replaced it with a black 3 Series BMW sport, and finally with a black E500 Mercedes Sport, left-hand-drive with Dutch plates, a real beast. I would deliberately park on yellow lines to annoy traffic wardens and pick up tickets. When anyone asked about the unusual number plates, I told them I had taken it from someone who owed me money. In this world it was all about reputation, and criminals love to gossip. They would do my work for me by bigging me up to their cronies.

I made Stanton objectionable even down to his taste in music. My car had a booming sound system through which I played hardcore rap such as NWA and the Wu-Tang Clan. My favourite was *Enter the Wu-Tang (36 Chambers)* and many years on, I still enjoy the odd blast of 'Protect Ya Neck' or 'Severe Punishment'.

I dressed well, never scruffy, though I had several tattoos. Long hair was de rigueur at the time and I grew a ponytail nearly down to my waist. My choice of suit was a black collarless number by Hugo Boss, often worn with a black polo shirt. Prior to a meet, Jo would lay out all my kit for me and always check the pockets. The worst terror for a UC was being caught with documents or identification; you are never going to talk your way out of that. A car I once drove had been used by another UC, and in the side pockets and glove compartment I found job briefing notes, pens and notebooks. It is surprisingly easy to overlook something incriminating, especially when you are in a hurry. My wedding ring had to go too: I would not be able to wear it until I finished as a UC.

I switched between two very expensive gold watches, both by Rolex, the luxury Swiss watchmaker. One was £175,000-worth of solid block sapphire and 18-carat gold, with square diamonds all around, and was apparently one of only five made. The other was worth £75,000 with a black onyx face set with pavé diamonds. They had been confiscated on other investigations. Criminals never fail to be impressed by 'a good kettle' and I would talk with my hands to make sure mine caught their eye. The top men always looked at your watch and your shoes, because if your footwear is scruffy they will dismiss you as a cheap clown.

My earliest occasional accommodation was a flat on Brunswick Quay, in the Surrey Quays area of south-east London, that Ray had set up for the use of several team members as required. I also put my name down on a council house waiting list, and eventually took occupation of my own flat on the third floor of a five-storey block in a down-at-heel area of Limehouse, east London. Built in a modern brutalist style, Ring House was an ugly, angular development of self-contained flats, with railed walk-around balconies and narrow, echoey stairwells. It was ideal. Once issued with a rent book, I could get a phone installed and use the address for passport applications and other documentation.

I lugged the bare minimum of furniture up the stairs, laid a mattress under the window to flop on, and put four heavy locks on the front door, the hallmark of a man who does not want people poking their noses in. It was important for my contacts to know that this place was not my real home, and I always referred to it in conversation as my 'office'.

My first six months were spent going out and being seen. When staying at the flat I would drink in the local boozer, an old, green-tiled, smoky pub by a railway bridge, where I could take my *Evening Standard*, have a beer and chat to the odd fellow drinker. I followed the horses, could talk racing and betting like a regular punter, and sometimes used the illegal bookies' runners that came in the local pubs. There was always hooky stuff for sale as well and I would often buy stolen goods. It all helped to establish my rep.

The British National Party was active in the area, which

was heavily Asian. It put up a candidate, Derek Beackon, for a by-election in Tower Hamlets and he was voted in as a ward councillor in September 1993, the BNP's first electoral success. His supporters would come in my local and start banging on about 'bloody Asians coming over here' but it was all talk rather than Battle of Cable Street stuff. They soon had me down as a local gangster and began nodding and saying hello. They did not strike me as very bright, but while I detested their politics they were not the people I was being paid to investigate. Instead I used my loose acquaintance with them to help build my legend and kept a few of their flyers ('BNP – FIGHTING FOR THE BRITISH WAY OF LIFE') in my flat. Beackon did not last long, as other councillors would not work with him and he was voted out within a year.

Though the only white person in my apartment block, I got along well with the largely Bangladeshi tenants. They must have marked me down as a bit of a bad lad but I was polite and courteous to them. One evening, a few years into my UC stint, I was on my way into the flat when a small Indian man appeared from next door. He told me conspiratorially that the police had been around looking for me. I thanked him and slipped him a score. That was my local security sorted; for several years, I kept Rav stocked with £20 notes and he kept me abreast of any unusual activity on the estate.

My real marital home was a three-bedroom, between-the-wars semi on an unremarkable road in a Home Counties suburb. My long hair, gruff manner, designer clothes and pimped-out car drew a mixture of mild contempt and amusement from my neighbours. Sometimes I accompanied Jo on the school run with our daughter, Jess, and could see the other mums looking at us thinking, *what's a lovely lady like her doing with a thug like him?* Some of them even grabbed their kids, as if I was about to start a fight. When asked what I did for a living, Jo would reply, 'I'm not sure,' which only added to the mystery. Even the teachers began to look on her with pity when we attended parents' evening.

Another legend-building trick was to have my fellow UCs send tourist postcards from wherever they were in the world, which I would leave around the flat. Eventually my collections included cards from New York, St Lucia, Curaçao, Malaysia, Singapore, St Tropez and the Algarve. They would usually carry cryptic written messages such as, 'All is well and we are both making progress with our local friends. It should be good by the time we leave.' Any crim reading that could only interpret it one way.

I thought deeply about how my character would behave in face-to-face or group conversations. Despite Stanton's spiky exterior, I used humour to disarm, distract or destabilise people. One technique was to co-opt lines from movies or songs. Sometimes I used a quip from Claude Rains in *Casablanca*: 'I'm only a poor, corrupt official.' It not only made people laugh but also conveyed a subtle meaning.

My favourite was a classic putdown from *Bad Day At Black Rock*, when Ernest Borgnine tries to pick a fight by loudly accusing Spencer Tracy of being 'a yellow-bellied Jap lover'. Tracy calmly replies, 'You're not only wrong, you're wrong at the top of your voice.' I used that several times to quieten loudmouths and it never failed.

If annoyed, I would use the word 'disappointed'. It was more effective than a blunter term. When I told people I was disappointed in them, I could see them thinking, *what the hell does he mean?* If the situation called for genuine menace, my phrase of choice was, 'I'll tear your face off.' Served up with an unblinking stare, it usually did the trick.

Sometimes my targets would lapse into deep slang, patois or jargon, depending on their background. The temptation was to talk back to them the same way, but that could easily sound inauthentic and give you away. Instead I would respond,

'Speak the Queen's, for fuck's sake, I can't understand a word you're saying.' Invariably they dropped the lingo.

But while planning, preparation and props are crucial, once you venture into the field you are on your own. There you have to rely on your wits and personality and your ability to read situations as they unfold. That cannot be taught; some can do it and some cannot. You go with gut instinct and play your cards as they fall.

One afternoon in April 1993, I found myself in the Renaissance Hotel in downtown Amsterdam. Opposite me sat a slight, dark-haired, bespectacled Scot in jeans, a fawn shirt and a blue quilted jacket. His name, he said, was Rob and he was selling heroin.

I had been sent by one of our operational drug teams. I didn't know the name of the job or much about it. I didn't need to. I was there to sound him out and see how far I could take things.

Rob wanted £100,000 a kilo. I bluntly told him that was a stupid price. After some dissembling on his part, I cut to the chase and asked how many 'pieces', or kilos, he had available. He would not say. I asked if it was white heroin. He nodded, and said, 'Chinese number four'.

In our world, China white was very rare. I had only seen it once before, in some Poste Restante letters when I worked in Birmingham; there were ten or twenty grams in each and it was so pure that if you hit it without cutting it first, you would die.

'How pure?' I asked Rob.

'Up to ninety-eight per cent.'

That sounded an unlikely level even for white. I asked again how much he had but he remained evasive. Instead he asked what I was prepared to pay. I told him £35,000 a kilo.

He looked crestfallen and asked if there was room to negotiate.

'That might be possible,' I said, 'depending on how much you can supply.'

He still refused to give a figure. I told him I would want regular drops, at least once a month, of ten kilos upwards. Rob remained fixated on price, saying £35,000 was far too low. I told him he would never make £100,000 a kilo and he should know that.

We continued for a while in the same vein but Rob was obviously unhappy and I was sceptical. Eventually I said there was no point in continuing, as we were nowhere near an agreement and no-one I knew would consider paying a hundred grand a kilo.

'You're wasting my time,' I said, and left.

Afterwards, the operational team asked why I hadn't strung him along. I told them that I knew instinctively this deal was not going to happen. The guy came across as a makeweight who probably had half a kilo of crap and was trying to ram it out for the best price he could. He could even have been a UC from another agency trying to trap a buyer. There was a further consideration: if your seller asks a silly price and you quickly agree, they start to suspect you. Sometimes being too keen is the worst thing.

I found a lot of this, targets that looked promising but did not pan out. It was not a problem. I was gathering intel, getting known on the drug scene and building my background. Even when a line of enquiry hit a dead end, it was all good. In fact, that was how we had devised it.

My Beta Projects colleagues were making their own inroads and would sometimes call on me to help out by playing a role in whatever scenario they had going. Again this helped bolster my own legend.

Little Tony got close to a very professional Jamaican crew in south London who were selling cannabis around the UK. They had managed to land a tonne in air freight, and Tony posed as someone who could get it out of the airport shed, where it sat awaiting collection, and take it wherever they wanted. He presented me and Harvey as reliable transporters who could move it for them once it was out of the airport. On Tony's recommendation, we were hired to collect the gear and take it by lorry to Toddington motorway service station on the M1, near Dunstable, to await further instructions.

We collected the lorry at a prearranged point. We could not see anyone in the vicinity but had no doubt the baddies would be watching us. As we got into the cab, the smell of grass almost overpowered us. We drove carefully, both to avoid a traffic stop and to allow our surveillance teams to keep up. We expected the gang to have their own team at the service station to check we were not followed, so all in all there were likely to be more cuzzies and baddies around than everyday motorists.

We drove into the lorry parking area and stopped in a visible spot. Everything seemed fine. But you cannot anticipate all eventualities. Just as I stepped down from the cab, a police motorway patrol pulled up alongside. This was not, so far as we knew, part of the script.

Two uniformed officers got out of their car, penned us in and began asking questions. Both our surveillance units and the smugglers must have been watching with a mixture of interest and dread as the cops asked what we were transporting. I had no choice but to lead them to the back of the lorry and lower the tailgate. The sweet aroma of 'erb hit our nostrils.

'What's in the boxes?' said the first cop, his eyes wide with excitement.

'Dunno,' I said, as insolently as I could. It was my last cocky comment. The cop whacked me round the head and I hit the back plate of the truck. He asked again, this time with more edge.

'Erm, I really don't know,' I replied.

The other cop took out a knife and punched it into the side of a box. The smell was now unmistakeable.

'Well?' he said.

I made a half-hearted dash to escape but was quickly restrained, as was Harvey. Out of the corner of my eye, I saw two cars gun out of the car park. *Our surveillance team has got its targets*, I thought.

Harvey and I were slammed against the van, handcuffed, thrown in the back, and driven to a nearby station for processing. After being booked in and relieved of belts and shoelaces, we were locked in separate cells. Mine had a bare bed-shelf and a steel toilet in one corner. It gave me a chance to get my thoughts together. I resolved to say nothing, as I had been trained, and let events unfold. Harvey, I knew, would do the same.

I was eventually taken to a room and interviewed by two detectives, who clearly had no idea who I really was. I stayed in legend, answering 'no comment' to every question and acting in a churlish, belligerent manner. Eventually they slung me back in the cell. Harvey got the same treatment.

After several more hours, punctuated by the standard crappy meal, I was hauled out for further questioning. As I was led to the interview room, I heard cheering. The block was full of Luton Town football hooligans arrested after a mass brawl. Word had spread that a bigtime cannabis lad was on his way and the hoolies gave me a roar of approval. I took the plaudits as I was led on – and got slapped again for my trouble.

The questions restarted. About half an hour in, one of the cops left to take a phone call. He came back, sat down and said, 'You can relax now. Your mate is safe.'

This time my ignorance was not faked; I did not know what he meant. He explained. It turned out that Tony had been whisked off by the bad guys in a Porsche when they saw the cannabis being seized. They had driven so fast that nobody could stop them and our surveillance teams lost them.

Fortunately the gang had all agreed that the bust had been down to rotten luck and had soon let Tony go without suspecting him. He had managed to ring our bosses, and they in turn had finally contacted the police station to tell them who we really were.

Harvey and I were given a cup of tea and released. It transpired that the police who busted us had been acting on an anonymous tip from Tony. They were not told who we were, just that our vehicle was carrying drugs and they should stop it. Our bosses wanted to have the load seized without disclosing our identity.

My handler ensured that I was released 'on bail' with paperwork showing I had been charged with a serious drug offence and I subsequently made sure that people I wanted to impress with my criminal credentials learned of my very public arrest. Having been held in custody and charged, there could be no doubt that I was anything other than 'at it'.

Of course I was never prosecuted. The charge sheet answered any questions while I was on bail, and eventually I could say the matter had been dropped because the CPS could not prove I knew of the load, I was just a hired driver. Again, it all helped the legend.

Harvey and I helped on another operation against an organised crime group operating out of a commercial premises on a West London industrial estate. Our covert entry team wanted to get in to wire it up, and needed a secure base nearby. We scouted the area, found that the unit next door was available and rented it. Posing as a couple of wideboys who were using the premises for their own dodgy activities, we came and went at all hours without arousing the suspicion of our targets, who simply assumed we were as dodgy as them. Our entry boys were able to use the unit to receive the feed from their hidden cameras and mikes, which they monitored in real time while keeping a hotline open to our HQ. When a team finally raided the unit next door, we watched it all unfold onscreen.

In all of our deployments, the lead officer was paired with a handler who was also a trained UC. The handler was the face of the UC to the operational teams. They took on all responsibility, from your welfare to ensuring your family are kept apprised of where you were. The ideal handler is skilled at dealing with people and defusing volatile situations, balancing the demands of the operation with the needs of the UC. It is a tricky job, requiring tact and diplomacy.

In my career I would have four handlers. Harvey handled me on jobs in the Middle East, Curaçao and Venezuela. He was cautious, methodical and gave precise deployment instructions. Keef handled me on a job against a Colombian cartel, an area in which he had expertise due to his own financial exploits. But my two main handlers were Elvis and Sheen. Both were exceptional, and we became close friends.

The biggest thing the handler has to deal with is the ego of the UC and mine was no exception. It was up to the department to handle my intel wisely and ensure that my cover was secure and it was up to my handlers to keep me on the right path. We would discuss each step of an infiltration at length, weighing up the pros and cons of any planned course. My handlers would then shuttle between me and our bosses, Ray and Nick, and constantly re-evaluate the terrain I had to navigate. They became my guardian angels and I trusted them with my life. On several occasions, they took enormous personal risks to ensure that no harm came to me.

Our families grew close. Both Elvis and Sheen would keep my wife briefed about my whereabouts and how I was. She had worked on the front line for HMCE herself and understood what I was doing. I often sought her advice, and in that sense we became a team. Without her, I couldn't have achieved anything like I did.

Some officers did not tell their families anything, either to protect them or out of misguided machismo. I found this awkward when we got together socially, as we would have to tiptoe around certain subjects that a wife had not been told. I often found that the wives knew a lot more than their men realised.

But my closest relationship in Beta was not with any of my handlers. It was, remarkably, with a man widely feared as one of the country's biggest crime overlords. A man capable of killing in cold blood, whose name was often spoken in whispers and whose tentacles reached into the furthest corners of global organised crime. He would become, essentially, my partner in the most extraordinary criminal intelligence operation ever attempted.

8

THE ACOLYTE

O*peration Acolyte was a novel, high-risk venture not just for the Beta Projects but for British law enforcement as a whole. For the first time, a specially trained officer would descend into the darkest depths of the underworld simply to find out and pass back whatever he could – for as long as it took. There was no specific task or mission. It was an open-ended operation, reliant on the courage, resourcefulness and wit of the man selected.*

That man was Guy Stanton.

Acolyte's particular focus was the heroin trade, which was of great concern to the authorities. By the late eighties several inner-city areas of the UK were suffering heroin 'epidemics'. Glasgow, London and especially Liverpool and its environs endured high levels of addiction and overdose, with the latter dubbed 'Smack City' by the press. As street prices plunged and abuse soared, politicians and commentators warned of a national crisis.

Most of Britain's heroin came from the opium fields of the Golden Crescent, the growing region that curves through Iran, Afghanistan and Pakistan. It first arrived with Iranians fleeing the Islamic revolution of 1979. They were quickly succeeded by traffickers from Pakistan, who learned to refine opium into morphine base and then diamorphine, or heroin, in makeshift labs dotted around the tribal zone of the Northwest Frontier. They mobilised an inexhaustible army of impoverished couriers to carry their powder to the West in passenger luggage or on merchant ships, oblivious to the long imprisonment these 'mules' faced if caught.

By the end the eighties, however, the biggest traffickers came from Turkey, the bridge from East to West. Turkish crime groups could acquire Golden Crescent heroin at source and send it into Europe overland rather than by sea or air. This meant they could move bigger and more frequent loads. Utilising the diaspora in cities like London and Amsterdam, the Turkish mafia was logistically unique in that it controlled both ends of the smuggle: the export from Turkey and the import into the user country.

What most alarmed both the police and HMCE was the size of the loads being intercepted, up to 250 kilos at a time by the early nineties. These were unprecedented quantities, indicating that illicit heroin had never been more readily available. And that meant more misery in the consumer countries, where property crime rocketed, driven by users seeking money to buy their fix.

'Turks' was actually a catch-all label for a number of different groups. Some were indeed Turkish, some were ethnic Kurds and some were Turkish Cypriots. Others were not Turkish at all, but Greek or Greek Cypriot. Historically some of these groups were implacable foes but in the drug trade they repressed their enmity. Business came first.

In the UK, the main crime firms buying from the Turks were based in Liverpool. Sharp, unscrupulous operators who saw vast profits in smack, they would cut it and sell it not just in their own city but across whole swathes of Britain and Ireland. One of Stanton's tasks was to uncover the links between London Turkish traffickers and these Merseyside *distributors. HMCE would use his knowledge, along with other lines of intelligence, to collate a comprehensive jigsaw of the supply chain. They would then aim to disrupt it and, ultimately, to bring the top players to justice – hopefully without putting their main source in peril.*

There was one high hurdle to overcome. While HMCE was very good at targeting active smuggling organisations, infiltrating Turkish organised crime was regarded as all but hopeless. The Turks, Kurds and Cypriots who made up this group were too suspicious, too savvy and too culturally different for British law enforcement to penetrate, their spoken dialects too obscure to understand. There was a sense of Mission Impossible.

Stanton, however, would have an 'in'. It came through the ID's most valued, but also most problematic, informant. He was a man Stanton had never heard of, let alone met, such was the sensitivity of his role, but he was known and widely feared in underworld circles. Stanton would have to go down the same mean streets as this man in order to meet the heavyweights of the business.

I had been an undercover officer for nearly eighteen months when, one morning, I received a call from Branch Ten boss Nick Baker. He told me we were going to meet an informant he was running. I had no idea what was being planned, but that lunchtime I accompanied Nick to the Thames Bar in the Tower Hotel, near Tower Bridge. With us was another officer who was to witness and note the introduction.

Already sitting in the bar was a heavily built man of about sixty, with a full black beard showing flecks of grey. He wore a suit and tinted glasses and filled one corner of a sofa. After handshakes and pleasantries, he turned to Nick and said in a quiet, strongly accented voice, 'He'll do. At least he doesn't look like police.'

Nick explained that I would be working with this man for the foreseeable future. A Greek Cypriot of brutal cunning, he was our best informant and knew hundreds of villains. His nickname from youth was 'Keravnos', which roughly translates as 'Thunderbolt'. He had led a thrilling and charmed life, almost an action-adventure fantasy. I was told that he had survived being shot on at least four occasions. On the streets of North London, he was known as a longstanding godfather. Indeed both my firm and the police had, at one time or another, been after him for any number of alleged serious crimes. Yet his intelligence had led to the seizure of hundreds of kilos of drugs and the jailing of numerous smugglers and dealers.

The problem was that, as an out-and-out rogue, he was prone to embroiling himself in the evidential chain, something defence lawyers could spot and use to undermine a prosecution case. But then choirboys don't make good informants. Nick also knew that he sometimes missed important details because he was not a trained investigator. I was to accompany him and make decisions, informed by my knowledge of the law, on what was permissible and what might be evidential.

Keravnos was born in a small village in the Troodos mountains of Cyprus, a highland area of dense woodland. His father, a forest ranger, died when he was only seven. He hated school, once fleeing into the hills to live rough after assaulting a teacher, and as a daring, troublesome young man was recruited into EOKA, the armed resistance group that fought to free the island from imperial control in the fifties. His first action was a blazing gun attack on a British garrison protecting a complex of copper mines. He became a trusted fighter, involved in shootings, bombings and multiple skirmishes, and his willingness to kill brought him to the attention of EOKA's military leader, the former Greek Army general Georgios Grivas.

Keravnos was eventually captured by the Brits after a fire-fight and by his own account was brutally tortured. Finally, half-dead, despairing and disillusioned, he was quizzed by Captain Lionel Savery, an outstanding military intelligence officer who favoured more subtle methods. Savery, who I am proud to say I came to know well, persuaded him to defect – although Keravnos's actions were always ambiguous – and eventually to join a secret platoon of turncoats known as 'The Toads' to gather information for the Brits.

Keravnos and Savery took to the wilds to hunt down members of EOKA, many of whom had killed British troops and their families. When Savery was himself shot in an ambush, Keravnos carried him to safety, saving his life. This forged a lifelong bond between the two men.

At the end of the Emergency, which concluded in 1959 with a peace agreement and the formation of the Republic of Cyprus, Keravnos and other Toads were spirited away to the UK and put on a pension for their service. In his absence one of his brothers was shot dead by masked men in a Limassol market, possibly as retribution or possibly because he ran a lucrative trucking route that EOKA wanted to take over.

A wild man was unleashed on the streets of London. Within a few months of his arrival, Keravnos had shot a Cypriot café owner through the window of his premises in what appears to have been a protection racket. He was convicted and jailed for four years for wounding with intent.

Emerging from prison into the Swinging Sixties, Keravnos opened a casino. This attracted the attention of Ronnie and Reggie Kray, who offered him protection for a regular fee. His refusal sparked a simmering war that lasted several years. He refused to back down and the Krays eventually left him alone, which enhanced his growing notoriety. Keravnos also got married, for the second time (he had first married when young), to a member of the Afghan royal family. She was as adventurous, and as tough, as he was, and as a couple they travelled the world getting in and out of the most outrageous scrapes.

Keravnos had only one aim: to make money, usually at someone else's expense. Along the way, he somehow gained access to some of the world's most influential people. He smuggled tobacco with the Camorra crime syndicate from Naples, and was briefly held hostage by the dictator Idi Amin while up to mischief in Uganda. He was also present in the home of Pakistani prime minister Zulfikar Bhutto when Bhutto was arrested in a military coup. Keravnos, who met Bhutto through a scheme to open a casino in Karachi, was held in custody for six weeks before his release. Bhutto was tried by the Pakistani Supreme Court, sentenced to death and executed on the charge of plotting to kill a political rival.

At the end of the seventies, Keravnos decided to venture into the booming drug trade. He had seen how lucrative it was, having occasionally been employed to enforce debts for a major Green Lanes heroin boss. Then a friend told him of two Americans with a lot of cash who were looking to buy smack in London.

Keravnos suspected they were DEA agents but, as was his wont, went along with the scheme to see if he could profit. He met the pair in a West End hotel and told them he could supply two kilos but would need payment of £20,000 upfront. Astonishingly the agents – who were indeed DEA – fetched him the cash in a holdall, thinking they were about to trap a major dealer. Keravnos told them he would be back with the drugs in an hour. He promptly took a cab to the airport and caught a flight to Spain with the money and his wife. The DEA was furious.

Keravnos planned to enjoy his new windfall but, true to form, soon found himself locked up in a Spanish prison for threatening to kill a local man during an argument. Inside, he befriended a young Moroccan who indiscreetly told him about a planned cannabis smuggle to Canada. Keravnos called his old army mentor, Lionel Savery, who passed on the tip to the authorities, and the Canadians seized two tonnes of hash.

Keravnos saw the future. Released from prison, he was taken by Savery to meet two HMCE investigators, one of whom was Nick Baker. They said they could pay him well if he worked for them as a criminal informant. They would also talk to the DEA and smooth over his problem with them. So he became a top-level snout.

The Cypriot conflict, London gangland, protection rackets, drugs and crooked politicians were just some of the stories that swirled around Keravnos. It was impossible to know how much was true. He certainly had connections but was often economical with the truth. HMCE decided the risks were worth it. It was decided to place me alongside him to gain intelligence on his underworld connections. The eventual aim was for me to make my own way in that world without his help.

On a cold evening in early 1992, I joined Keravnos at a restaurant he owned in Kilburn High Road. It was the kind of small, intimate place that stayed open into the small hours, with authentic food, bouzouki music and a bit of plate-smashing at last orders, and was a safe venue for my first full outing. Nevertheless my handler parked close by, ready to link up with me afterwards and note everything and everyone that I had seen and heard.

Wearing a heavy overcoat over a suit, I felt like I had walked into a sauna. The sight that greeted me was like the villainous bar in the first *Star Wars* movie. Low lighting, tables with bottles of Johnnie Walker whisky and moody groups of men sitting in clouds of cigarette smoke, deep in conversation. Keravnos greeted me like a long-lost son and proceeded to introduce me to various rogues. He told them I was the son of an old friend, now dead, and everyone seemed to accept this without question. From then on, if anyone asked I would tell them I had met Keravnos through my dad, before his demise in Holland.

Among the men of note I met that night were Mehmet K, a Turk with alleged drug connections who was later killed in mysterious circumstances, and Paulie, a sly, scruffy Greek Cypriot with a shock of henna-coloured hair who was up to all sorts of larceny. They were the first of an extraordinary cast of colourful characters.

A few nights later, I met Keravnos again with one of his nephews, Big Andy, and another relative, Jack Kiri. We were going to visit a club he had once owned that had an unlicensed casino in the back. He had lost the club some years earlier to a rival, which still niggled him. We were going there, he said, to meet a gang who had a couple of kilos of heroin left over from a lorryload, which they were looking to sell. This was partially true but Keravnos had a second motive.

'We are going to hit the spieler tonight,' he said. 'The roulette table.'

'What do you mean?' I asked, a little alarmed. 'Are you going to rob it?'

'No. We have got our bloke behind the roulette wheel and we have a magnet controlling the wheel, and we are just going to keep winning.'

A Trojan gambler by nature, Keravnos was engaged in a war with the club owner over his recent losses there and was hellbent on screwing the place. Jack and Big Andy would play at a table where the croupier had been bribed to place a magnetic device on the wheel. Not being very technical I never got to the bottom of it, but basically the punters placed their bets, the wheel was spun, the magnet was turned on and the ball fell onto the specified number.

At least, that was the plan. I went in and watched what

happened with horrified fascination. Jack sat down at the table. He was a big lad and, perhaps because of nerves, was sweating heavily. He took an assortment of items from his pocket while trying to find a handkerchief to wipe his face. One of the items was a bunch of keys, which he placed on the table.

The keys immediately flew to the roulette wheel, where they stuck fast. The magnet had obviously been activated.

Amazingly, nobody else saw this. But worse was to follow. Jack was so intrigued by what had happened that he seemingly forgot why he was there. He reached out, recovered the keys and laid them again on the table, only to watch them fly once more in the direction of the wheel. He did this twice before the pit boss spotted him.

'Oi!' he shouted. 'What the hell?'

The place erupted. In no time, it seemed everyone in the club was involved in a mass brawl. As chairs, tables and glasses flew, Keravnos seized the opportunity to try to grab any cash in sight. He failed, and I had to bundle him out while the battle royal raged – after all, I wanted to be able to use this place in future.

We re-joined Jack and Big Andy at another venue an hour later. They were bruised and miserable. The casino bouncers had roughed them up, taken their money and flung them into the street. They had also pummelled the croupier. Keravnos demanded to know what had gone wrong. I could see that no one wanted to admit what had happened, least of all Jack. 'Well, that was a waste of time,' concluded Keravnos.

This was to be my new working environment. It was Fred Karno's Circus really, a lot of the time.

We started to frequent spielers in Hornsey and Green Lanes, the heart of London's Turkish community. Most looked like greasy-spoon cafés from outside. Inside they might have a little counter serving coffee and sweetmeats and tinned lager, with newspapers lying around on Formica tables. They were a mainstay of the local underworld, a hangout and a meeting place and somewhere to chew the fat.

Green Lanes itself starts in Hackney and leads north for about six miles, making it one of London's longest stretches of road with a single name. It is also used as the name for the surrounding area. According to tradition, first a community of Greeks settled there. Then the Turks came in and many of the Greeks moved out to Cockfosters and Hadley Wood and the M25 ring. Then the Kurds moved into Hackney and the Turks moved up and took Palmers Green – though it still has the highest number of Greek-Cypriots anywhere outside Cyprus – and other areas.

When I first joined the department, a seizure of a hundred kilos of cannabis would have been huge and a kilo of heroin spectacular. By the time I started as a UC, we were finding a hundred kilos of heroin in one hit. Now, no distributor could afford, or wanted, to buy that much at once. Besides the upfront cost, keeping such a stash secure would have been a nightmare. So when the main traffickers brought in a big shipment, they offloaded it in smaller parcels of perhaps five or ten kilos to a number of mid-level distributors.

I let it be known I was always in the market for five kilos of any load coming in. It was a good ruse, meaning I was often one of several dealers who were party to a big importation. If my information then led to HMCE intercepting the load before it could be broken up, no-one could isolate me as the snitch. It also allowed me to ingratiate myself with the gangs involved and find out what other business they had in hand.

Apart from spielers, my regular haunt was a club Keravnos owned in Euston called Fantasia, where we would usually join a table of solid men with deep voices, big guts and thick moustaches stained by heavy smoking. They always had at least one bottle of whisky on the table. I would be introduced as 'Guy', then Keravnos would go round the table: 'That's Tony, Nick,

Tony, Tony, Nick.' You had a table full of 'Nicks' and 'Tonys', because no-one was going to give their real name. Which was a problem, as I wanted to identify them. The usual topics of conversation were football, girls, food, clubs, gambling and the standard of the coffee. No-one discussed 'gear' unless a run was imminent.

Most of the drug bosses, or *babas* in Turkish, would not trust their own granny and I walked a tightrope of suspicion. But an incident one morning in a Green Lanes café confirmed that I had been accepted. I was hanging out there, minding my own business with a coffee and a newspaper, when a mid-level heroin distributor, who I knew only by his first name, burst in with a holdall and came straight to my table.

'There's three kilos in there,' he said, breathlessly, indicating the bag. 'Can you keep hold of it?'

My inner customs officer wanted to nick him there and then. Three kilos was a lot of gear on the street, and for me to guard it and then return it not only went against every instinct but also carried public risks. Suppose a user later died from shooting up some of it, or someone was shot or stabbed while buying or selling it?

I had discussed such a scenario at length with my managers. They knew it would blow my cover if I acted, and the whole point of Operation Acolyte would be lost. I was there to play the long game. My bosses and I would tread a thin line between investigation and complicity, but this was the new approach we had decided on.

I looked the lad in the eye and gave him a nod. He dropped the bag and was gone.

The gear was collected from me in the same café less than an hour later. All I could do was note the people and the surroundings and describe the holdall later to one of our intelligence teams. Importantly, however, word got around that I was a stand-up guy – as much as anyone was in the drug world.

There were still no fixed rules regarding my infiltration. The parameters were laid down in guidelines, not law. My governing principle was to learn as much as I could. How I did that was not prescribed in black and white; there was a lot of grey. At first my role was to see and hear, reporting back everything I could. In each page of my daybooks, I would write down what had happened that day and the details of every phone call and conversation. Sometimes I scribbled on hotel stationery or even torn envelopes, if I was in a situation where I could not carry a notebook and had nothing else to hand.

I did not know what our operational teams were doing with my info and they generally did not know about me – any intel I passed on would be sanitised through Beta Projects to protect me as its source. Basically, I was a secret informant, albeit one on a government salary. My material might lead to a scoping operation, enhanced surveillance or an application for telephone interception. But I was rarely told.

Drug gangs are constantly wary and will use any means to protect themselves. I learned first-hand that all they really want is money and power. This can make them easy to manipulate. Above all, almost every one I encountered had a hidden weapon: they informed to the authorities. The old adage of honour amongst thieves is a blatant lie. When things get hot, or to damage a rival, they will sell out anyone. Conversely that leads them to trust no-one, especially when they encounter a new face.

To maintain cover, I had to be a convincing villain. And not just some low-level gofer; I had to be a main player. My method was to meet them where they felt most secure. That meant casinos, near-beer bars, brothels and Turkish cafes, all places where it was relatively easy for them to suss out normal surveillance. An undercover cop sitting at a roulette table, cautiously playing red and black with a little pot of chips while trying to watch everyone around him, would be easy to spot and the baddies would just walk away. I began to live nocturnally, going out at nine o'clock at night, coming back at five in the morning and sleeping till noon. It was hard to get used to but I had to live the way they lived.

Keravnos was my way in and I came to know him like an uncle. He had three sons by his first marriage. All were built like brick shithouses and sometimes worked as bouncers at Fantasia. When they were short-handed, I would join them on the door. Soon I knew much of the clientele on social terms and was able to report who went there and who they met. One key face was Philly F, whose family were Palmers Green café owners. I learned that Philly was a major underworld armourer, who supplied weapons to an array of hoods.

A lot of business was done in casinos and I began to spend long evenings there, particularly the Sportsman, the Palm Beach and The Stakes in London, and the Genting down in Brighton. The big drug players all tended to show off – Keravnos too – and loved to be adored and served, so they were happy in casinos where the customer is king, especially if he is splurging cash. Keravnos and his wife had been involved in casinos for years and in their heyday had a lot of money, but they burned through it like it was paper. He was himself a colossal gambler, and I would sit and watch him with a mix of awe and trepidation. One night in the Palm Beach I saw him win £63,000 in a short spree. That was much more than my yearly wage. He blew it all in the next hour. Easy come, easy go.

I would play roulette and blackjack at a much lower level. In fact I often played to lose, putting down £50 and hoping that I got slowly wiped out. It was less hassle to lose, as any winnings had to be detailed in my undercover account, which was an administrative pain. I would rather dribble away a small amount over the course of an evening, conscious that I was gambling with government money. Casinos also afforded me a level of protection against any potential allegation of corruption, as all the tables were covered by CCTV and suspicious activity by an officer would have been easy to prove.

I picked up the nuances of how to behave at a table like a regular punter. There is an etiquette, like tipping the croupiers at the end of a good run. You look out of place otherwise. Eventually Beta Projects even sent officers on a Dutch-run training course built around visiting casinos, but I already knew the drill.

The gaming houses catered for a cross-section of society, a real melting pot. You met famous people, sports stars, criminals and their associates, lots of Middle and Far Eastern characters who love to gamble, businessmen who dealt in cash. Much of what the gangsters did was for show. They had this exaggerated, mafia-don view of themselves. Food was very important. We would sit down for massive meals, ordering loads of dishes, with Keravnos taking charge and barking at waiters. The casinos had private restaurants and were often used for meetings.

Only one time did Keravnos offer me money. He had been away somewhere and had a big win and handed me $1,000 in an envelope.

'I don't want that,' I said. 'You mustn't offer me money. I'll have to notebook this now and report it.'

I handed it back to him, notebooked it there and then, and was getting ready to drive off when he threw the envelope into my car through the window, like a kid. I took it home, sealed it and later took it up to Nick Baker in the office.

He wasn't trying to bribe me. He simply thought that, as he'd had a good run, it was fair that I should share his spoils. I continually had to make clear to him that I was a customs officer, not one of his cronies.

We had some flash-points, usually over silly things. He liked to dominate, but I wouldn't hesitate to go back at him and argue him down. I sometimes used to joke to Nick Baker: 'Keravnos has a soft spot for me – I think it's a swamp.'

Once, I drove to see him at an apartment he kept in Brighton marina. He had some Arab visitors over and was planning to entertain them that evening. After we had talked, Keravnos said we were going to the casino, and would I drive? I was, as usual, dressed: black suit, black polo shirt, spit-shined shoes. Keravnos went into his flat and emerged wearing an orange trilby hat made of straw, a loud check jacket and yellow trousers.

'Where are you going?' I said.

'We are going to the casino,' he said, puzzled.

'Not like that you're not.'

'What do you mean? Don't tell me how to dress.'

Tongue-in-cheek, I said, 'I know people round here and I can't be seen with you dressed like that. You look like you've been let out of an asylum.'

He ranted and raved but eventually went back inside, re-emerging in a smart grey suit and black shoes. But as we walked to the car, he produced the orange trilby and stuck it on his head, like he had won a little victory.

Though he loved to dominate, I could not let him call the shots. Bottom line, he was an informant, betraying those around him, feeding their confidences through me into our system. I wasn't with him a lot of the time, he would ring me when something was afoot and then introduce me to a new target. I became fairly sure that, away from me, he was doing things he shouldn't. I later heard that instances of this were picked up on our phone taps. If so, I would not be told. I never knew whether he was actively committing crimes or was calling things on just so that he could tell me. It was a fine line. If he asked someone for gear, was he creating the crime, which might undermine any future prosecution? We had to be very careful.

For many years the Met suspected Keravnos of wholesale heroin dealing. One police intelligence report claimed that he ran a café in Green Lanes and was 'suspected of selling drugs and gambling and holding firearms on the premises'. From my point of view – and I got closer to him than anyone outside his family – he was not capable of being Mr Big. He did not have the mentality of the classic Turkish heroin baron; he was a wild, undisciplined Greek, albeit one with a colourful history and a high profile. The Turks were much more circumspect and methodical, and thought long-term. While they knew him and sometimes dealt with him, they never trusted him.

In my time dealing with some very dangerous men, he was, however, one of a small number who I felt were capable of killing a stranger in cold blood. He was never afraid, never bothered. Nor was he worried about serving time, having been in prisons around the world. I was lucky; he liked me a lot. I did feel that if I was ever exposed, he would stand with me, not least because he would be protecting himself as well.

Among the many notorious men he introduced me to were the Baybasin family. I met Huseyin, their leader, several times, always on the street; he never went to rooms or cars for fear of being taped. Well known to international law enforcement, the Baybasins were at that time on the run from Turkey and were offering information to HMCE and the police in return for British passports. Huseyin was arrested not long afterwards in Holland after a multi-national operation and was jailed for life, although he has always denied the charges, claiming he was fitted up by the Turkish secret service. Who knows? His brother Mehmet later went down for thirty years for conspiring to import cocaine with a Liverpool crew.

I also met some of the notorious Arif family from the Old Kent Road area, who made their reputation as violent armed robbers. One of them sent a lad to Amsterdam on a drug run while I was dealing with him and I overheard a conversation about it. I passed it back to the ID, who rang the Dutch. They located and searched a car we had identified and found seven kilos of smack in the boot. They then watched it until two men came along and they had two holdalls with another two kilos each. The Arif brother I was dealing with, supposed to be the toughest of them all, went berserk when he heard, but never suspected me – he thought another lad in his team had turned snitch. I didn't do much with them though, as they were already under heavy police scrutiny.

Similar were the powerful Adams crime family in north London. I met a couple of the brothers but never worked against them because so much resource was already being targeted at them. Anyway it was a fool's errand, as they knew they were under constant watch.

The smartest boss I came across was a young Turk called Ayhan, who lived just north of London. He had extensive links to Merseyside and was suspected of moving huge amounts of heroin there, but was so clever that for years we struggled to get near him. He would never use a phone in his house or even the local payphones, instead driving for twenty minutes or more just to make a single call from a 'clean' kiosk. He was also one of the first to make extensive use of disposable burner phones. He never used his own name but usually went by 'John'.

Our heroin teams developed a deep respect for his guile. His downfall, as with many of them, was that he stayed in the game long after he should have made his money and quit. He was eventually jailed for fifteen years for conspiracy to supply, by which time he had been at it for years. He was said to have benefited by more than £3 million but that was just for the case he was tried for and was a gross underestimate in my view.

Keravnos opened other doors for me in Liverpool, which led to various players. One was 'Liverpool John', who was connected to every name on Merseyside. Another, my first tangible hit there, was a mid-level distributor called Tony Murray. A rough-and-ready Scouser with thick curly hair and a moustache, he had been knee-capped years before after crossing a rival and was registered disabled. He also had damaged kidneys and had to drink water constantly because of it. He once spoke out in the press after the death of his nephew from an overdose, calling drug dealers 'the scum of the earth', but was himself pushing heroin, which he regularly bought from the Turks to distribute in the north.

Keravnos introduced us in London. Murray told me how he would travel down in a series of cars pre-parked at various motorway service stations to thwart any surveillance. The second time I met him, he let slip that he had a trade on the go and it was being taken north on the train by a courier. I managed to get to a phone to alert my handler and the courier was arrested with three kilos at Runcorn railway station. Murray was later nicked himself and heroin worth £1 million was seized. He was jailed for twelve years. I never met him again, but heard that he returned to his ways after leaving prison and got another twelve stretch.

I met an even bigger target one evening at Keravnos's house, where I was introduced to this heavily built, mixed-race guy with a Liverpool accent, accompanied by a couple of street soldiers to watch his back. This was the infamous Curtis Warren, the rising star of the drug world and the *bête noire* of HMCE. Known in Scouse slang as the 'Cocky Watchman' for his constant vigilance, he had been arrested in 1992 as one of the team behind a 900-kilo importation of cocaine smuggled inside ingots of scrap lead. The ID was convinced that Warren and a businessman called Brian Charrington had set up the deal directly with a major Colombian cartel. However, at the pretrial stage it was revealed that Charrington was an undisclosed police informant, and the charges were dropped.

Warren's drug wealth would subsequently land him a spot on the *Sunday Times* Rich List.

I found him a curious character. Obviously powerful within his circle, he made clear that he did not smoke or drink, almost like a boast. He was obviously intelligent and in another life might have made a successful, if ruthless, tycoon. But beneath his calm exterior ran an undercurrent of menace. He was a new acquaintance of Keravnos, so it was a cautious meet and no trade was discussed. On reporting back, I was told to keep a watching brief and that our operational teams had matters in hand.

We met again soon after at a grubby Greek taverna in Lark Lane, Liverpool. It was another inconclusive meet where Warren mostly discussed who was out to kill him. A gang war was raging in the city and some of his friends were in the thick of it. Not long afterwards he departed to Holland, where he felt safer but was arrested and jailed for running a prolific smuggling operation. I had no role in his downfall, which was largely down to Dutch wiretaps.

It was also on Lark Lane that I met one of his rivals, from a notorious family of lunatics from the south end of Liverpool. They were in conflict with Warren's mob. This nutter came into the same café with a Heckler & Koch MP5 submachine gun under his coat. I had to report it as soon as I could safely make a call, as it was a military-grade weapon and the police needed to know.

Some felons were actually likeable people. I would hang around with them before and after meets, shooting the breeze. Sometimes I borrowed money just so that I could pay it back on time and with interest, establishing myself as trustworthy and reliable. I even helped some of them collect debts, so they could see me at my most menacing. When a Scouse loon called Crazy Tommy had his house firebombed, I learned that a number of people suspected I had done it. I did nothing to dispel the rumours; it was great for my image.

I slipped into their lives, doing a favour here, driving someone there, supplying mobile phones to this guy, providing a car for that guy, becoming their go-to fixer. The main thing in Operation Acolyte was that nothing bad happened to someone that could link directly back to me. That would have been the end of my usefulness. If someone had a shipment taken out, or a lieutenant arrested, they would attribute it to good policing, bad luck, or betrayal by someone else. I knew it was probably my intelligence. But suspicion never stuck on me.

Sadly in the drug business you can't avoid hotheads. I generally swerved those who were prone to random violence, irrational jealousy or carried heavy chips on their shoulders, as they were a waste of time and energy, but it was not always possible. So I devised ways to keep them in their place. I had to show I was not to be messed with, even though the last thing I actually wanted was to go toe-to-toe with some headcase, as it would do nothing to progress the job and even less for my well-being. It was a tricky balancing act but I came up with ways to face down aggressors and defuse flashpoints, often through humour. One reason I was selected for the work was that, while I can have a fight, I had a knack for disarming people with talk. My mum and dad's families had grown up alongside some heavy criminals and I had learned how to chat to them.

A confrontation one night in the West End of London, however, emphasised the thin line I was walking. I was invited to a restaurant where a party of Scouse gangsters were meeting a contingent of London drug dealers. Over thirty faces gathered there in a part-business, part-social capacity. I was quietly sipping a brandy, keeping my eyes and ears open, when in walked a young lad carrying a bag. Pale and pasty-faced, with bad acne, he looked like he survived on a diet of fish and chips. He clocked me, marched right up and stared into my eyes.

'I don't know you,' he announced for everyone to hear.

The table where I sat fell silent.

I had been dreading this moment, a direct face-off. Everyone in the restaurant was watching. I knew I had to see off this skinny runt, and forcefully. I summoned the spirit of my dad's old neighbour, Pete, and stared hard into his eyes.

'Well you're lucky, 'cos I don't fucking know you.'

The temperature in the room fell to freezing. I stayed locked onto his stare but spoke to the whole room.

'What the fuck is going on?'

A well-known London face stepped up and came between us. 'It's alright Guy,' he said, his voice low and tense. 'The boy knows everybody around here. If you were Old Bill or something, he'd know about it.'

I maintained my stare, knowing I had to deal with this in a way that would banish any question marks about me. The lad had to be put in his place.

'You may not know me, mate, but now I know you,' I said loudly. 'And I'll make sure I know everywhere you've been, everywhere you're going to be and everyone you talk to. And if anything goes wrong with me' – I let the words hang, for dramatic effect – 'then I'll come looking for you. Personally.'

I was surprised at the venom in my own voice. So was he. If possible, he turned even paler.

'Erm, sorry, pal,' he stammered. 'I was only saying, like, I didn't know you. I didn't mean anything by it.'

There was a long, awkward silence, until the London face again intervened.

'Don't worry kid, it's alright, this is Guy. Go and do your business and let's forget all about it.'

The lad delivered his bag of what looked like a large amount of cash to one of the men at the table, then left without so much as a glance back. I carried on like nothing had happened, but my guts clenched. *Did this boy have something on me?* I reminded myself that paranoia can eat into your soul, and carried on with my dinner.

I later learned that, despite his scruffy appearance, this lad was said to know every face in the underworld and acted as a kind of spotter, sussing out anyone who seemed iffy or out of place and pointing them out to his paymasters. The twinge inside me took a long time to subside. It confirmed that there was a limited amount my handlers could do to protect me and that, ultimately, I had to build a bulletproof persona.

At the same time, I had to ensure that Stanton never came home with me. Fortunately I found that as soon as I dropped off the car, took off the Rolex and the suit and accounted for my wad of notes, it was as if I had disrobed from that character, physically and mentally. I never had any problem stepping back into my own skin. Jo helped by instantly getting me back into a domestic routine. I love the gentle pursuits of cooking and gardening and she would have a list of humdrum household tasks at the ready. The fastest way to bring me back down to earth was changing the baby's nappy. It never failed: one minute cock-of-the-rock, the next, nappy-changer in chief.

Jo also let me indulge my other passion, collecting casualty medal groups from the British Army, Navy and Air Force. The research involved was a great relaxant. I admire the uncomplicated heroism that such medals symbolise. The recipients, many of them very young, were rewarded for acts of bravery that were clear-cut compared to the ambiguous, treacherous world in which I operated. I was certainly not expecting any medals.

Nor did I ever account for becoming a murder suspect.

Mehmet K ran a café-spieler in Palmers Green. An ethnic Kurd, he had a reputation for violence and was much feared. He and Keravnos knew each other well and he was one of the first people I met when I moved into that world. Keravnos said he was a mid-level dealer.

One morning in March 1994, I went with Keravnos to meet the brother of another trafficker, who ran a shop in Green Lanes and apparently owed Keravnos money. They spent a heated hour arguing about this alleged debt, to no conclusion. Hence Keravnos was in a bad mood when we moved on to call on Mehmet at his club, the Star Musikal.

Again it kicked off. Keravnos and Mehmet ended up having a fearsome row out in the street while I stood by, scowling. It was again over money owed, the kind of ruck Keravnos was always getting into. It was not physical but shouty and threatening, 'I'll kill you', that sort of thing. We eventually left in our car.

A few hours later, a hitman walked into the Islington café where Mehmet had gone to play backgammon and shot him dead.

Keravnos and I were soon credited on the grapevine with his murder. Naturally the police took an interest. I told them what little I knew. The speculation only lasted a short while, until intelligence indicated that Mehmet had ripped off a rival dealer. But it served a purpose, enhancing my reputation once more.

Mehmet's killer was never caught. More than a decade later, the *Times* reported that he was assassinated by a hitman working to the orders of Turkish intelligence, who hated him for his active support of the Kurdish independence movement. I had no knowledge of that, but it seems plausible. He certainly moved in a murky world.

After his death, there was a spate of Turkish-related killings all over London. Deadly force had until then been rare among the Green Lanes *babas*, who treated the drug trade as business and avoided needless turf wars. But violent divisions in Turkey, particularly between Turk and Kurd, were finding an echo on the streets of north London. At least eight deaths over the next three years would be attributed to the Turkish-controlled heroin trade.

Aged twenty-two and showing off my HM Customs and Excise blazer to my proud mum. Little did she suspect the secret work I would go on to do, very much out of uniform.

With my then-boss Dave (right) on a trip to India to investigate a major fraud. It was my first taste of foreign adventure and of the corruption that often accompanied it.

In my earliest incarnation as an ambitious London gangster, with then-fashionable ponytail and shades. I later chopped off the hair and razored it down.

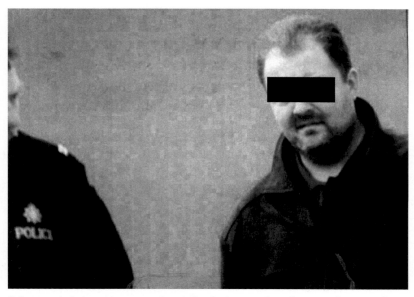

Being arrested at a motorway service station for transporting a large consignment of cannabis resin in a van. The local police had no idea I was working undercover.

An identity document for my regular companion Keravnos, the ferocious Greek-Cypriot exile who led me down into the depths of the heroin underworld.

The *Falcon*, an ageing trawler that we converted into a salvage vessel, off the coast of Yemen during its voyage to collect a huge consignment of heroin. Operation Gurkha established the Beta Projects covert unit on the global stage.

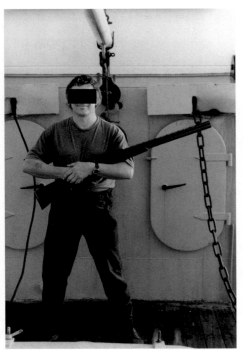

Big Pete, skipper of the *Falcon* and a former SAS sergeant major, with his rather large gun. It came in handy to deter both pirates and recalcitrant crew members.

With Elvis (left), one of my two main handlers, while on a trip to train the Jordanian police in undercover work. Beta Projects became recognised for excellence all around the world.

Sharing a brew at sea with my fellow UC Chameleon Boy. He had a nose for mischief and an effortless ability to switch sides during team arguments.

The boys on boat: Chameleon, Charlton and Eccles before one of our lengthy drug-running excursions. These lads could get themselves into trouble just by doing nothing, but you could not wish for better colleagues or companions.

The immediate aftermath of the street shootout I survived in Otrabanda, Curacao, while working undercover for the Dutch police. I made a sharp exit after diving behind a car.

The disguise I had to adopt to give evidence in a high-security Dutch courthouse for the trial of the same cocaine gang. It must have worked, as the defendants failed to recognise me in the witness box. Their boss freaked out when he learned who I really was.

Staking out Veracruz harbour in Mexico and the merchant ship *Castor*. It was carrying one of the biggest cocaine shipments ever seized at sea, on behalf of a Colombian cartel. I hung around the docks posing as a British businessman looking to salvage wrecks.

Heading to Constanza, Romania, where I maintained an outlet for my fake shipping business. I worked across four continents and numerous countries, and would often send my Beta colleagues postcards, which they could use to enhance their own legends.

Meeting some of the late Ahmed Shah Massoud's men in the Panjshir Valley, Afghanistan, while working as a private investigator after my customs career ended.

Taking time out to cool my feet in the Afghan heat. For a working-class lad from West London, I've had a pretty interesting career — and survived a few scrapes.

Another one of the victims I knew as 'Redhead' for his scarlet hair. He was shot in north-east London while sitting in his car in a traffic jam. Someone walked across the road and put two bullets in him. I suppose he was not hard to recognise. So tense did the atmosphere become that a number of criminal trials were moved to the high-security Woolwich Crown Court because of the fear of an armed breakout, especially if the defendants had links to the Kurdish terrorist group PKK. HMP Belmarsh links directly to the court by an underground tunnel, so prisoners could be escorted securely.

Operation Acolyte never had a clear endpoint. The nearest it came to a climax was my involvement in one of the biggest heroin seizures ever, in the midst of this shooting spree. In late 1995, the police and the ID were working on intelligence that a Turkish group was planning to import up to 500 kilos, an unheard-of amount for the UK. Keravnos and I learned that a number of London dealers had been already been promised ten kilos apiece, at £17,000 a kilo. Another guy we knew was in for twenty kilos. At least half of the batch was expected to go up to Liverpool, where the spot price for dropping it off was higher, at £20,000 a kilo. There was talk of some 9mm handguns and ammo being part of the deal, so we knew this gang was dangerous, and a Scotland Yard tactical firearms unit was put on standby.

I also heard that one of the suppliers had 100 kilos of cocaine available, at £28,000 per kilo. I made him a cheeky offer of £24,000, but he knocked me back. Keravnos and I were, however, asked by the group to supply a van to move some of the heroin, the sort of logistics my Stanton character specialised in and which made me useful to organised criminals. We had our 'in'.

We duly got them the van, but at the last minute heard that instead they were going to transfer the shipment from a lorry into two cars, a white Porsche and a black, four-door BMW.

I ran to a phone and urgently called my handler. 'It is being broken down now,' I said. 'The gear is in an underground car park in the Docklands area of East London, being transferred to two cars.'

The cavalry charged in. They took out the BMW as it left the car park and a Peugeot linked to the same gang some distance away. In total they seized 165 kilos, and the raid made a huge splash in the next day's newspapers, with pictures of a senior officer proudly posing by the BMW. What was not reported was that the Porsche got away, we believed with at least 250 kilos in the boot.

Eventually the *babas* began to openly complain about our successes. One night I was with a group of them when a major trafficker called Sami asked me, 'Have you ever come across "The Other"?'

'What do you mean by "The Other"?' I asked.

'Customs,' he said. 'Don't let them get on you, coz if they get on you, they do not let go.'

I had to stifle a laugh. But it showed we were getting to them.

Acolyte was open-ended and ran for almost a decade. I must have supplied hundreds, if not thousands, of pieces of intelligence, some of the highest quality, some little more than informed gossip. It all helped us to construct a uniquely detailed picture of the drug underworld and fed into numerous investigations.

Yet it was only one of the operations I was working on.

9

ARABIAN NIGHTS

In late spring of 1993, I flew to Dubai with a handler.

Several years before, Keravnos had secretly facilitated the arrest of a Pakistani trafficker linked to the biggest seizure of heroin ever made at Heathrow Airport. The man's two sons, who we suspected were heavily involved in the trade themselves, had since sworn to find out how their father had been caught. Keravnos stayed in touch with them and managed to introduce me to them through a third party, a relation of his Afghan wife. But he made it clear that once he got me in, the rest was up to me.

I arranged to meet the sons in the Hyatt Regency in the Deira area of Dubai. The place was not so built up then; the coastal Sheik Zayed Road was empty and the best hotels were on the Creek or in Deira. We met in the opulent, split-level lobby. They were warm and friendly, but quickly asked about Keravnos and how well I knew him. They warned me not to trust him and said that, though they had no proof, they suspected he had betrayed their father.

I said I was not close to him, and briefly described my background in shipping and transport. 'But now that you have said that, I'll be very careful around him,' I said. 'And if you don't trust me because I know him, and would rather not meet again, no problem. I wouldn't blame you.' That seemed to satisfy them. We arranged to reconvene for dinner.

That evening we sat down at the Seafood Market restaurant in the Meridien Hotel, out near the main airport. Specialising in fish cooked 'Far Eastern' style, it was the most fashionable joint in the city. The sons were relaxed and effusive. They were also keen for me to meet a black-bearded Pakistani in a cream-coloured *shalwar kameez* sitting nearby. He beckoned us to his table, and it turned out he spoke passable English.

The brothers introduced him, with a show of deference, as Haji Ayub Afridi. He was often known, they said, as Haji Khan, with the name 'Khan' signifying a leader or boss. They told him I was an Englishman with money and connections, nothing more. We joined him to eat.

Afridi did the talking. He was loud, domineering and bombastic. He asked pointed questions about my transport routes by land and sea, then barely bothered to listen to the answers. He disgraced himself by drinking whisky straight from the bottle, but didn't care. He acted like he owned the place. When the waiters brought out his main course, a magnificent sea bass on a huge bed of cous-cous and grilled vegetables, he grabbed it with both hands and tore into it whole.

In between mouthfuls, Afridi had no qualms about sharing his own exploits. He was, he said, a drug smuggler – the best. He boasted of having moved enormous shipments of up to three tonnes of heroin from his fortress home near Landi Kotal, on the Afghanistan–Pakistan border. He would escort such loads with a fleet of armoured vehicles and claimed his compound – more of a palace, really – was virtually impregnable.

If Afridi was to be believed, he was a major international player. I made sure we exchanged contact details before I left.

I did not know it but I had just met one of the world's biggest narcotics traffickers. Afridi's tribe held sway over the Khyber

Pass, in the lawless North West Frontier region, where the Pakistani government had no legal right to operate without the permission of local leaders. The Afridis controlled the smuggling of both drugs and arms there, and he was their chief. The authorities had once found seventeen tonnes of hashish at one of his warehouses in Balochistan. Yet in a country rife with corruption, this had not stopped him from being elected to the Pakistani National Assembly, though he had recently failed to retain his seat.

Afridi was, in the heroin world, equivalent to Pablo Escobar or the Ochoas in cocaine. He was the top of the pyramid. There was no-one higher.

I met him again before returning to the UK. We talked in general terms about markets, logistics and transport but it was hard to pin him down on specifics. He had so many schemes going that he was too preoccupied to commit to anything with me, a stranger, at that time. Or too canny.

I passed back all I learned about him and the two brothers, and was surprised when no further action followed. I was wrong about this – my intel was being used, but there was no need for me to know. As the UC, I was rightly kept in the dark. In fact, my meetings had reinforced suspicions about his global activities among numerous agencies, with the Americans in particular taking a keen interest.

These meets showed the level that Keravnos could get me access to. They also sparked, indirectly, the operation that would establish Beta Projects on the global stage, when the contacts made on that trip to the Middle East led me to another team. I first met minor members in various London casinos and clubs. Not wanting to seem over-eager, I was polite but somewhat dismissive of these boys. I did make sure they knew that I knew Afridi and similarly powerful 'businessmen', which they reported back to their masters. No doubt they were impressed.

The upshot was another flight to Dubai with an introduction to two traffickers based there. Mohammed and Babalua were looking for someone to transport a tonne of heroin to Europe. If true, this would easily be the biggest single load HM Customs had ever stopped. I was to offer my services, saying – not exactly truthfully – that I had a vessel that could carry the load. When Beta was first envisaged, the aim was to reach the stage where we could infiltrate the upper levels of the drug trade. We expected this would take time and probably a large number of in-and-out, bust-buy jobs to boost our credibility. But with this one extraordinary operation, we could jump several steps and go straight to the top.

I was accompanied to Dubai by both a handler and my boss, Ray, in legend. Ray booked into a separate hotel and was careful to keep his distance. He was there to meet senior embassy staff and officers of our Secret Intelligence Service (SIS), usually known as MI6. They had the in-country resources to cover my meets with the targets, and connections with any local spooks and senior officials we might need to tell. SIS gave Ray the impression that they had seen it all before, though this may have been bluster. We had certainly never done anything like this.

Our targets sent a chauffeur to collect me at the airport. A small, wiry Arab, he was very talkative and asked a lot of questions, for a driver. He even said at one stage that he would like to work for me. Dropping me off at the Hyatt Regency, he said his boss would be along to see me that evening, and sped off.

As I waited in the lobby that night, I was approached by the same man. He had changed into expensive clothes and carried himself with a self-assurance not evident before. It turned out that he was in fact the boss, Mohammed. He liked to pose as a driver so he could take a look at any new contacts personally and weigh them up. It was a nice trick.

We went for dinner, where he introduced his partner. Babalua was a Pakistani, well-groomed, bespectacled and studious in manner. Privately educated in the Home Counties, he spoke impeccable English, and in my dealings with him I would never see him lose his temper. But he was authoritative and clearly used to giving orders.

Mohammed and Babalua said they had access to vast quantities of drugs. They talked of one or two tonnes of refined heroin and up to forty tonnes of cannabis resin. If I could get the right vessel out to a pick-up location, the transport contract was mine.

That was the first of a series of meets in the Middle East over the next few months. Their heroin shipment needed collecting from the Makran Coast of Balochistan, the largest of the four provinces of Pakistan. A long, thin coastal strip of bleak semi-desert, the Makran is sparsely inhabited, with just a few strung-out fishing villages and small ports linked by a single jeep track running east–west along the shoreline, backed by a wall of arid mountains. It is nearly 6,000 nautical miles from the UK.

Our plan was to sail a boat around France, Portugal and Spain, across the Mediterranean, through the Suez Canal, down the Red Sea and into the Gulf of Aden and the Indian Ocean. Two dhows would bring the drugs out to agreed sea coordinates and cooper to our boat.

I was the boss of the shipping group. My character was rude and arrogant and liked people to see his wealth. He was also savvy and streetwise. I played him that way. Mohammed and Babalua, for all their intelligence and cunning, fell for it. They *wanted* this deal to happen.

Once safely back in the UK, Ray organised a round of meetings with senior officials from the military, the Foreign and Commonwealth Office and the security and intelligence services. He needed certain clearances and to make extensive health and safety assessments. The job began to expand.

As the country's foreign intelligence service, SIS had been looking for a new role after the end of the Cold War. In 1991 the Soviet Union had collapsed and the hammer and sickle had been lowered for the last time over the Kremlin. The routine work of the traditional spook vanished almost overnight. At the same time, organised crime had become truly international. Given that SIS already lent support to law enforcement in British dependent territories, they now made a strong pitch to extend that role. This meant moving onto HMCE's turf. We didn't mind. There was more than enough work to go around and they could bring assets to bear that we could only dream of.

After much deliberation, we decided to approve an investigation unlike any that had been tried before. Operation Gurkha was approved.

Our first step would be the purchase of a suitable boat. Big Pete would skipper it. He was a hulking northerner and as hard as tungsten nails. A tale was told that he once went undercover into a rough South London pub run by the fearsome Arif brothers. They were holding a family celebration and when a bloke went past with a tray of sandwiches, Pete, feeling peckish, took half the tray. One of the party went over and asked him what the hell he was doing, but Pete looks so mean that even the Arifs let it go.

He was partially deaf, the result of an incident during a parachute jump, and mumbled when he spoke. This gave him an unsettling quality, as no-one had the bottle to ask him to repeat his words. A superb skipper, he would come to look down on the rest of us with a mixture of fatherly love and overwhelming pity at our lack of seamanship. As the saying goes, it might have been our mission but it sure as hell would be Pete's ship.

He and I went to a boatyard in Gdansk, on Poland's Baltic coast, to check out some promising vessels but could not find what we wanted. We next visited Urk, a windswept fishing port in the Netherlands. I'm no expert but Pete knew what he wanted and settled on an old but sturdy beam trawler. We duly bought the *Falcon* and converted it into a working salvage vessel, equipped with cranes, diving apparatus (we were all PADI-trained) and a large rigid-hulled inflatable boat, or RHIB, which we could use to run gear from ship to shore. Oily and rusty, loaded with grimy machinery and a rattling generator that belched black smoke, she was perfect.

In April 1994 I flew to Oman for six days of further negotiations with Mohammed and Babalua. My handler, Elvis, and Ray again came as my shadows. The plan evolved. I set up a front business in Oman, where we would dock after making the pickup. There the *Falcon* would offload the drugs, which would be put in a container and shipped to the UK via Dubai – or so our targets were led to believe. They would travel to the UK to oversee the unloading, at which time we would arrest them while the authorities in Dubai picked up any of the group still there. We could seize and secure the illicit cargo somewhere along the way.

The unprecedented venture required sensitive, top-level talks with the Dubai and Omani authorities, whose permission we needed to proceed. The ID's deployment of UCs and handlers had to be approved by our chief investigation officer under authorities reviewed every month. The Foreign Office also insisted that the British ambassador in every country involved with our boat's journey be made aware of the operation. A Royal Navy frigate was tasked with monitoring our trawler throughout its voyage from over the horizon, in case of emergency. The commitment in manpower and materiel was substantial.

Finally but crucially came the selection of the crew. Beta was able to provide a number of UCs with sailing experience. For security reasons, it was decided that they would be joined by several elite, highly trained specialists employed by the Ministry of Defence. Their involvement was strictly hush-hush. All I can say is that they were top-notch operatives.

It was late spring when Elvis and I hopped over to Cyprus to meet the *Falcon*, which had passed through the Strait of Gibraltar, crossed the Med and docked outside Larnaca. We wanted to check that the ship and crew were well and to orga-nise the proper permits for them to navigate the Suez Canal, before flying on to Dubai. The Arabian Sea and the Indian Ocean were still a long way off.

Working the run with Big Pete was Eccles. Another good seaman, Eccles never learned which fights to pick and waded headlong into every debate. I think he secretly harboured designs to run the ship. This presented him with two problems: Big Pete, and Big Pete's gun. The latter was a pump-action shotgun, legally held on board to deter pirates – and mutinous crew members.

They were joined by Pigpen, Sheen, Mungo and Chelsea. Pigpen was the other trained skipper on the team, a skilled helmsman and navigator. Sheen, big and balding, had raced yachts as a hobby and acted as a deckhand and convincing heavy. Mungo was another lump, and with his thick Geordie accent and bashed-up face, could deter most opposition. Chelsea was a small, sharp Londoner. They were a good crew.

Elvis and I entered the dock that evening and saw Pigpen coming down the boat's boarding plank. 'How's it been?' asked Elvis.

'Fine, old boy,' said Pigpen. 'A bit bubbly in the Bay of Biscay but mostly calm.'

He looked filthy, which was normal on a boat. More alarm-ing was a septic boil, angry and red, on the side of his neck. Any serious ailment could delay their passage.

'Look,' Elvis said, 'we'll go into town and find a restaurant. Get the lads together and follow us in.'

As we headed to a good eaterie I knew near the old town, I could see Elvis had fallen into deep thought. 'Did you see that boil on Pigpen's neck?' he asked. 'You know what this means?'

'No, what?'

'Scurvy,' he said conspiratorially, 'the dread of all sailors when a long time at sea.'

I'm no doctor and no real crewman either, but scurvy – really?

Half an hour later, the whole crew was drinking cold beer at the restaurant. Elvis had been away to make a phone call and came back looking worried.

'Look lads, we might have to delay as it looks like Pigpen has caught scurvy.'

'What?' they said in unison.

'Scurvy,' said Elvis, sounding like Black Dog from *Treasure Island*. 'The curse of the sailor on a long voyage. Don't worry, I've ordered fresh vegetables and lime juice from the dock stores. We'll see no one else catches this scourge.'

'What are you on about?' said Big Pete.

'Look at Pigpen's neck,' said Elvis.

'Oh, that,' said Pigpen. 'Sorry to disappoint you, old thing, but this isn't scurvy. I was coming back through the dock the other night, well pissed, when I fell into a barbecue left on the dock. The leg of the barbecue flicked up and stabbed me in the neck. I didn't feel a thing, as copious amounts of rum had dulled my brain and other body parts. The stab wound turned septic and now it's a boil.'

'Boil?' said Mungo. 'Howay with ya, it looks like a second head.'

'The man with two brains,' chipped in Eccles.

'One's enough for him,' I said. 'Where are you going, Elvis?'

'To cancel that order of lime juice and veg,' he said, scuttling away over the dock.

The following day I went to find a local shipping agent who

could supply our papers to traverse the Suez Canal. I stopped at the shabby office of one Khalid Ibrahim and rang the door-bell, which in itself was an act of bravery: two bare open wires sparked and sizzled, accompanied by a wisp of smoke and a smell of burning.

Mr Ibrahim answered the door. He wore a suit that had once been white, and looked like one of the shadier characters from *Casablanca*.

'Hallo, sir,' he said. 'As-salamu alaikum.' *Peace be to you.*

'As-salamu alaikum wa rahmatullahi wa barakatuh,' I replied. *May the peace, mercy, and blessings of Allah be with you.* I knew it was courtesy to return the greeting in a proper manner. 'Mr. Ibrahim? I'm Mr Stanton, owner of the Falcon. I rang yesterday.'

'Ah yes, yes,' he said, showing two prominent gold teeth. He led me into his office. 'What can I do for you?'

'I need to complete papers and permissions to transit the canal.'

'Let's see.' He fished out some forms. 'Two of these, one of these and three of these. That'll be four hundred and thirty-eight Cypriot pounds.'

'I don't want to buy the canal. I just want to get my ship through.'

Mr Ibrahim smiled again and handed me the forms. 'Fill these out.'

While I completed the paperwork at a table, he made tea and sat opposite me. 'Where is your ship going?' he asked.

'Into the Gulf. We are salvage specialists.'

'Oh,' he said, looking at me curiously from over the rim of his cup.

'I'm on a bit of a tight deadline, so anything you can do to speed things up would help.'

'Do you know I love England?' he responded. 'I love your Queen.'

'Do you?'

'Yes, especially pictures of her, they are always nice to see.'

'What type of pictures?'

'Little purple ones, with "twenty" written in the corner,' he said, smiling even more broadly. 'It's very nice to see those pictures. About five of them and you will find you will make your deadline.'

This was how business was done. You either accepted it with good grace or got nowhere. Mr Ibrahim was a slick operator, and could mug you with a smile, but in the end you both got what you wanted. I paid him the extra £100.

The *Falcon* took another three weeks to reach Oman. I flew ahead, suffering the indignity of the Emirates airline's business class. Meanwhile the boat crew was augmented by four more men: Squid, Trawler Dan, Smartie and Topper. They were 'lent' to the operation by the MoD and had extensive sailing experience. Their attitude, skills, professionalism and courage would become a constant inspiration.

Squid's weakness was his devotion to Newcastle United football club; he loved them even more than Mungo, a bona fide Geordie, did. Dan was very much at home on the high seas, having worked on trawlers in his youth, and nothing fazed him. Smartie was an engineer who would prove over the next few months that he could always coax one more trip out of the ageing *Falcon*. Topper was their boss and an all-round top bloke. Their obvious familiarity with boats made for strong cover. They were also authorised to carry guns and stashed an arsenal of weapons on board, just in case.

As the *Falcon* crept through the Canal and into the Red Sea, the going was slow and the heat relentless. Sheen suffered the most. He had just started a long-term relationship with the woman who was to become his wife, and had accepted this job on the understanding that he would not be gone for long.

As it turned out, the whole team would be away for many months, interrupted by short returns to the UK.

Early one morning, they put in at a port in Yemen to top up with fuel, fresh water and food, intending to be quick and to pass unnoticed amongst the traffic sailing in and out. Pete expertly manoeuvred the *Falcon* into a berth on the harbour wall, then climbed onto the dockside, telling Squid and Sheen to contact the freshwater bowser and load on more water, while he dealt with the landing paperwork at the port authority.

When Pete returned, he looked in consternation at the spot where he had left the *Falcon*. All he could see was the bridge and two masts rising from the water. His boat was firmly settled on the harbour bed.

At the subsequent mini-ships court martial held by Big Pete, Sheen fessed up. A rusty, 1,000-tonne water barge had come alongside, belching black smoke. The Arab crew shouted over, asking how much water was needed. Squid and Sheen did some quick calculations and reckoned on two tonnes. The bargemen threw over a large-bore hose, which Sheen connected to the water tank in the cargo area. Squid steadied the hose with his foot and signalled to the barge to start filling.

After several minutes, Smartie noticed that there was water all over the deck. Sheen went to check below, opened the hatch and saw the fridge float by. Using his seamanship skills, he determined that this was odd and there should not be more water inside the ship than outside. The barge had loaded the water so quickly that our tank burst, flooding the boat. Luckily it was not too deep down and the lads were able to get off before she sank.

To exact revenge on his crew, Big Pete sent them around the dock to find a pump capable of re-floating the boat. Someone remarked they were the only salvage team to have to salvage their own vessel.

I kept picking up snippets of these and other shenanigans.

At one stage, so I was told, some sort of military conflict broke out in Yemen. The lads were alerted by a message from the Royal Navy frigate HMS *Cornwall*, telling them to clear out sharpish, and as they were leaving Aden fighter jets roared overhead and bombed some nearby oil installations. The story grew in the telling to them braving shells exploding all around.

It got so that Ray Pettit, back in London, came to dread answering the phone. Not long after the shelling incident, he took a call from Big Pete. It went something like this:

'Where are you?' said Ray.

'We've left Oman.'

'I thought you were staying there for two or three days?'

'Ah, it's a long story, Ray.'

'Pete, what the hell's happened?'

'I'll tell you later.'

It turned out that they had been drinking in a bar – Oman is not one of the 'dry' countries – in their reeking scruffs when some locals took exception to them. The next minute they were in a mass brawl. It was no contest. They left four of the locals unconscious and had to flee before they were all chucked in prison.

My role was rather less taxing, at least physically. As head of the organisation, owner of the boat and negotiator with the Pakistanis, I had to act the part. Hence I moved between various five-star hotels, including the Hyatt Regency Dubai, the Galleria in Deira and the Gulf Hotel, a classic old colonial pile in Muscat, Oman. Some had Olympic-sized pools, several restaurants and chauffeur-driven courtesy cars. I felt that the lads, on the other hand, should project the image of an over-worked, underpaid boat team. Their billets would have to reflect that.

Still, I worried about them. So one morning I set off with Elvis in our rented Jaguar to make sure they were in a good, solid two-star hotel. The drive took two-and-a-half hours across desert. As we pulled up at a rather rundown Hotel Alhambra, the bedraggled figure of Sheen wove towards us. He had been found guilty by Big Pete of trying to sink the ship, was missing home and his new love and, worst of all, had only one paperback to read. He lurched up to the car like Ben Gunn, his bald head sunburned and his eyes glassy.

'How are you then?' I said, lowering the window an inch. Steam drifted from the car as the cold air-conditioning hit the fierce desert heat.

'Let me in,' said Sheen, looking a bit wild.

'Can't do that,' I said. 'You'd mark the seats.'

'I need cold air.'

'Love to help, but what would this do for your cover?'

'Fuck my cover!'

'What are you reading?' I asked, changing the subject. 'Looks like an encyclopaedia.'

'It's my paperback. I've been swimming up and down the pool and it's sucked up lots of water.'

At this point a camel sauntered over and began to nibble Sheen's book.

'Got to go,' I lied. 'Elvis is allergic to camels.'

We spun the Jag round in the car park, hurling up dust and stones, and left Sheen forlornly holding his half-chewed book, mouthing expletives to his dromedary friend.

Eventually the lads were in range to make the collection, only for Mohammed and Babalua to ask for a delay. Apparently shipping the drugs from the northern tribal area of Pakistan to the Makran coast was causing them unforeseen problems and it took a few more weeks before all was set for the collection run to the rendezvous point off. Dhows were to bring out the heroin and load it at sea onto our vessel. At least, that was the plan.

Unfortunately a tropical storm struck. Our vessel managed to make the coordinates on time but the dhows were beaten back. We were unable to wait there for long enough for them to retry, and the run was aborted.

Most of our crew were sick and the ship needed work to repair the pounding she took from the heavy seas. I flew again to Dubai to arrange a new handover date. We decided we would hide the drugs in fish boxes on our way to Oman. They would then be put in two containers for onward shipment.

The lads eventually made the run again – and again there was no-one there to greet them. They stayed in situ for several days, sailing around and scanning from coastline to horizon, but nothing appeared and they were forced to abort.

I attended yet another hastily-arranged meet with the smugglers in the Emirates. They gave an inconsistent battery of excuses, ranging from gear being ripped off, to the death of the team leader, to a failure by their land-based supply team. Though not party to all of the intelligence being gathered on them, I felt they were genuinely trying. The narcotics trade is fraught with difficulty and setbacks are the norm. Fortunately I had negotiated that Mohammed and Babalua would pay the crew's wages and fuel, so it wasn't costing HM Treasury as much as it could have. This proved that they were serious, as they would not have put money upfront otherwise. They reassured me that all was well, and the run was back on.

Two months later, we finally thought we had cracked it. SIO Ray flew to Dubai once more to link up with my handler, while I dealt with Mohammed and Babalua's team. Given that the heroin would go first to Oman, I decamped there to prepare for its arrival. Nick Baker ensconced himself with SIS at their London headquarters to monitor the operation remotely, and would not leave the building for several days. Our boat was in the Indian Ocean, ready to collect.

Yet once again the Pakistanis failed to deliver. Their dhows could not load up, they said, because of too much military activity on the coast. I never found out whether they were untruthful, unlucky or just incompetent. According to our intel, their drugs may actually have been detained by corrupt local military whom Babalua had neglected to pay off. We feared that the heroin would disappear into other, smaller smuggles. We could also no longer justify the prolonged presence of a British warship as cover. After an agony of waiting, our biggest ever seaborne operation was stood down.

Our frustrated and exhausted crew were directed to turn the *Falcon* back to the UK. They had spent almost nine months with the boat by the time they got home. Given the circumstances, they performed remarkably. The privations and boredom of sea travel affected all of them but they never once called it a day.

Success has many fathers, they say, while failure is an orphan. Custom House became the scene of a major debrief to account for all the naval vessels and others assets used. The job had cost a fortune and the spooks couldn't understand what had gone wrong. We had to explain that this was the norm when dealing with criminals. Failure in an operation, such as a case too weak to take to court, was not necessarily a problem for us. If we took out some gear, destabilised an organised crime group or gathered reams of intel that could be useful in the future, that was still a result.

In any case, all was not lost. Mohammed and Babalua insisted they still wanted to ship the drugs. I told them my salvage boat was no longer available, so they hatched a new plan to send two shipping containers from Karachi to the UK via a circuitous route. But violent religious unrest in Karachi, which led to scores of deaths, once again scuppered their plans.

Keravnos stayed in touch with them and helped the pair put together another scheme, involving antique statuary from Afghanistan. These valuable figurines and icons had been kept in private hands in Kabul. Now the owners needed money to escape the civil war there and were desperate to find buyers. A group of Indians in London were prepared to receive the arte-facts on their behalf, and Keravnos somehow inserted himself as a middleman between them and the antiques trade. Sensing a big payday, he convinced the Indians that he could find the right buyers.

The world of antiques is replete with chancers and fraught with dubious deals. We suspected that these artefacts had been stolen from religious sites and had considerable historic value, even though they were accompanied by apparently genuine licences and papers of authenticity. It was also logical to suspect that Mohammed and Babalua would use them to conceal the heroin we had failed to pick up off the Makran.

In late 1996 their container arrived at Felixstowe. A customs rummage team searched it. Finding that the figurines appeared to have the correct paperwork only made them more suspicious and they drilled into some of the statues. It soon became clear, unfortunately, that there was nothing hidden inside and the figures were genuine. Amazingly, given the nature of those involved, it was a legitimate deal. The goods were released to the Indian receivers before any more damage was done. Keravnos helped them sell them and did nicely out of it: one piece went for £85,000. No heroin was found.

Patience is a virtue, and our luck finally turned. Soon afterwards, we learned that Babalua had sent yet another con-tainer, and our rummagers descended on Felixstowe again. Hidden amid a consignment of clothing destined for a London address were five tonnes of cannabis, worth an estimated £16 million. It might not have been the heroin we wanted but was a bumper job nonetheless. Babalua, it seemed, was able to produce drugs but not to control how they got to market. That was his weakness.

We briefed the newspapers that the seizure came from a tip-off, and there was nothing in the reporting to suggest we had infiltrated the organisation. Babalua called me soon after, still not suspecting me, and said he wanted me to take over his group in Dubai, which was now in complete disarray. He was in London and we arranged to meet. He admitted the seized gear was his and said he was getting out. We did not have the evidence to tie him to the cannabis, and still wanted the heroin, so we strung him along to see if he might lead us to it. He left the country.

Before we could develop things further, Mohammed, Babalua and most of their organisation were arrested by various authorities in the Middle East and Pakistan for other offences. They disappeared into the system and I never heard from them again. Countries like Pakistan, Oman, the UAE and Saudi Arabia have the death penalty for drug trafficking, and I did hear an unconfirmed report that at least one of them may have suffered execution. After more than three years, our own investigation was stood down.

Operation Gurkha was long, expensive and dangerous, and tied up some of Beta Projects' best people for months, but the enthusiasm of all those involved never waned and its repercussions were profound. It proved we could do long-range projects and work in lockstep with the intelligence services and the military, and that international boat jobs were feasible on a grand scale. 'Makran made Beta's name,' Ray Pettit believed. 'The Canadians and the Dutch couldn't do that kind of operation, even the Americans couldn't do it, but we showed we could.'

It proved that Beta could perform effectively worldwide and laid the foundations for relationships that would bear fruit over the coming years. Not long afterwards the key agencies involved, together with various police organisations and the National Criminal Intelligence Service, formed the Organised Crime Operations Group. This secretive body would meet every few weeks in Westminster to identify crime groups to attack and to coordinate resources against them. It had some spectacular results.

In a further postscript, in 1995 Haji Ayub Afridi surrendered to the US authorities, having previously been indicted for smuggling fifty tons of cannabis to the USA in the late eighties. He was also accused of laundering millions of dollars. He came forward, he said, to prove his innocence. Afridi served a relatively short prison term and returned to Pakistan on his release. 'I wondered what sort of deal he had struck with the Americans to get such a short term, and who or what had he given up,' recalled Guy Stanton.

In Pakistan he was re-arrested, and in 2001 it was reported that he had been jailed for seven years in Lahore for smuggling 17.5 tonnes of hash seized at the Hub Dam fifteen years earlier. Again his incarceration did not last long. Further reports said he had absconded and fled to his Khyber fortress, others that he was released after the 9/11 attacks. One newspaper report claimed that he was 'central in moves to bring together the shattered Afghan warlords, whom it is hoped will ... be able to assist in the tracking down of Osama bin Laden'. He died of natural causes in 2009.

Operation Gurkha had another unforeseen consequence. Elvis, Sheen and Stanton all spent long months away from their partners at the height of the operation. The year after they came back, all three had babies.

10

TAKING STOCK

Following the failure of the Operation Gurkha heroin pick-up, I cadged a lift on a lorry being driven to southern Spain by Charlton, my fellow Betrayer. A forceful South Londoner with a view on everyone and everything, Charlton was our best HGV driver. He would criss-cross the UK and continental Europe, taking drugs or cigarettes hidden inside for gangs whose trust he had won, under the cover of being the owner-driver of his own rig. If his loads were taken out by our firm or the police, and the conspirators arrested, he claimed he was an innocent employee transporting what he thought was legit cargo, and the targets rarely suspected him of betrayal.

On this occasion he was heading to Malaga for a pick-up. I was working a separate case and needed to get to Gibraltar to meet a source promising access to a Moroccan-based group of hash and baccy smugglers. After a long journey involving much mickey-taking and office gossip, Charlton dropped me off and I caught the ferry as a foot passenger to Gib.

I was actually mixing two jobs. The first was to cultivate my source, who came from a well-established smuggling family. Illegal cigarettes were becoming a massive problem for the Exchequer and Gib was a major source of supply, and he was able to introduce me to some of the people behind this market.

The second, which involved crossing back over to Spain, was to hook up with a different gang working in cannabis. They were unusual in that their boss was female, something almost unknown in the male-dominated drug world.

'Martha' was well known to our firm, having been prosecuted in the past. She was believed to be planning a run of two tonnes from Morocco into Spain and then on to the UK. I had been sold to her as someone who could help. We met at an al fresco restaurant with a charming sea view at Rincon de la Victoria, just east of Malaga. Martha was slim and dark, with hard features. She sat with two men. One had the build and look of a bodyguard. The other was besuited, fit-looking and very aware; he was, I guessed, the money man.

I decided to get under Martha's skin from the start. Feigning ignorance, I sat down and addressed myself directly to the money man. He immediately became uncomfortable. As I ploughed on his unease increased, while Martha looked distinctly annoyed.

Eventually he blurted out, 'I'm not in charge, she is.'

'What?' I said, playing the misogynist. 'You've got to be kidding. A "sort" in charge? What is the world coming to?'

Martha butted in angrily. 'You want to deal, you deal with me.'

This was good. Instead of appraising me, she was trying to impress. I waded on.

'Sorry, love,' I said, leaning back with a patronising air, 'but shouldn't you be home cooking and looking after the babies?'

Her team were now stuck between wanting to jump me for my rudeness, and fear of scotching the deal for their boss, who was boiling with anger. I knew I was pushing hard but recalled the saying: *He who angers you, conquers you.* That was my aim.

'I have just lost half a tonne at sea,' she hissed, fire in her eyes. 'Half a tonne, that is the level I deal at.'

'Well don't that beat all. You're the first boss I've met who boasts about *losing* gear. Sorry, darling, but I'm out of here.' I stood up and made ready to go.

'Sit down,' she barked.

I did. We started over and I wasn't questioned about a thing. The shock of my insult to her authority had been too much. She concentrated on telling me how big her team was, who they were and what they had done. It was a very informative chat.

I passed on all the details to my handler, but before we could progress the case, the Spanish police arrested Martha. It turned out they had already been working up a case against her. Still, it had been a useful trip.

Knowing that I had cadged a lift there, the bean counters at HMCE were keen that I should save a flight fare home. Fortunately the *Falcon* had just made a legend-building run off Cap Spartel, the cannabis collection capital of the world, which was sometimes so busy that ships would queue to meet the small craft bringing out hessian-wrapped bales of hashish. The crew were due to sail home but made a detour to Gib to pick me up.

I found them docked at the South Mole, the breakwater in the southern section of the harbour. I was nominally the *Falcon*'s owner, so there was nothing suspicious about me going on board, but I waited until late evening so that few people saw me.

The next day, a kindly old lady tottered up to the vessel. We had been readying to sail and the engine room was filthy. I was sitting on an upturned bucket, smoking the stub of a cigar, black with engine dirt and with my hair tied in a scruffy ponytail. If someone had dropped a match I would have taken half the dock with me.

In a dowager voice, the old lady asked if we could recover some jewellery that she had lost over the side of her boat, a huge private yacht moored some way down from our tub.

She wrinkled her nose the nearer she got to me and I could see her eyes misting. Washing on the ship was discouraged, it kept inquisitive visitors at a healthy distance. All we usually cleaned was our teeth. When standing down from a job after weeks at sea, we would often burn our clothes rather than try to wash them.

The lads, all trained divers, duly recovered her tiara, though how they found it in the murk remains a mystery. The lady repaid us with crates of beer sent over from her floating gin palace and we gave ourselves a pat on the back for keeping our cover so expertly. That was the last pat for some time as normal service was resumed.

The following morning we left the harbour in clear weather. The two true seamen aboard were Big Pete and Eccles. The rest were amateurs: me, Charlton and Chameleon Boy. I never claimed to be a seaman. If any of my targets asked if I was, I would reply, 'Of course not, I own the bloody things. I don't know the front of a boat from the back, I get people to do that.'

Unlike Charlton, who was always right and would hear no arguments, Chameleon picked up his sobriquet for effortlessly switching sides during any debate, to the extent that he became a card-carrying member of every faction in the team. He also had an instinct for mischief. They were a sound bunch, each different but that's what made them good covert operators. No one would ever guess what they really were.

The bickering was always in good spirit and kept us going during long, boring hours of slow sea travel – and I mean slow. The boat's top speed was ten knots but Pete was ordered to keep it at a sedate four knots to save fuel. This was guaranteed to drive him mad, and the combination of certain crew members he regarded as useless, and the enforced speed limit, ensured he was mad a lot of the time. Sometimes we moved so slowly that I felt I could drop over the side and swim faster.

By the next morning, as the *Falcon* crashed through deep-green rollers of the Bay of Biscay somewhere off the Portuguese coast, he was even more sullen. Somehow the restocking of the cooking gas cylinders had been overlooked.

'I can't travel all the way back to Blighty without hot food, or at least a cuppa,' complained Pete. 'What are we going to do.'

He, Eccles and I were sitting morosely in the galley. On watch were Chameleon and Charlton. 'I'm sure I checked the gas supplies when we left port,' said a sheepish Eccles.

'Look,' I said, laying the sea chart over a table, 'let's do a quick detour into here, Porte de Sine. I'll pick up some supplies and hunt up some replacement gas canisters. What do you think?'

Within the hour, the *Falcon* was anchored a mile out and Pete and I were in the RHIB heading for shore. Porto de Sines was a large port and we attracted little attention. I picked up bread, beer and sardines. We normally dined on gallons of tea, instant noodles and Mars Bars, so fresh fish was welcome. We also scoured the harbour for gas canisters, without success.

As we prepared to leave, I noticed some dock workers welding repairs to a crane. 'How much for the gas canister?' I asked them, waving a bunch of twenty escudo notes.

'How much you got?' said the gang boss.

'A hundred and sixty escudos,' I said.

'Funny,' said the gang boss. 'This canister cost a hundred and sixty escudos.' What a coincidence.

Pete and I lugged it onto the RHIB. We both had a nagging doubt whether oxyacetylene was the proper replacement for calor gas, but who would know the difference?

Back on board, we put to sea. While the lads busied themselves around the boat, Pete and I climbed onto the galley roof with the canister, which was too big to go inside. We pulled the oven gas line through the aft galley window to connect it.

The boat was rolling and keeping balance was hard but Pete managed to push the gas hose onto the connector. It made a loud hiss and then cut off.

'Let's tighten the grip on the hose line and turn on,' I said.

At this point the safety seal on top of the canister pinged off. A light aluminium cap embossed with the words 'Danger: do not use if seal broken' arced through the air and vanished over the side of the boat.

'That's not good,' said Pete.

'I suppose not, but only you and I saw it, so no harm done.'

We lashed the canister to a small roof mast. 'Get into the galley and check that the canister is connected to the oven line,' yelled Pete to Eccles.

'Okay,' shouted back Eccles. 'It's all connected.'

Pete and I opened the gas valve. 'Turn it on and light her up,' I shouted.

There was a muffled thump. The roof of the galley came up in a large bulge. Its white paint cracked and turned a dark brown. Then the windows blew out. A small flame flickered at the end of the lead where the oven used to be.

'Oops,' said Pete.

We scrambled down just in time to meet a dazed Eccles coming out of the galley.

'What the fuck happened?' he said woozily. His face was black and there was a smell of burning, with a trail of blue smoke curling up from his hair, as if he had a lit fag behind his ear. 'I heard you shout, then there was a blinding flash.'

'That would be the oxyacetylene blowing up,' I said, hoping he would be suckered by my honesty.

'Oxyacetylene?' shouted Eccles. 'Oxy-fucking-acetylene? Where's my shirt and trousers?'

'You'd better lie down,' I said. 'You look a little hot under the collar.' Wisps of blue smoke continued to rise from his head as he trudged up the deck.

'Looks like cold food all the way home,' said Pete.

Such was life on the boat with the boys. We spent much of the time laughing.

The Beta Projects headquarters had by then been relocated, along with much of the ID, to Custom House. Grade 1 listed, it sits on the north bank of the Thames, in the heart of the City, and is considered to be one of London's finest Georgian buildings. Beta was first stuck in the basement, before later moving to the third floor on what became the building's secure wing.

It may have been a magnificent pile, but as UCs we were not allowed in. Indeed we could not enter any official site without permission, and even then had to be driven in the boot of a car or the back of a van, so no-one could see us. So when, a few months after my trip to Gib, we held a conference to assess the progress of Beta Projects and to plan its further expansion, it was held in an off-site location that could never be connected to HMCE.

On a Monday morning in mid-November, the Beta Projects officers and a small number of guests met in secrecy in a conference room in the north of England. It was their third such gathering in the three years of Beta's existence and, with the team now established full-time, the most important yet. It had originally been intended to hold such meetings every six months, but operational demands on the UCs made that impossible. Winter was the best time for them to get together, when boat smuggles dropped off. The purpose was to review progress and plan for the future.

ACIO Nick Baker welcomed the ID's overall boss, Chief Investigation Officer Doug Tweddle, and other senior managers, including the deputy in charge of intelligence and the principal for administrative support. Arranged around the room were Beta SIO Ray Pettit and twenty-one members of his team, both undercovers and handlers. They included

Guy Stanton and the colleagues nicknamed Charlton, Big
Pete, Elvis, Sheen, Pigpen, Chameleon, Keef and Little Tony.
Representing an array of skills, experiences and personality
types, they were a disparate group – to a degree. Only one
was female and one black, a reflection of the limited pool
from which Beta Projects drew its UCs at the time.

Also present was the SIO of Branch 8, responsible for the
drug liaison officers, or DLOs, based abroad. A lady from
the Secret Intelligence Service sat quietly, taking the occasional note; Beta was now working regularly with SIS. Others
present included two officers from the division's Technical
Support Unit; a lawyer from the Solicitor's Office; the officer
who led Omega, a tiny, secret unit within Branch Ten that
liaised with the security and intelligence services; the team's
accountant; and Keith Jones, their psychologist.

Though largely informal, there was a sense of gravity to
the proceedings. Just a month earlier, two officers from the
Met's SO10 branch had been shot and badly wounded while
working undercover in Birmingham. They had been sent on
secondment to West Midlands Police to buy crack cocaine,
but their targets had turned the tables and tried to rob them at
gunpoint. Both had to be medically discharged from the force
and would receive hefty financial settlements. No-one at the
conference needed reminding of the dangers of the job.

The first to make a report was Keef, who had recently
returned from a two-week training course with US Customs.
Largely classroom-based, its most valuable component, he
said, was how they taught UCs to cope with stressful situations. The Americans also explored psychological techniques
like assessing and using body language in their interactions
with criminals.

The emphasis on psychology, particularly for the well-
being of the UCs, was something Beta Projects took seriously.
Baker and Pettit were aware of the danger that their officers

might experience a form of Stockholm syndrome, the emotional state in which hostages develop a sympathetic bond with their captors. In the undercover world it manifested itself through long-serving UCs adopting the traits of their alter egos and behaving like the criminals they were investigating. There were known cases of FBI agents being unable to switch off their false personas and committing serious crimes, while one Canadian UC was said to have become so confused after giving up his legend that he could not talk to anyone but his dog. Regular testing, would, it was hoped, spot any problems before they arose, and Stanton and the others had periodic psychological reviews.

Our psychologist was a decent chap and would talk to all of us individually in private. He took great pains to look for evidence of what he called 'seepage', where the UC looked and sounded fine but was breaking down inside. Every so often you would have a very dark session where he would ask if you were you feeling depressed or had thoughts of suicide. He was also always looking to see if you were lying to him. Some UCs start to lead the life of their legends, while hiding it from their handlers. When I was Stanton, for example, I would think nothing of tipping fifty quid in a casino or high-class restaurant. But I would never do that in real life.

Some believed these assessments to be a waste of time but I never met an invincible UC in my entire career. Some just coped with pressure better than others. The handler was crucial here. Not only were they your interface with the outside world, they were also watching for signs of unusual behaviour: withdrawal, being too flash, drinking too much, paranoia. No-one was immune.

Going home and switching off was a problem for a lot of UCs. We all had different ways of diffusing stress. Some liked to go running or to the gym. I had my medal collecting and my garden. Little Phil, our Scouse odd-job man, unwound by visiting galleries and museums. He sometimes even arranged meets there, as it never occurred to villains that art galleries are the most CCTV'd places in the world.

Next, one of the covert method-of-entry team spoke about anti- and counter-surveillance and the use of personal disguises. Customs UCs rarely used disguise, unlike the spooks of SIS, although Stanton would later wear one when testifying in a Dutch court case.

Two senior officers then discussed liaison with the security services and working with HMCE's own drug liaison officers, or DLOs, abroad. Beta Projects officers had licence to roam and were increasingly finding themselves in locations all around the world. Their DLO colleagues in each country were briefed before deployment on the work of Beta and would turn out to be indispensable allies.

If you were going into a place for the first time, you wanted to know exactly what you might be up against. The DLOs had vital in-country knowledge. Conversely, they needed to know what you might get up to, as they were acting on behalf of HM Government in a sovereign foreign state and would take the flak if things went haywire. They were also an interface with local law enforcement. If you suggested a plan to them, they could advise if it was illegal in that jurisdiction or if the place was too corrupt for it to work. You might then devise a 'black op' instead, which they have to explore through other channels with the ambassador and SIS. That course was never taken lightly. You can't just pop people into another country and do what you want.

The DLOs could never replace a good handler, though. At the conference we discussed an early foreign deployment in which we had used a boat and the DLO ended up handling the job. We decided that was wrong, you had to have a handler out there in person.

Foreign travel was also great for legend building. If I was meeting traffickers in, say, Dubai I would deliberately phone criminals in the UK or Europe for a 'chat', mentioning where I was and perhaps the pedigree of the people I was with. Likewise I would sometimes have colleagues phone me from abroad while I was at a meet in the UK, to impress the people I was with.

Beta eventually set up transport firms with the German and Dutch police. If we needed a Dutch UC to play a role in London, we could call on them and vice versa. There was lots of mutual cooperation and they were all great partners. Our financial man, Keef, also linked up with a Dutch counterpart to show him the tricks of the dodgy money trade. They ultimately opened a business together in Amsterdam, offering financial services to narcos. A lot of what we did was actually taken from the Royal Canadian Mounted Police, who were at the cutting edge when it came to creative undercover work and fake businesses.

Budget controls and the keeping of accounts were discussed and the meeting allocated various administrative tasks to each officer. They would have to perform these on top of their undercover work. Guy Stanton was responsible for acquiring and maintaining all of their many passports; some UCs had half a dozen. Little Tone covered Beta's input to CEDRIC, the HMCE computer system for collating and disseminating intelligence. Charlton looked after their vehicles and liaised with the DVLA. Elvis took office equipment and IT. Harvey was responsible for their cellphones and for maintaining legends at the Contributions Agency. Keef kept the major banks and the Inland Revenue sweet.

We bought an office under the name of a cover company, and a cavernous warehouse where we kept cars, ocean-going RHIBs and other kit, all top-notch; it does no good to have sleepless nights about the quality of your equipment. Thanks to Ray and Nick, nothing was cheap or shoddy. They never cut corners. The trawler was our best flash asset but we also had two yachts, one usually based in the Caribbean, the other Gibraltar, with crew living on them, sailing around and offering their services to traffickers.

Stanton frequently flew business class and I became so well known on the Emirates airline that they would put out a bottle of champagne for me when I boarded. I often flew overnight and, as I don't sleep on flights, would use the quiet time to read in peace, sipping a glass of bubbly. American Express eventually wrote to say that I was spending between £10,000 and £20,000 a month, much of it on flying teams in and out of the Middle East and putting them in hotels. Stanton was already an AMEX Gold holder but they offered me a black Centurion card as well, reserved for their most exclusive clients. Flashing it in front of bad guys worked wonders for my legend.

We had lots of props. All of mine were real. You couldn't claim to be a player while wearing plastic shoes and a fake watch, driving a Fiat Twingo. Some of the cleverer criminals feign poverty – Pablo Escobar was shot dead in an old shirt and flip-flops – but they are rare. The normal rule is, if you've got it, flaunt it.

Maintaining an affluent front had its downsides. Once, working in Ramsgate, Kent, I popped into a public toilet, took off my Rolex to wash my hands, and walked out leaving it on the sink. I didn't notice for an hour, and thank God when I rushed back to the loo it was still on the sink, all £75,000 worth. That would have been a hard one to tell Ray.

When I first got my other Rolex, worth £125,000, it was too small for my wrist, so I took it to a London jeweller to have an extra link inserted. It was obvious when I dropped it on the counter that the assistant was used to a more genteel type of client. He examined it nervously and said, 'It will cost five hundred pounds.'

'Good. Get it done quick, I'll be back in an hour.'

When I returned, the shop was much busier, which set off my suspicions. I wondered if the kid had called the police, believing the watch was stolen, and I was about to be arrested.

'I'm Mr Stanton, I left the Rolex here earlier today for a link.'

'Hold on,' said the lad, 'the manager would like to talk to you.' *Here we go*, I thought, *this is a nicking*.

When the manager came out, however, he rushed to greet me like an old friend.

'Mr Stanton! So pleased to meet you. What a beautiful watch! I've only seen one other like this in my life. Where did you get it?'

Henri Exton always told me to distrust everybody. If somebody admires your watch, you might later find that he knows someone at Rolex – who keep the serial number of every watch they produce – and is planning to check you out. We had this one down as a gift from my Arab employers, so the 'sheikh's' name was on the records. It was actually a secret loan from Rolex themselves.

'It was a gift from my Arab employers,' I lied.

'I guessed it was from the Middle East from the movement. Our Arabic customers like a ticking hand rather than a sweeping hand. It's magnificent. I believe there are only five of these in the world.'

'To tell the truth I don't like it, it's too gaudy for me.'

'Really?' His eyes lit up. 'What do you like?'

'Just a plain gold Rolex.'

'How about a white-faced gold Rolex and eighty thousand pounds for your watch?'

He meant it. Now my eyes lit up. 'Err,' I stammered, thinking, *could I take the money and tell Ray I lost the watch?* Instead honesty prevailed. 'That's very kind of you. But I don't think my employers would be very happy.' I was being more truthful than he knew.

'Of course. But here is my card in case you ever change your mind.'

Integrity intact, I left the shop, but the sum of eighty grand played in my head for weeks.

Ray would arrange any luxury goods that we needed. Cars we would usually buy, although the Dutch-plate 500-E that I drove was a seizure that the Dutch police lent to us. Cars might look flash but they can be cheap compared to top-end watches and jewellery.

Also discussed was the role of female UCs. Little Tone outlined an operation involving a number of female couriers supplied by the Regional Crime Squad, and the problems they had encountered. Chief among these was sexual harassment from their male targets. All of Beta's handlers at that time were men, and a main concern was how a male handler could adequately help a female UC to cope with sexual advances while working in character. The obvious suggestion was that Beta deploy female handlers in such cases, which would have the added benefit of making contact with the UCs easier, for example in ladies' toilets, where male handlers and targets could not go.

One of the male UCs joked that he was concerned because no advances of a sexual nature were made to him.

Beta had very few women. The problem was not that they did not want to deploy them, it was that criminal teams would not talk to them or take them seriously. I only ever met one smuggling team led by a female, which was Martha in Gibraltar.

While there have been cases of women being active in the South American cocaine trade, generally Turkish, African, Slavic and Asian traffickers were dismissive of women. We can be as woke as we like, but in the Turkish or Middle Eastern drug world they simply will not deal with a woman. Western enlightenment doesn't come into it; they are misogynists and their women stay in the background. I once watched a TV drama series that portrayed a female leader of a Kurdish crime group. Not a chance.

Though I never worked on a job with a female UC, I was certainly not in the camp of using them only as arm candy. My own wife was a long-term investigator in the firm, and I worked with women in other departments who were highly professional. And as UCs they have their own arsenal of skills and wiles and can be brilliant at leveraging ego in men. The police had some excellent female UCs.

But there was no denying the danger of entering an aggressive male environment and facing sexual pressure. That did not stop female deployments – and male UCs could face sexual advances too – but it was a serious health and safety concern. We found out after one operation that a female police UC had spent the night in one of the target's rooms. Whether she had sex with him or not, it was dangerous, and she was out of the control of her handler.

The more general question of sex on the job, for both male and female officers, was simple: don't do it. It was common sense. Any vice is a bad idea when you are working. You are there to obtain evidence and may have to speak to that evidence in court. If defence counsel find out that you have slept with your target, or the target's wife or girlfriend, they are going to make mincemeat of you.

Likewise if you took drugs with their client. What was your reasoning? You could just imagine the ripping you would get: 'Explain to the court, officer, were you in a fit state of mind when gathering this evidence? It's all very clear to you now but of course you haven't just smoked a spliff or snorted coke, have you?' The same with drink. We were taught to dump booze and we dumped all the time. You keep buying drinks but control the bottle on the table while everyone else is getting paralytic. My biggest vice was probably strong coffee.

I did go into brothels because they were good meeting places. Most of them were near-beer places, the kind of clip joints I had investigated as a regular officer. The baddies liked to go there and talk business, as it was difficult for a surveillance team to follow them in without showing out or being expected to pick up a girl.

Beta also had very few officers from an ethnic minority background. Our only black UC for a long time was Harvey. The police had a lot more. Ethnicity can have an advantage, in that your mere appearance can open doors in certain communities. At the same time, it can be deployed insensitively. For example, management might be tempted to deploy a black UC against a ragamuffin Jamaican yardie gang when in fact he came from a middle-class family and was unlikely to fit in. I could go up against the white underclass because that was my own background; I knew those streets and how those people talked.

The conference moved on to discuss a series of mundane but necessary action points. Limits were to be raised on the officers' credit cards, given the amounts that they were spending. Somebody suggested the UCs be authorised to make small buys of drugs in order to establish credibility. CIO Tweddle was supportive but wanted legal advice first. 'You were not going to nick anybody on a credibility buy,' said one of those present. 'The idea was to find out who was in charge of the person you were buying from and where they were getting their gear. You could also identify lower-tier dealers, who you

could pass on to local enforcement for future action.' The
wiring up of vehicles and premises was also aired, for which
the Technical Support Unit was responsible. Many UCs also
wore devices to record evidence, initially the pioneering
Nagra reel-to-reel recorder, small enough to be taped to the
body and concealed under clothing.

The Nagra was a standard piece of kit that recorded in
greater clarity than other devices, even the later digital ones.
It was not muffled when you played it back. Some didn't
want to wear one because it was risky but I felt they used that
as an excuse. The more successful UCs were those that taped
the most and I wore one as much as I could. If you are going
to engage you need evidence, otherwise what's the point of
being there? Obviously if the situation is too dangerous and
you expect to get rubbed or stripped down, you have to leave
the recorder and make notes afterwards. But the more you
get your targets making admissions on tape, the less need for
you to testify in court. Often we would play them the tape
after arrest and they would throw up their hands and plead
guilty. It is hard to continue a denial when the tape is clear
evidence.

I usually taped my Nagra to the small of my back or my
groin. The microphone leads were the problem, as they had
to come up over your body to pick up the sound. We later
adopted a system called Falcon, with tiny microphones in
pagers or phones. The Nagras were superseded by a transmis-
sion kit, with a microphone and someone nearby carrying a
receiver bag to pick up the conversation, then by digital kit,
which was much smaller and lasted longer.

The closest I came to being caught was when a London
gangster insisted on patting me down in the street. I opened
my shirt to show my bare chest but refused to go any further.
Given that we were in a public place, he accepted this as fair.

My Nagra was actually in my shirt, so he missed it. The Turks were subtle, they would come and give you a big hug while patting your body for any lumps. To be fair they were often looking for shooters, not tape recorders.

At around this time, the ID was invited to join the International Undercover Working Group, which brought police forces together from all over the world to share experiences and coordinate. An informal body with no central office, it met twice a year, often in attractive locations such as New Zealand and South Africa. The invitation was accepted. Assistant chief Nick Baker attended for the ID and met managers of similar rank to discuss issues such as cooperation and legislation, although he was the only customs officer in what was otherwise a police body.

For Beta Projects, Ray also hosted semi-regular team meetings once every couple of months at our secure premises. These brought everyone together to see what they were up to, have some face-to-face time and air any grievances or complaints. The only excuse for non-attendance was if you were deployed. You could bring everybody up to speed on what jobs you were on and let off steam at the same time.

In reality, team meetings often descended into a combat zone. Poor old Ray faced a load of egos all screaming and shouting *I want this, why has he got that car, why wasn't I invited on this job?* He would do his best to placate us but it was a thankless task.

As more candidates came forward for the team, we also changed our recruitment and training. We would hire outside offices to conduct interviews, then run candidates through a three-day preliminary course, mainly in-tray exercises to see how they coped and find out what their skillset was and what their stories could be.

At the same time we decided that, although the courses run by SO10 and Omega in Manchester were great, they were not giving us what we needed on the customs side. A lot of customs work takes place abroad, where we faced different issues than domestic cops. They are not holiday trips, you are away in a false name, under false documents, and have to consider the laws of the host nation and the diplomatic niceties. We ended up devising our own training more suited to our needs.

By then I was running flat out. Operation Acolyte was going strong but Stanton was also moving through other layers of the underworld. Almost every week brought a new meet, a new scenario, a new game I had to play. And the drug trade kept churning more furiously than ever.

11

IN DEEP

The Hotel Torrequebrada, a brash beachfront leisure complex and casino in the Costa del Sol resort of Benalmadena. I was in the lobby to meet a Dutchman called Jan.

He had rung the day before from Gibraltar, was travelling to Spain and wanted to talk business. I agreed to meet but said it had to be soon, as 'the season' had just begun and I was very busy. Jan knew what I meant – the cannabis-sailing season starts in the spring when the weather improves and the seas are calmer – and said he was keen to crack on.

At 9.30 a.m., a tall, clean-shaven man in jeans, leather jacket and gold jewellery walked into the lobby.

'Jan?'

'Yes.'

We shook hands. 'Do you mind going somewhere else?' he immediately asked.

'Sure.'

We walked outside to a gold-coloured Mercedes coupé with a thin man in the front passenger seat. He had dark, cropped hair, a heavy shadow and the deep tan of someone who spent his time in the sun. But when he said hello, his accent was pure East End Cockney.

We drove for ten minutes to a marina and found a small bar for coffee.

'So what are you after?' I asked.

'We're looking to sail a load to somewhere off the Irish coast,' said Jan. 'We need you to take it onto your boat, over to the UK, and run it inshore in a Zodiac.'

'Doesn't sound like a problem. But I need to know who I'm giving it over to.'

The tanned Londoner cleared his throat. 'That'll be me,' he said. 'The gear's mine.'

I nodded but said nothing, letting them lead the conversation. Jan said my boat would come alongside his at sea to take on the load. The Cockney and I looked at each other and both burst out laughing.

'My boat would smash yours to bits, mate,' I said. Far better, I went on, to sail out to coordinates in the Atlantic and use a small craft to cooper the gear between the two main vessels. I would then sail the load back to another pre-arranged point off the English coast and from there would motor it ashore to the Cockney's reception team.

'There'll be a lot of fine details,' I said. 'Codes for us to use, signals, timings, positions, money transfers. But that's not up for discussion now. I'm here to see if we can strike common ground. If all three of us are happy after today, we can meet again to seal the deal.'

They agreed.

'Do you still live in London?' asked the Cockney.

'Nah. Retired to the Home Counties now.'

'Kent?'

'Being a bit nosey, aren't you?'

He laughed. At that point another customer sat down on a chair behind us and seemed to agitate them.

'Why don't we walk and talk?' I said.

Relieved, the Cockney stood up and the three of us set off

on a short stroll around Benalmadena marina. Jan pointed out several yachts that he claimed were his. One, with green-and-white markings and a red ensign, was in the process of being sold, he said, but if the sale fell through it would be the one he would use for our run.

'Where have you traded from before?' asked the Cockney.

'The Middle East mainly.'

He asked about smuggling routes from that area and if I could introduce him to any sellers there.

'I could, but not at the moment. We need to know each other better.'

'Can you transfer gear from there to the UK?'

'Not a problem. But, no offence, mate, I'm not that happy about you asking so much about me.'

'Sorry,' he said. 'I can just see some big possibilities. Gotta sound these things out, don't ya?'

As we walked on, Jan indicated two more boats moored together: a yacht and a large motor cruiser. He said they were his too. 'Both can carry three tonnes,' he said.

'Maybe they could both go to the rendezvous point,' said the Cockney. 'Could your ship handle that?'

'It could. Would the load be in twenty-five lumps?' Hash was often packed in 25 kg parcels known as lumps.

'Yeah.'

'That's fine. My boat's got nets and a crane that can lift one-and-a-half tonnes at a time from smaller boats.'

Jan next pointed out a so-called cigarette boat, a low-slung, high-speed racer of a type often used to smuggle cigs across the Strait. He said it had 850 horsepower and was one of his best. If he was to be believed, he had an entire fleet.

The Cockney asked, 'Do you mind meeting next time in London?'

'I'm not too happy inside the M25. What about the Midlands?'

He insisted on London, and eventually I consented to meet at lunchtime on May 1 at the Tower Hotel, near Tower Bridge, which had a small, intimate upstairs bar.

'Problem for me,' said the Cockney, 'is that if we have too many meets, next thing is we are all looking at a conspiracy charge. If we get smudged together, that's it.'

'I make you right,' I said. 'And while we're on the subject, can neither of you use the phone to contact me.'

'Sure,' said the Cockney. 'Don't worry about it. I've got a mate called John, and he never knows when to shut up. We were working on a thing, and every time he said "Morocco" over the phone, I had to throw mine away. England is the worst place to do business,' he continued, warming to his subject. 'The Customs are shit-hot. If they get an inch on you, you're dead.'

I agreed.

'Fifteen months ago, I lost an entire crew down in Cornwall,' he said. 'They're all in Exeter now, doing a long time.'

I knew about this mob, a proper South London firm that my colleagues had taken out as they unloaded four-and-a-half tonnes from a fishing boat. The ringleaders got a dozen years each.

'Bit different in Holland,' said Jan. 'I'm appealing against a sentence there at the moment. I got six months for two-and-a-half tonnes.'

'No kidding, that'd be worth a twelve in the UK,' I said.

'Dead right,' said the Cockney. 'I think the government's going to legalise cannabis anyway. Then they can tax the fuck out of it, like they do everything else.'

I laughed. 'Well, since it's still illegal for now, let's stay careful.'

The Cockney asked if it would be possible for my landing team to drive the load ten miles inland before handing it over, rather than do so by the shore, and said he would pay up to three per cent more for this.

'No, I'm not happy with that. All the risk will be with me.'

'But I don't want my people to see your boat or where you are landing,' he said. 'That's your business. What about if you take a van from me, drive it to the landing, load it, then drive it back?'

'That might be possible. We can firm up a plan later.'

'Well, if we can come to some deal, I'll be very happy,' said the Cockney.

We walked back to the car. I again took the back seat again and we headed to the hotel.

'Back in England, I'm more paranoid,' said the Cockney, twisting around in his seat. 'At home I go everywhere on a bike and no-one can get near me without me noticing. You'll see, when we next meet I'll be blacked up in all my biker leather. Conspiracy's difficult to prove in Spain but dead easy in England.'

He asked again about the placement of his coastal team and 'not plotting my boys right next to the beach'.

'We can discuss all this later when we've settled on a price and firmer date,' I said, determined not to drop my knickers on the first date.

I got out at the hotel and we shook hands. 'See you in London,' I said. 'Stay safe.'

'I hope we can do business,' was the Cockney's parting shot. 'You've got just I want.'

Back in my room, I grabbed some sheets of hotel notepaper and quickly wrote a full account of the meeting in ballpoint to pass on to my handler.

The Cockney and Jan didn't turn up for the meet at the Tower Hotel. I never found out why.

Three months later, in late June, I sat in a rented office at a business premises on Avenue Louise, a main thoroughfare on the south side of Brussels. The office was newly furnished and had smoked-glass windows for privacy. Opposite me was a fat, bespectacled Liverpudlian called Terry, who had been introduced to me by an intermediary. My role was to provide transport for a cannabis shipment and a safe slaughter where it could be broken out of its cover load and removed to storage.

Terry looked quite dapper in a dark suit. The same could not be said for the man with him. 'This is Harry Boy,' he said.

They were obviously friends but looked startlingly ill-matched. Harry Boy was six feet two with the build of a journeyman heavyweight and a face to match. He wore an electric-blue tracksuit of a material that generated so much static his hair stood up. And what hair it was, a long peroxide mass, almost polar white, of tight curls. His huge gold neck-chain could have anchored a battleship, and on each arm rattled an array of chains and ID bracelets. His massive feet were encased in pure-white trainers.

'How do,' said Harry Boy.

'Alright, pal,' I said. 'Sit yourself down.'

Terry faced me across a table, while Harry Boy stood at his shoulder.

'What we are looking for,' said Terry, 'is transport and a safe place for a slaughter.'

'Yeah, slaughter the load,' said Harry Boy.

'Above all,' said Terry, 'it's got to be safe, out of the way and not known to many people.'

'Yeah, not known to people,' echoed Harry Boy.

'How big's the load?' I asked.

'Why do you need to know?' asked Terry.

'Yeah, why do you need to know?' came the echo.

'If I'm providing transport, I need to have some idea of where, when and how,' I said, truthfully. 'I wouldn't want to be left holding my dick and nothing else on the day.'

'Understood,' said Terry.

'Yeah, understood,' repeated Harry Boy.

I finally snapped.

'Look, mate,' I said to Harry Boy, 'can you shut it? It's a bit off-putting hearing your echo every time your boss speaks.'

'What!' roared Harry Boy. 'I'm Terry's advisor. He don't move without my advice.'

'Lucky you don't advise him on how to dress.'

Terry barely suppressed a smirk.

'What do you mean?' demanded Harry Boy.

'Well, look at you. You're dressed like a pimp.'

'Pimp!' shouted Harry Boy. 'Pimp! My wife picked this out for me.'

'Well then she's cheap,' I said.

That was a serious insult and I half-expected Harry Boy to explode. Instead he turned red, then purple.

'This outfit,' he gurgled, 'matches me shiny.'

'Your what?' I asked, knowing full well that it was northern slang for a gun.

'Me shiny, me shiny,' he repeated, starting to pace around the room. 'Me gun is the same colour as me tracksuit.'

'So you've spray-painted your gun, I mean your shiny, to match your clothes? The paint must really help it to shoot well.'

Harry Boy was finally struck dumb. It was perhaps dawning on him that a matching tracksuit-and-firearm ensemble was not a great look. Throughout our exchange, Terry sat wearing a half-smile. I'm sure he knew I was teasing Harry Boy.

'Harry, Harry,' he finally said, 'go stand over there and don't keep interrupting.'

I returned to the matter in hand and Terry and I discussed in broad terms the load, the wagon I would provide and the slaughter. Harry Boy moped in front of the smoked glass, where he could see his reflection.

'What's the matter with me trackie?' he said to himself, in a sulky tone. 'It's top class. My wife got me this. That guy hasn't got a clue.' Still muttering, he turned and came over again to remonstrate further. I decided to nip this in the bud.

'Look, mate. This is going to get nasty in a minute, so don't fucking go there. I've had enough of your bollocks.'

He stopped in his tracks but opened his mouth to protest.

'Harry!' barked Terry. 'Shut it.'

Terry and I looked at each other and burst out laughing.

We got down to business. Terry had a crop of two tonnes of sinsemilla, a strong, seedless cannabis, ready in Jamaica and needed transport to the UK. I offered him two options, both by shipping container: we could either slip the entire container past customs in the UK via my corrupt port contacts, or remove the drugs discreetly in a rip-off while the container awaited clearance at the docks.

The first option, I said, was less risky. But the 'box' needed to be 'dry' and not a 'con-air' or a 'reefer', by which I meant the goods should not be in a chilled or frozen container. Throwing in a bit of jargon helped establish my bona fides.

'What size loads have you handled in the past?' asked Terry.

'Probably the biggest I've done was seventy-three tonnes. One of sixty-eight tonnes. So your two tonnes won't be much of a problem.'

Terry took this manfully in his stride.

'You'll need to sort the paperwork from Jamaica,' I said.

'No problem,' he said. 'That's all in hand. I'm more bothered about the British end. The UK's a fortress. Which port is going to be best for you on this?'

'I can get your load through Thames port or Felixstowe.'

Terry grinned. 'I'll call you Mr Felixstowe, then. What's the price?'

'It'll cost you a hundred quid a kilo. Two hundred grand for the lot. If you want a rip-off, it'll be another fifty large on top, as my people will be taking a bigger risk.'

Terry switched to small talk while he mulled over my offer. Then he suddenly asked who I knew in Liverpool.

'I do know people in Liverpool,' I said, 'but what has that got to do with anything?'

'I'm just trying to put your mind at rest, pal. You might feel better about this if you knew we had a mutual acquaintance.' He switched tack again. 'I had fifty kilos of gear in Ghana until recently, but I moved it up to Amsterdam. I made a loss on that but I did it to show my Ghanaian suppliers that I mean business. The big problem for them is that they make virtually nothing on gear in Europe, they get a much better price in the UK.'

By 'gear' he meant cocaine. This was getting interesting. For coke I said I could offer him a rip-off by air, and we discussed the best type of cargo to hide it in. 'Avoid perishable goods,' I said. 'Rice or spices are okay.'

'I didn't think they were common loads,' he said.

'I'm afraid you don't know much about this trade, then. Just make sure your people control the loading at the Ghana end.'

Terry seemed confident about this and said the gear would be loaded by 'the head of Ghanaian customs'. Knowing some African countries, this was not far-fetched. He then asked about the arrival airport. I said Heathrow was best.

'I thought the flights went only to Gatwick from there?'

'Well you're wrong again. Flights go from Ghana to both Heathrow and Gatwick.'

I had the feeling he was testing me by asking questions he already knew the answers to. He said he had at least fifty kilos of coke ready, which would go for around a couple of million in the UK, depending on purity. I quoted him £150,000 for my services. 'My fee will be paid cash-on-delivery on arrival of the goods. I don't ask for money upfront as most people can't afford it.'

He said he did not know how the coke had got to Ghana but believed it might even have been grown there, as the mountain conditions were the same as in Bolivia. This was unlikely. I did know that West African states were starting to be used as transit points on the smuggling route from South America to Europe, and suggested sending my own people to Ghana to act as a link. He wasn't having that, saying he would have his people there.

'Okay. But I will need to know as soon as the aircraft carrying the gear is on its way. Your people will have to be calling in as they wave goodbye to the plane on the runway.'

'No problem.'

As we concluded, I said it had been an easier meeting than I expected, as Terry seemed to have much of the work sewn up. He said he liked my directness and plain talking and asked if it was possible to meet again in the UK. After some debate, we agreed on Corley Services, on the M6 motorway near Birmingham, at six o'clock in the evening. Terry would call me with a day.

We shook hands and he and a somewhat downcast Harry Boy left. I had not been taped up, so I used the notepaper of the Holiday Inn at Brussels Airport to scribble down my account.

Terry rang a week later, and said simply, 'Tuesday.' We duly met in the restaurant on the northbound side at Corley. This time there was no Harry Boy but a new face, a cool, self-assured black guy who Terry introduced as Cliff. He politely asked if I'd had a good journey and where I had travelled from.

'East London.'

Terry wanted to know if I could handle his sensi by air freight from Jamaica, and said his people were 'straining at the leash' to send it. I said I would need to speak to my people, and asked what was happening with Ghana.

Cliff took over, saying there was a slight delay there which he was going to sort out, and asked what I thought would be the best cover load. I said that garri, a kind of flour made from cassava, was a common export.

Cliff nodded. 'He's right,' he told Terry.

'It should be packed in strong sacks, either hessian or plastic,' I said.

'That will be no problem,' said Cliff. 'Are the flights from Ghana cargo-only?'

'No, they're normally cargo and passengers mixed.'

'What papers will we need?'

'It will be better if the load is manifested.'

'But would you be able to recover the paperwork when the load arrives?'

'Sure, I can do that.'

Cliff switched back to the Jamaican sensi, saying it would probably be hidden in canned goods or a large load of ginger, and asked which port would be best for the container to go through.

'I've already told Terry, Felixstowe suits me. I've got good control there.'

He asked me for the names of shipping lines out of the West Indies. I mentioned the Harrison Line and a couple of others. They were all part of a consortium, the New Caribbean Line, that carried most of the loads from that part of the world.

'Well if we can't do it by air, we'll certainly do it by sea,' said Cliff.

I told Terry to ring me the next day with a yes or no. Both he and Cliff assured me they were happy with my transport price of £100 a kilo for the grass and Cliff said he appreciated my frankness.

We went over the details again as we walked back over the motorway bridge. Cliff then said he had to make a call, while Terry walked with me to the car park.

'Did you come in a red BMW?' he asked, all innocent.

'Right car, wrong colour. You don't give up, do you? Keep trying.'

We shook hands and were about to part when Cliff reappeared.

'What would be the best airline from Ghana?' he asked.

'Ghana Airways into Heathrow. Their cargos go into a separate warehouse rather than the British Airways one, which is harder for me. Terry suggested Gatwick but that's not possible, it's all BA.'

'How often do Ghana Airways come into Heathrow?'

'Monday, Wednesdays and Fridays.'

'Right, we'll use them,' he said.

We all shook hands again and I drove off.

Terry phoned a couple of days later. Again he kept it brief: 'Yes or no?'

'Not at the moment,' I replied. 'But I might be able to in six to eight weeks.' I was at that time embroiled in another major case.

'I've just got one question,' he said. 'Front or back?'

He could only mean whether the load should be placed at the front or back of the container for removal. 'If I understand you correctly, it's the back,' I said.

I didn't hear from them again for weeks. Then one lunchtime Cliff rang, wanting to meet. We agreed on Corley Services again, on the southbound side.

This time Cliff turned up with two new blokes with strong Scouse accents but no Terry. He asked if I minded going elsewhere, as his friends were 'very unhappy on this manor'.

'I don't mind where we go,' I said, but my thoughts were racing. *What was going on?*

We squashed into a Ford Escort and drove south, turning off at the A444 and stopping at a Welcome Break pub on a roundabout. Once inside, Cliff said he was ready to do business. His 'puff' – no 'charlie' this time – would be in a box and would be in the region of eight tonnes. 'I've just been out to Jamaica and everything's ready,' he said. 'My relatives are handling the load.'

'What will the legit cargo be?'

'Pots and pans. You know those large cooking pots made of steel? They go for twenty-six quid a throw in the Midlands.'

'So where do you two come into this?' I asked, looking at his accomplices.

'I'm going to be in charge of the slaughter,' said one of them.

'Who's sorting his wages?'

'I am,' said Cliff.

'And where's Terry?'

'Terry's been nicked,' said Cliff. 'In Cyprus. Doing a paper fraud with some Cockneys. Bad news, really. Still, it'll cheer him up if we can get this sorted.'

One of the men said he had recently been to South Africa in the hope of moving thirty-five tonnes to the UK. If true that would have been one of the biggest cannabis smuggles ever. 'I took a team there but we couldn't pick up the gear,' he said. 'Would you be able to help?'

'Let's get Cliff's run out the way first and then see where we stand.'

Cliff said, 'I'll be going out again the week after next, and should have the bill of lading ready for you in two to three weeks.'

We had a back and forth about who was going to phone who and about being careful over the blower. 'The Old Bill listen in and use devices to follow cars,' said one of them conspiratorially.

'I hope they haven't been following you tonight,' I told him.

All three laughed. We wrapped up, they drove me back to Corley and we parted.

At the end of September, fully three months after my first meeting with his organisation in Brussels, Cliff rang again. His voice was strained.

'What's the problem?' I asked. 'You sound worried.'

'No, no, I'm okay. I just need some questions answered.'

'You do, or is it your two mates?'

'Them,' he admitted.

I flipped. 'Who am I dealing with here? You have brought in two new faces, now they want to ask all sorts of questions, and that could give me a problem.'

'There's no problem. I'm in charge and you'll be dealing with me.'

I calmed down and told him to ring me back with a time and place to meet.

Two nights later, we met at the Holiday Inn in Birmingham city centre. Over orange juice and Perrier – strictly business – I asked Cliff what the problem was.

He again said, unconvincingly, that there was no problem but that when they had left me the other night they had thought of a couple of questions. One was how would I get the box out of the dock.

'By truck.'

'Do I need to pay duty?'

'What are you talking about? I'm going to be ripping the box off, so you won't be putting any paperwork in at the UK end.'

'Okay.' We talked more about logistics, then he asked if I would be able to remove information from the port computer system.

'That's my business,' I said. I also said I expected my people to be with his when the box was open, so they could confirm the size of the load and ensure I was being paid the correct price. 'I expect you to rip me for a small amount,' I said, 'but don't get silly, and tell your mates I won't be happy if they act stupid.'

'I'm a straight dealer,' he insisted, sounding insulted. 'There won't be any problems like that. If this one is a success, I'd like to drop a load of gear in with the next one.'

'Okay, but that'll cost you two grand a kilo.'

'I hope you are not upset with us,' said Cliff.

'I just want to know who I'm dealing with.'

'It's me.'

'Okay, but be careful. How are things with Terry?'

'Still inside. The Cypriots have put his case back and he's a bit depressed. Tell you the truth, he got very slack and tried to go it alone. That's why he got caught.'

'Not sure I like the sound of that. Tell Terry he better remember who he has been dealing with. I don't want any problems brought to my door.'

'Look after yourself,' said Cliff.

'Likewise.'

Again things went quiet, until one evening Cliff phoned and asked if I could meet him in Amsterdam. I asked if there was anything wrong and he said cryptically that there was someone he wanted me to meet. We set a date for the following week and I booked a flight.

We met in a hotel. Cliff explained that now we were so close to carrying out the trade he had brought along a man who would, if it was necessary, be able to tell if I was genuine. He made a call and five minutes later came a knock at the door. I was surprised to see a Liverpudlian drug dealer called John walk in. We'd had dealings in the past and I knew he was very cautious. I had once met him at a McDonald's restaurant and he had insisted on walking all around the building checking for cameras.

'Hello, John,' I said. 'What's all this then?'

'Nothing heavy, Guy. Cliff here just wanted to make sure you were right.'

Cliff was obviously uneasy about something but I had no idea what I might have done to arouse his concern. It soon became clear that I had done nothing wrong, this was just Cliff's regular way of dealing. When all was ready to go, he would bring along a third party to question his counterpart, as a kind of final stress test. On this occasion it just happened that I knew John.

John chatted for half an hour. I noticed he was careful not to ask about the load, but did ask Cliff if I was providing the slaughter. Cliff said that it was a bit more than that, but seemed a little shocked that I knew John. We said our good-byes and arranged a final meet in London in a couple of weeks.

Just as in my previous encounter with Jan and the Cockney in Spain, I never heard from Cliff, Terry, Harry Boy or any of their team again. For weeks after, I agonised over what I must have done wrong. Had some 'tell' given me away? Would it betray me again in the future? I went over and over my actions but could not pinpoint what had gone awry.

It was a couple of years later that I ran into John again and learned the truth. He admitted that he had warned them off by telling them I was going to rob them of their load. I was flabbergasted. I asked him why on earth he would say that, as I had never hurt him or his crew and he had mucked up a good payday for me. He shrugged and said, a little ruefully, that he was down on his luck at the time and had earned £500 for warning them. He had lied for a measly 'monkey', but said he had been desperate.

No matter how well things are going, something always comes along that you cannot foresee.

12

MAXIMUM GANGSTER

There are no rules in the drug trade. Start making assumptions and you will soon be proven wrong. The meekest men can be the toughest, while the most assertive can be the least effective. At the top end of the trade, bling-laden idiots like Harry Boy were rare. The best were as discreet as hedge fund managers, and every bit as acute and ruthless.

One of my most interesting connections came out of a quiet meet at a country pub in rural Norfolk. There I met Linval, a small Rastafarian in his mid-thirties who said he wanted to import a large load of cannabis by container.

'What do you call large?' I asked.

'About six tonnes.'

My legend for this job was someone who could control the illicit movement of goods through the docks. Such facilitators are very valuable to drug gangs, and much sought after. I said it would cost him £100 a kilo to get his load in and asked how urgent it was. He said they were due to crop in Jamaica and he hoped to have six to eight tonnes of Northern Lights, a strong herbal cannabis, by the end of October, just a few weeks away. He wanted it before Christmas for the festive holiday market.

I said I could easily control his container at Felixstowe. But I didn't want my time wasted. 'If you are not serious, say so, and we'll leave it until you have a proper idea of what you want.'

'I'm serious,' he said. 'But I represent a group and I'll have to talk to them before we move any further.'

He promised to be back in touch and I watched him drive off in a BMW 7 Series with personalised plates, a bit conspicuous for a drug dealer. The meeting had taken no more than twenty minutes.

For whatever reason the Christmas load was not forthcoming, and it was a full six months before our second meet was fixed, at the Hilton Hotel at Stansted Airport. An operational team pre-booked a room for me on the first floor and our technical support unit wired the room for sound. I arrived in plenty of time to be briefed by them and collect the room key.

I went down into the hotel bar to see Linval standing with three strangers. Once I heard them speak, I marked two down as Londoners, including one introduced as 'Fred'. We moved from the bar to a nearby table, where we kibbitzed about the weather and my Rolex, which worked its usual magic and gripped their attention.

Fred said we were to wait for two more men, one of whom, Frank, would be in a wheelchair. Years earlier he had been shot in the back, shattering his spine and paralysing him from the waist down. 'He's embarrassed about meeting in public,' said Fred.

I clocked a light-blue Peugeot pull up outside, and soon after, a heavily-built guy in gold-rimmed spectacles came in and walked over. This was Frank's driver and minder.

'Frank doesn't want to meet in the lobby,' he said. 'Can we go up to a room?'

'I've already reserved one on the first floor,' I said.

We all went up and I let them into the room. The minder in gold specs arrived last, pushing Frank from the lift in his wheelchair. A mid-forties West Indian in tracksuit and training shoes, he was well-groomed and clean-shaven. In his lap he carried a bag of rolling tobacco and Rizla papers.

'Can someone fetch me a drink?' he said, very quietly and with a slight lisp. One of the group scurried off. 'And turn on the telly or the radio. You never know if these rooms are wired.'

Once he was happy, Frank turned his attention to me. 'You know, I rarely come to meetings in places like this,' he said. 'Too public.'

'Really? I like meeting in public, cos I've got nothing to fear. I'm just a businessman having a meeting.'

'Well, I'm very cautious.'

Time for a bit of Stanton. 'If you're that cautious, why are there five people at this meeting that I don't know?'

There was a short, uneasy silence.

'I see your point,' lisped Frank. Then he slipped into a mini monologue to establish his credentials. 'I'm old firm. Everyone knows me. I've been here since 1954, met a lot of people, been inside a few times and don't ever want to go back. So we're going to take this nice and slowly.'

'I agree. That's the best way to do things. So what can I do for you?'

Frank said he believed that I was an 'importer'. He had gear ready in the West Indies but had not found an agent who could import it. He believed I was such a man.

'You've got me totally wrong. That's not what I do.'

He seemed surprised and glanced sharply at the others.

'I'm not in the importation business,' I continued. 'I can rip containers from the docks. I thought that was why you were here. If you're looking for an importer, you need to look elsewhere, and I'll be on my way.'

Frank allowed that there were still possibilities in what I was offering, and asked what I could do.

'I can steal your container from the dock and deliver it wherever you want.'

He said he was interested but wanted to discuss matters. Really he wanted to probe me. He claimed to have everything under control in Jamaica but would need a bill of lading to consign the load to the UK. He asked if I knew what he meant.

'Of course. But your container will be accompanied by a line bill and that will have all the details I need.' A line bill was similar to a bill of lading but issued by the carrier. 'What size box will you be using? Twenty or forty foot?'

Frank seemed unsure. He asked if I knew what cargo normally came from Jamaica, to use as cover. I suspect he knew and was testing me. I mentioned canned goods, cooking oil and beer, but made it clear I wasn't there to set up his load for him. I did offer some advice.

'You are better to use dry boxes, not reefers or con-airs.'

'What do you mean?'

'Reefers are deep-frozen containers and con-airs are used to carry chilled produce. The logistics of using either is difficult because you would need to be importing either fresh or frozen produce, and importers who do that tend to be regulars. If your people came in as new faces, that might create suspicion.'

Frank gave a hollow chuckle. 'The last thing I want is problems with the Customs and Excise.' He lowered his voice. 'Customs will go straight back to my supplier in Jamaica if it all goes wrong. They are devious people. They put tracking devices on containers if they find gear inside. And their surveillance is hard to pick out, very hard. They use bikes and all sorts of different vehicles.

'Let me stop you there, Frank. No offence but I'll be honest, I'm uneasy about a man who seems to know so much about Customs and their methods.'

'Listen, man,' he hissed, 'I've had to learn about them. They're my main problem. No-one's more cautious than me. I have people on the lookout all the time.'

'I don't believe you. I'm now sitting at a meeting with six

people, all of whom know what we're taking about. That's not very security conscious to me.'

'He's right,' interjected Fred, unexpectedly.

I gave him a hard look. 'And what's your role here, pal?'

'I'm a mediator for Frank,' said Fred. 'We go back a long way. And Bob and Linval are my sons-in-law, so I know they're sound. But I always worry about big men like you. You look police.'

I knew from experience that it was often not the main man who was most suspicious – he *wanted* the deal to go ahead – but his number two. Fred was making a typical second-in-command move, trying to subvert a possible threat to his position while showing his worth to his boss. I had to put him in his place.

'I always look out for the opposite,' I said. 'Small blokes. With ponytails or dreadlocks, who no-one would think were coppers. Like you.'

Frank looked at him as if to say, *he's got a point.*

'But I've known you for years,' Fred protested. He was spooked. Good.

Frank resumed control. He said he had been in the sinsemilla trade for a long time. 'In the early days in England you could only get one form of gear, it was called chew brown. It was hard to import large loads. We used very crude methods. We would wait near the dock area in Jamaica, flag down a lorry on its way in and offer the driver twenty grand to load up our box. If he didn't agree, we would force him at the point of a gun. It usually worked but we couldn't do it long-term.'

He went on to say he could have me harmed if things went wrong. It was turning heavy.

'I'm not in that my-dad's-bigger-than-yours game,' I said. 'Threats don't bother me. Let's get back to business. What do you want?'

'Bottom line, I can guarantee a large load from Jamaica. Can you promise you can get it out of the dock?'

'Yes. But no-one can guarantee anything a hundred per cent, not even you.'

'Can you get into the container to rip the gear?'

'I normally rip the entire box. Stealing just part of the load is too risky.'

'I'd prefer just to take the gear out, because I don't have anywhere to store a forty-foot box. Can you handle a piggyback?' He didn't expand, but I took him to mean sneaking their gear into an inbound container owned by somebody else.

'Well, again, it's risky,' I said. 'You'd have to break the seal on the container to put it in, and that would give you away. You also have to bear in mind the extra weight.'

'I know that. We'd take contents from the container first and use the gear to replace it, so the weight would be the same. I prefer dealing that way.'

'Well to me that's a big risk. Another danger is, the real owner of the container has it cleared and removed before I can get to it.'

'Can you get control of it quickly?'

'Once I have it hidden in the stack, I'll be okay. How big is the load?'

'Large,' was all Frank said. Maybe he didn't actually know. 'We have to build up some trust between us before I can tell you that and we can work together. I need to know a bit about your background. I can offer up loads of people in the UK who can speak for me.'

I had to decide quickly how to play this. 'Let me put my cards on the table. I work for a team out of the Middle East. My main trade is moving stuff out of there by ship. I've done it for many years, and I'm very, very good at it.'

'I've worked out of Pakistan doing the same thing,' said Frank.

'No you haven't. As I see it, you've never done that in your life.'

Frank gave a mirthless smile.

'I can introduce you to my employers,' I went on. 'But I warn you now. Once they've got their hooks into you, they will never let go.'

'Colombians don't frighten me.'

'Who said anything about Colombians?'

For the first time, Frank look worried. I left my words hanging.

'Do you own a boat?' he asked.

'I do.'

'I wish we'd met a couple of months ago. I needed a boat then.'

'That's my main trade. This rip-off part of my business is just a sideline.'

'How hard do you find it, sailing gear from the Middle East?'

'That side of my business is not on the table at the moment. But if you want to take that further we can discuss it at a later date.'

'Yeah, I would like to. We can do that one-on-one.'

Frank then took a little lump of brown resin from his pocket. He said it was charas from Pakistan. 'I know people who grind this up into a power, one of them uses a cement mixer, then they add ghee and make a paste, which they shape into quarter-kilo blocks.' It felt like a little pre-planned scene, again for my benefit. He was a sly one.

He returned to the subject of Felixstowe, saying he knew it well and had been in and out of there many times. 'I know how difficult it is to get gear out of there,' he said pointedly.

'Well I know Felixstowe very well, Frank, and I know what I can and can't get out of there. What are you trying to say?'

He smiled his thin smile, then changed the subject again.

'Can you help us get stuff through any airports?'

'I can't. And I have to say, I'm amazed that you seem to be able to move stuff absolutely anywhere. I'm beginning to have my doubts about how serious you are.'

The others all laughed, as if I had said something preposterous.

Frank pressed for a definitive price for my services, but I held off until I knew more about the size of the load and the method of smuggle. Finally I quoted him by writing '£100,000 = 1T' on his tobacco paper, meaning a hundred grand per metric tonne, or £100 a kilo. If he kept that scrap of paper, it could be strong evidence in any prosecution.

'That's a good price,' he said. 'Almost too good.'

'It's a fair price. I don't want to hear any rubbish like how you'll pay me a grand a kilo, because I know you can't afford it, no-one pays that much. At my price, one genuine ten-tonne job and I'd have a mill in my bin, I'm happy.'

Frank seemed to relax. 'When would you want to be paid?'

'I'll be with you from the time my people deliver the gear, and after that you'll have twenty-four hours, because I know you are going to ask for time to pay. You won't leave my team's sight for twenty-four hours, and to avoid any embarrassment I expect full payment after safe delivery. My people will also check the weight to confirm the price. Payment will be in cash, obviously.'

'Okay. Can we meet on my turf next time? I find meeting in public embarrassing. You can't see it, but I have to wear a colostomy bag.' He added, 'I can guarantee your safety one hundred per cent, nobody can go at you while you're with me.'

'Okay. Your manor next time.'

I got up and shook hands and said I would wait for his call.

Our meeting had taken two-and-a-half hours and been unusually tense. I was drained, and glad to lead the way downstairs. That's when things almost went horribly – and very painfully – wrong.

I went to the reception desk and said, 'I want to pay and check out of room 106.'

The receptionist looked at her computer screen and said, without stopping, 'Oh yes. Customs and Excise. With the discount, that comes to …'

I froze. The urge to run for the nearest exit was almost overwhelming. Instead I turned as slowly and casually as I could, expecting any moment to feel a fist in the face – or worse. To my great relief, the lads had not stopped behind me but were already leaving by the revolving door twenty yards away. They had not heard a word.

I asked the receptionist who had made the booking. She said it had been done through HMCE's official hotel budget so that they could get a discount. *Effing idiots*, I thought. The operational team had clearly followed normal procedure and gone for the group rate to save the department money.

That would have taken some talking to get out of. Somehow I don't think I would have been believed.

Frank, it turned out, came from a notorious Birmingham family. One of his relatives had been shot dead in Jamaica. Another, a woman, was said to have bitten the nipple off a female police officer during an arrest. Our Birmingham office had been investigating some of them for years.

I never heard back from him. Perhaps he didn't like my suggestion that he stay with my people until payment, essentially as a hostage. A control freak, which Frank clearly was, would also not have liked that I was a self-confessed ripper. If I could rip off a container, I could rip off him. That's what he would have done. Needless to say, from then on the handler or UC made all their own travel and booking arrangements.

Standard Beta Projects practice was to shift the opposition from one UC to another. Jobs often began with an informant, who might introduce one of us to a crime gang as a driver or boat owner. The first UC would meet them but at some stage would make an excuse to pull out and introduce them instead to 'a pal', another officer. He might then pass them on further, to a third UC. By then we had gone so far down the line that we had 'cleansed' the original informant. When the bad guys were finally nicked, they could not decipher where things had gone wrong. They would not know that, rather than one weak link, the whole chain had betrayed them.

In that spirit, I was introduced by my colleague Keef to a couple of old-school South London enforcers who had moved into the drug game. Keef met them through his money laundering work, and learned that they were looking for someone to 'rip off' suitcases of cocaine arriving at UK airports. He suggested me. My intention was to get to know as much as I could about their operation, then pass them on to yet another UC, Charlton, as the person who actually controlled the airport rip-off team.

Late one winter afternoon, Keef and I found ourselves waiting to meet them out in the open air near Hays Galleria, on the south bank of the River Thames. The museum ship HMS *Belfast* was moored nearby. When the pair approached, I recognised one as an experienced armed blagger called Mick. He was about fifty, medium build, clean-shaven with grey curly hair and a strong South London accent. Dressed scruffily, he had a distinct mark on the pupil of his left eye.

His smaller companion he called Roy. He was a bit younger, with swept-back hair, short, in rumpled clothes. I wasn't sure if their dishevelled look was deliberate, to avoid giving any impression of wealth, or if they were just naturally scruffy.

Roy began with the immortal words: 'Do you know who I am?' I truly didn't. But he was keen on rhetorical questions. Before I could answer, he commenced bigging himself up. 'You know how much my house in Hadley Wood is worth? Three-hundred-and-fifty grand.' He nodded to himself at how good it sounded, and said it again more slowly: 'Three. Hundred. And fifty. Grand.'

'Really?' I said. 'I've got half that on my arm.'

As Roy's eyes darted to the Rolex on my wrist, I took the opportunity to deliver another jab. 'My place in Surrey is worth three-and-a-half mill. Now can we cut out all the bol-locks and get on with it?'

I almost felt sorry for him. From that point on, Roy dropped the front. He was actually a nice geezer, a sort of chirpy Cockney. He would greet people with a bit of fake boxing, like the hoodlums in the film *Midnight Run*, and was likeable, funny and loved a few beers. Undoubtedly a hard man, he did not display that side of himself unless he felt threatened.

Mick said they had a 'guaranteed' shipment of coke ready to leave Bogotá, Colombia, and wanted to know if I could facilitate its arrival in baggage. I said I could. After a back-and-forth about them checking me out and vice versa, Roy asked where I could 'do the business' for them. I said Heathrow. I asked if it was coming direct from Colombia, as that was easiest for me to handle. He agreed but asked if it might also be possible from elsewhere, saying he liked Saint Martin, a half-French, half-Dutch island in the north-east Caribbean. 'I can use tourists as cover,' he said.

We discussed the relative merits of direct flights and stop-overs. They both complained that they had often been let down in the past. I said all they had was my word. We moved on to weights. They were talking thirty to fifty kilos. I said fifty was very heavy for the method they wanted.

'Is there a limit?' asked Roy.

'No, but heavy bags are harder.'

'I heard the weight limit was twenty-five kilos,' he said.

'No, but bags over twenty-three kilos are marked as heavy for safety reasons. Any overweight bag will be marked up clearly and that won't be good for you.'

Roy said he was worried that we could be cops. I said I feared the same about him, but the only way we could be sure was to walk away and forget it. He didn't want that. Instead he asked how I felt about them and invited me to meet his wife and kids and to look at the house he was so proud of. I declined, saying that if the cops were scoping his house they would see me as well. He nodded.

I told them my price was £50,000 per bag and if they had fifty kilos they would need two bags. Could they afford it? Roy said money was no problem.

'Everyone says that,' I replied. 'If we begin business, when will it happen?'

Roy said he needed to speak to his man to let him know what was happening and to get an idea. He would be meeting him that night. They asked how I could guarantee delivery.

I said again that they only had my word but that my people cared only about money and not the product they were carrying. 'At the end of the day either trust me or don't. I'm not bothered.'

I asked who was in charge, Mick or Roy. Mick said he was, but in my view it was Roy, as he led the talk and I spoke mostly with him. I told them that my people delivered from A to B only, with no detours, and would need to meet the 'faces' they were collecting from and delivering to.

Mick asked how we would contact each other. I said I didn't use phones, so we should plan our next meet now. After some debate I relented and gave them a mobile number – any calls they made to it would be useful evidence. We agreed to always meet at the same time and place, so all we needed to say over the phone was a date.

Roy continued to express concerns about security, volunteering that one of his boys had recently been shot while making a money drop, but said he had a 'good feeling' about me. 'How do you feel about us?' he asked.

'Alright, as far as it goes.' They could make of that what they wanted.

We agreed to go twice a week with fifty kilos in two bags. I also promised to check out the Saint Martin flights. We said cordial goodbyes and walked off in opposite directions. I had managed to get a full recording of our chat.

Mick rang a few days later to say he had been doing some 'homework' on the deal, and asked for a meet next day. We agreed on 5.30.

He didn't turn up.

He rang the next day and we had a big argument about who had been waiting for who. Mick claimed the meet had been set for five and he had been there from ten past. I said he was talking crap and I had been waiting there for ninety minutes. 'I had someone with me who could have helped you and I looked stupid because you didn't show,' I complained. I laid on the temper a bit and Mick eventually gave a grudging apology. We agreed a new date the following week.

At 5 p.m. on the allotted date I was back by HMS *Belfast*. Mick turned up with a skinny, scruffy mate he called Ken. I did not know him and told him to leave, which he did. I told Mick that I was annoyed he had brought along a stranger, just as before, and as we ambled in the direction of Tooley Street, I asked why he always had another face with him when we met. He said he hoped I could form a rapport with his people. I warned him not to do it again.

He asked for the name of my man who would organise the rip-off. I said it was Charlton and he had done this type of work before. I said I was in import-export and my dealings were on a much larger scale than him, but Charlton would provide a good service. I also told Mick that if he messed things up with Charlton, it would go badly between him and me.

Mick said things would not go wrong at his end. He repeated that he was not a 'cozzer'. He even opened his jacket and invited me to search him. I declined but he insisted, so we gave each other a pat down. This was the occasion when I had my Nagra hidden in my clothing, so I opened my shirt to show my chest and torso but then said, 'I ain't going any further out here, pal, it's too cold.'

He was apologetic. 'You can't be too careful,' he said. 'Old Bill use wires.'

'You've been reading too many crime novels,' I said.

We ducked into a café-bistro and ordered coffee. Mick said he could get the bags on in Bogotá and it was 'a hundred per cent'.

'Nothing is a hundred per cent,' I said.

'I've got a pal in Colombia called Lucio who'll put the gear on. It'll be a direct flight, Bogotá to London. The bags will be tagged and he can mark them if we need to.'

'What with?'

'Union Jack stickers?'

'You must be joking,' I said. 'Why don't you just write "cocaine" on the side?'

He laughed. 'Perhaps Union Jacks aren't a good idea. Fifty grand doesn't seem a lot for you and your mate.'

'It's just for him.'

'So what do you get out of it?'

'Goodwill.'

'How do you mean?'

'If it goes well with him, it might lead to a lot more business between you and me. We could be very useful to each other.'

He seemed to get excited at this.

'Will you be receiving the bags?' I asked.

'No. I'll be nowhere near the gear. But only Lucio and I will know what's in the bags.'

He said not even Roy would know when and where the deliveries would be. He also told me his personal profit was £280,000 per run.

We left the café and walked up the street to Potters Field Park nearby. Mick asked if Charlton might be open to a small 'tester'.

'I'll pay ten grand for a dry run,' he said. 'I'll send a case with just a signed bit of paper in it, to test your mate's system.'

'Ten grand is a lot of money for an empty case.'

'Yeah, but I prefer to wipe my mouth for that, if it means the system works. Anway, would your mate be able ...'

'Hang on, hang on. This all seems a bit too easy to me. You seem to have everything set up, except for London.'

'Yeah? And?'

'It's too easy. I'm not happy with this.' I started to button up my coat. 'I'll have to think about it. Something feels too cushty.' I made to leave.

'Hold on. Can't I just talk with your mate. See what we can work out?'

With a show of reluctance, I rang Charlton there and then and set up a meet at the usual place, beside HMS *Belfast*, for two days' time. Before leaving, I warned Mick not to be late again and said that if we smelt anything wrong, we'd be gone.

'Nah, look mate, I just hope we can get all get along better and stop being suspicious of each other.'

'We can only do that when we're in business. Let's see how things pan out.'

Mick said he was going to a hotel bar for a drink. 'Everyone knows me there,' he said. 'Why don't you come?' It did not seem very sensible, so I declined. We shook hands and parted.

Just as Keef had first set up the meeting between myself and the two targets, now the plan was for me to hand them on to Charlton. He and I were on time for our meet but once again Mick arrived late, flustered and explaining that he'd had problems parking his car. I ignored this, introduced Charlton, and the three of us walked along beside the river. Charlton acted lairy, saying that if anything felt wrong, he would be gone.

'Do you want to make money or not?' said Mick. He was no lightweight and we could only push him so far.

'I'm just laying my cards on the table right from the off,' said Charlton. 'That way, we avoid any problems in the future.'

'Alright. I've got a bag of twenty-five kilos going from Bogotá to Heathrow and I need you to take it off. I can do it any way you want, and there's fifty grand in it for you. I can even give you a photo of the bag.'

'I'll need the flight number and bag tag details, if there are any,' said Charlton. 'Will it be checked-in baggage?'

'I'm not exactly sure how it's getting onto the flight,' said Mick, 'but it will probably be checked-in luggage, because I know it is going to be monitored all the way to the UK.'

'In that case the weight can't exceed normal baggage allowance,' said Charlton. 'If it does, it will be sent through to the freight terminal and be treated as unaccompanied baggage.'

'I know all that. If that happens, it'll ruin our chances of getting the bag.'

'Okay,' said Charlton. 'But you must follow the instructions I give you.'

Mick insisted his people in Colombia knew what to do and said he was 'one million per cent certain' they would deliver. 'But is there any way to test the system?'

'Yeah. Guy said he has already discussed this with you. How much are we talking?'

'Around ten grand.'

'What'll be in your tester bag?'

'A bit of paper.'

'You don't need an organisation to do that. My kid could do it. Don't you think ten grand's a lot for a bit of paper?'

'I'll just have to swallow that.'

'Any test I do will be proper, and it will cost you twenty-five.'

Mick and Charlton began to argue over the merits of sending a tester and neither of them looked like backing down. I decided to leave them to thrash it out and strolled off towards Hays Galleria.

After a while, they walked back to me. Both had calmed down and Charlton gave Mick a pager number. We made small talk about the cold weather and said goodnight. It was 10 p.m.

Charlton took over from then on but the job, like so many, ran down a dead end. They managed to put a case on a flight, and Charlton ripped it off, but it only had clothing inside. We were never sure if it was a tester or if the London crims had been ripped off by their suppliers in Colombia, but for whatever reason they did not come back to us. Mick later went down for other crimes.

I was too busy to worry about it. By this time I was running at full speed just to stand still. One day I might be in the Pink Floyd coffeeshop in Amsterdam West, listening to the funk rock of Mother's Finest while discussing lorryloads of hash with a Dutch gangster; the next, sitting in a trailer park caravan poring over a shipping map while haggling over half a tonne of coke with a firm based in Portugal. A lot of these teams talked the talk but couldn't walk the walk. They claimed they knew how to rip on containers, or cooper between boats, when they didn't have a clue. I swear some of them were picking my brains, trying to get me to teach them how to smuggle. That was a bit beyond the call of duty.

Each high-level meet, however, gave me increasing confidence that Guy Stanton was now accepted at the top table of the drug underworld. This was confirmed one day by an unlikely source. I had driven down to the south coast to meet one of our boat crews and arrived at the dock to see Big Pete and Eccles laughing over a piece of paper. 'You should read this,' Eccles said, and passed it to me.

It was an HMCE suspect movement report, routinely kept on people we had reason to suspect, and it was about me – or rather, my alter ego. Apparently Stanton was suspected of large-scale smuggling by none other than my own firm. My

UC status was a deep secret known only to Beta Projects and a handful of senior officers. Here was proof that my cover was working: my own side did not know who I really was.

What tickled the lads most was the description of me and Little Tone, in his legend as 'Joe Walker'. Six weeks earlier, we had travelled to Gibraltar for a meet. Tone is small and thin; I am not. This had struck the customs officers who had stopped us on the way out. Their report read:

Suspect: Guy Stanton
Suspect: Joseph Walker

Both the above are suspected of being engaged in arranging the transportation and financing of large shipments of cannabis from Morocco to Spain and the UK.

Stanton is known to own or have part ownership in several small vessels (GWT 150 to 300 tonnes). He has been the subject of departmental interest for the past year-and-a-half. Known to be ostentatious and aggressive, shows obvious signs of wealth and is known to be surveillance aware. Warning, he will deliberately confront any suspected surveillance.

Stanton is 5ft 10in, hair thinning at the front with the back pulled into a long pony tail, very heavy build (fat), approximately 135 kilos. Dresses smart suits with ostentatious gold jewellery, drives a black 7 series BMW. Stanton may live on a smallholding near Roberts Bridge, Hastings. The ownership of the farm is being investigated.

Joseph Walker is believed to be Stanton's financial advisor. He has been observed travelling with Stanton on several trips to Morocco, Gibraltar and Spain.

Walker is 5ft 4in, very thin build, 63 kilos, long dark curly hair and a small moustache and a heavy smoker. He wears cheap suits and has a bad perm. Believed to reside outside the UK.

I felt the description of me was a little unkind. They were dead right about Tone's bad perm though.

All of these assignments produced a wealth of intelligence and a steady stream of leads for the operational teams or for foreign, partner law enforcement agencies. Many of them also revealed the fundamental frustration at the heart of the Beta Projects mission: failure was normal.

True success would be to wrap up an entire organisation.

13

THE LONG JOB

In the summer of 1995, a fishing captain named Baird MacKenzie was offered £800,000 to take a boat to sea, pick up twelve tonnes of cannabis, hidden in fish boxes, from another ship and land it in Scotland. MacKenzie told the police, who put him in touch with HMCE.

With their encouragement, he travelled to London to meet the gang, and in a pub was given a mobile phone, a football programme to use as the basis for encoding messages, and an atlas showing roughly where off Morocco the pick-up was to be made; the exact latitude and longitude would be given over the phone. He was also told that the Moroccan police had been bribed.

The amount was reduced to three tonnes, for which MacKenzie would receive £300,000. He was to take the cannabis to the coastal town of Troon, where it would be loaded onto two vans, one to go to Glasgow and one to London.

HMCE told MacKenzie to go along with the plan and Beta Projects supplied him with a fishing boat, Cirrus 2, and an undercover crew. The boat was to be brought first to Torquay, Devon, in readiness but MacKenzie told the gang it had been damaged by bad weather and needed repairs, a delaying tactic to allow time to equip the vessel and plan the operation.

Under the command of an officer code-named George, and with three other UCs and MacKenzie on board, the boat eventually sailed from Milford Haven, loaded with 100 fish boxes. At Cadiz, George and MacKenzie met some of the gang, one of whom was to sail with them. They were also given a geographical position off Morocco and a call sign and code-word to use when they were met at sea.

At the prescribed location, Cirrus 2 met another boat and a cargo of hessian sacks containing 'soap bars' of cannabis resin was transferred and placed in the fish boxes. Cirrus 2 then sailed to Troon and off-loaded at night at the fish harbour. Gang members were putting the boxes into a hired van when they were arrested.

The three tonnes of resin was estimated to have cost the gang £1 million to buy in Morocco. Split into end-user quantities, its value was put at £15–£20 million. Mackenzie testified against the gang and was said to have made legal history as the first witness in a Scottish high court trial to be relocated abroad, for his safety.

The case had all the elements of a classic Beta boat job and ran relatively smoothly from start to finish. As one Beta Projects officer remarked, 'We had become very successful at going to Lorache lighthouse and picking up a couple of tonnes of Moroccan. That was shooting fish in a barrel.' But another, separate job running in parallel with it, and involving Guy Stanton, would become far more complex and threaten the lives of some of Beta's best operatives. Officially named Operation Yeager/Jaeger, it would become known as the 'Long Job'.

The Long Job started out small. A police UC had come across a little firm looking for a boat to cooper cannabis from Morocco. The cops alerted us and Beta Projects was brought in. Eccles was chosen to front the job, his first role as the lead. He would be introduced to the firm as someone who could lay on a yacht and crew to collect their gear from another boat and sail it to the UK.

Eccles began by meeting the original target, a bloke called Norman from Hayes in west London. Already known to the police, he was regarded as a heavy player and was always accompanied by a mate called Ricky. Eccles assured them that he could lay on an experienced, reliable crew. As talks progressed, word spread through the bush telegraph and more drug teams became interested in what appeared to be a genuine transport vessel. As a result, the job began to escalate as more was added to the original load.

I was drafted to join Eccles as his second-in-command. A little protection would allow him to get on with business, while I could field any mundane queries, help to keep a steady hand on events and intimidate people if necessary. I was also reffed up to the hilt by known criminals, which would in turn enhance Eccles's cred.

The gang called a meet with us to discuss logistics and to scout a drop zone for the cannabis. Their favoured site was on the Cornish coast. So it was that Eccles and I found ourselves waiting at a Shell service station on the A39 outside Falmouth. We were in my old blue 4.2 Jaguar XJ6, not too old and not too flash. It was also rigged to tape conversations.

At the appointed time, several cars pulled onto the forecourt from different directions, all full of men. This we had not expected, and we both jumped out, fearing an attack. Eccles scanned faces to see if he recognised anyone. We were up against more than a dozen blokes.

'Who do you know?' I said under my breath.

'None of them,' said Eccles.

'Well give me a face, quickly. Anyone.'

'Him,' he said suddenly, nodding towards one. 'That's Norman.'

I shouted, 'Norman!'

'Yeah?' he replied. 'Who are you?'

'I'm with Eccles. What's all this? Who are all these comedians?'

'Oh,' he said, 'we've had a bit of luck.'

It transpired that other teams had heard about the scheme and were buying space on the boat for a share of the gear. It had become a multi-combine load and apparently they were all turning up for this meet.

'Never mind that,' I said. 'This is ridiculous, all standing round like a bunch of clowns. Let's get out of here.'

Norman led a convoy to a pretty thatched pub at Penelewey, outside Truro. As we parked, I asked Eccles if he wanted me to go in with him. He rightly said he would go alone but would raise a shout if the meeting got too hot. In he went.

It turned out there were at least three separate teams, all ready to invest in the shipment. Eccles found it difficult to sit with the main men without others intervening and chipping in, and after ten minutes, he emerged and called me in. He had been fielding a barrage of questions and felt the need for an assist. He also said that waiting in the pub had been two Dutch suppliers, which was crucial intelligence.

We went to the bar and I asked Eccles what he wanted to drink. As we waited for our pints of Stella Artois to be poured, a small, cocky bloke peeled away from the bunch and came over.

'Make mine a Stella too,' he said.

I knew I had to let these boys know we were not to be messed with, so I turned and gave him the Stanton treatment.

'Do I fucking know you? No? So you can fuck right off and get out of the fucking pub. Cheeky bleeder, scrounging beer off of me.'

He looked sheepish and went outside, telling his friends he was going to wait by his car. I looked at Eccles and whispered, 'One down.'

Eccles felt a little better, as we all did in a tight spot when a colleague joined us. We re-joined the group and he handled the technical discussion of sea co-ordinates and meeting points. In the meantime, I chatted to the different teams and tried to find out who was who. After a short while we were all good mates – except for me and the drink scrounger.

The plot was for the suppliers to sail the cannabis out of Morocco to coordinates in the Bay of Biscay. Eccles and his yacht crew would sail to meet them, and the cannabis would be swapped from boat to boat. For security the numbered co-ordinates would be given using a code, substituting letters for numbers. Such codes are commonly ten-letter phrases or words with no repeated letters. In this case the phrase was 'HORNY DEVIL', so H = 0, O = 1, R = 2, N = 3, all the way up to L = 9. The letters then replace numbers when the teams talk to each other.

It turned out that the real brains of the scam was David Huck, a veteran yachtsman who had first appeared in our intelligence files in the late seventies. He had lived a charmed life and never been convicted, having spent much of his time hanging around the Mediterranean before moving to Ireland to live in grand style in five acres beside Lough Derg. He also owned a house in Dublin, two homes in Ibiza and a restaurant in Portugal, and drove a classic Morgan sports car. In 1993 Huck had gone to ground after drugs were found on a boat he owned off the west coast of Ireland, and the Garda began to investigate the source of his wealth. It was another two years, however, before he came back into our orbit.

Huck was organising the smuggle and landing of the cannabis. Some of the load would go to Norman and Ricky and some to Huck's own distribution team, led by a guy called Ray. We also got the feeling that at least one other team was involved. Eccles had not only penetrated the smuggling crew but also had a link to the distribution gangs buying a piece of the action. This was looking very tasty.

Just a couple of miles from the pub was the crossing point of the River Fal at King Harry Ferry. Eccles and I took Huck's oppo, Ray, down there and we crossed and re-crossed on the five-minute chain ferry, while Ray scoped out a potential landing site. He was a sharp bloke who knew what he was talking about. I learned later that he and Huck went back many years and had survived some hairy moments at sea. There was no doubting their bottle.

There was also no doubt that the job was on. By comparing our notes and all the intel from other sources, our operational team was able to piece together who was who in the conspiracy.

The team that did much of the negotiating at the UK end was led by Norman and Ricky. A key aspect of UC work is trying to weigh up the opposition; in short, is your target all show or does he live up to his rep? Norman and Ricky were the real deal. Both in their early thirties, this pair had been around the block.

A second team, lined up to buy some of the shipment, was fronted by two brothers from Hull. They no doubt had their own customers waiting to buy from them.

A third team included Ray, Huck's right-hand man. We figured he led a wholesale distribution team for Huck's share of the load.

The fourth team was the delivery crew, who would sail the load from Morocco to our vessel outside territorial waters. This would include Huck himself, along with a fellow Brit, a Frenchman and a Dane.

Finally came a three-man pick-up team who would make the collection on land. They came from the Cardiff area, for some reason, and included the clown who had tried to cadge lager off me in the pub.

Over the next few weeks we gained a fascinating insight into how the opposition worked. Some of them began to big up Eccles and me as 'boys who can' even though they barely knew us. Like all crims, they exaggerated, and soon we were being described as 'a top team' who had 'done loads of runs before' and were very successful and totally trustworthy. This hype came from them, not us, and made our job much easier.

Our selected vessel for the trip was a modern Bowman 45, a popular ocean-cruising yacht. The crew was to be a mix of Beta UCs and officers supplied by the MoD. I was chosen to join them, as for once I was not the putative boss of the outfit, just one of the workers. I looked forward to the fun. We had now been operating in this field for several years and made a strong team. Despite the odd fall-out and even fisticuffs, we did our job well and had the results to prove it.

In early spring we sailed out of Queen Anne's Battery, Plymouth, the historic base for many a famous seafaring quest. Our goal was to meet Huck and his crew in the Atlantic on their yacht *Fata Morgana*, named after a form of mirage or illusion sometimes seen at sea. Given how elusive this boat would prove to be, it was an apt moniker.

It took several days to reach the rendezvous. The weather was dreadful, with heavy seas and blinding rain. Pigpen was in charge of the boat with Eccles his number two, then me, Chameleon and Whitey, another fine seaman from the same elite MoD unit as the guys who had worked on Operation Gurkha. They handled the yacht superbly through awful conditions. Nevertheless we were thrown around in the storm like a non-stop rollercoaster. I resorted to 'talking to dolphins' – our euphemism for seasickness – every hour or so, to no sympathy from the others. We abandoned all pretence at hygiene except teeth cleaning, and survived on Mars Bars and Pot Noodles, on the misguided theory that they tasted the same going down or up.

One night the yacht was tossed so violently that even brewing tea was impossible. At two in the morning, I clambered downstairs to my makeshift bunk, a wooden plank that you tied yourself to with part of a sail, like a bad hammock. Fumbling in the dark as the boat heaved and the wind howled, I made it to the loo, which was controlled by a pump. Having finished my business, and forgetting where I was, I pump-primed the loo. It promptly exploded, sending me through the door into the main cabin covered in excrement.

There was a few seconds of silence while everyone made a bid to reach a safe place. Then the laughter started. Soon they were all helpless with giggles. I went into a ten-minute rant about how we were not paid enough, how de-humanising it was and how no one understood us. Cue more laughter.

It went quiet again. Even the wind had dropped a little. I calmed down. 'Anyone want tea?' I said, as a small rivulet of shit slid down the side of my face.

After reviewing the situation over a brew, it was clear that Huck had been defeated by the weather and not made it to our rendezvous, so we regretfully turned for the long run home. Disappointment is something that all UCs have to adapt to. On complicated jobs, things often go wrong. The criminal teams are never as good as they think, certainly not like their TV or film portrayals. They have the same problems of any international business: obtaining their product, transport, trusting the people they are dealing with, finance. They also have to look over their shoulders for law enforcement, traitors in their midst, or violent rivals. This makes them so distrustful that even when they find the real thing, such as an apparently reliable boat crew, they sometimes refuse to believe it. Consequently jobs can fold without any logic, leaving the UC to contend with failure through no fault of their own.

In this case, the traffickers still wanted to go ahead. And so a couple of weeks later we set off on trip two, again sailing from Queen Anne's Battery into long rolling seas. Pigpen and Eccles were in their element as, day after day, the yacht rode up each wave, crested, and thundered down the other side, again and again. I took my usual position, hanging over the side speaking dolphin, sometimes joined by Chameleon.

We battled through to the rendezvous once more, only to find nothing but empty ocean. The weather turned even worse and this time everyone suffered, while I graduated to degree-level dolphin. Still we hung on for hours, wondering what to do.

Then a small aircraft appeared low over our yacht. It was one of ours. Eccles managed to call on our radio and the voice of Elvis, our handler for the job, came on to tell us that the run was off, as our targets had failed to set off. We turned around, put our bow into the oncoming storm and headed for home once more.

Undaunted, we tried again soon after. Trip three was, once more, out of Queen Anne's Battery into the Bay of Biscay. And once more the weather was vile, with huge seas and pins-and-needles rain. All that we could see of each other on deck was eyes peeking out of foul-weather gear.

Somehow we again made it to the RV point, and waited. I was on watch during a particularly nasty squall when I saw a large shape outlined against the gloom and called to Pigpen to come up, as it didn't look right. Indeed it wasn't. The shape turned out to all 10,000 tonnes of *HMS Cumberland*, a Type-22 guided missile frigate of the Royal Navy that was supposed to be hanging back to help us if needed. Her visible presence told us to return home. Intel had revealed that the *Fata Morgana* had once again failed to collect the hashish and sail out to meet us.

We were gutted, even more so when Elvis again buzzed us in a plane to 'make sure we were all right'. Knowing that he would soon be back in the UK with a pie and a pint did nothing to lift our spirits.

Following our return from the third aborted run, Eccles and I travelled to London to see Norman and Ricky to discuss why the delay. We met at Waterloo Station, from where they drove us out of town towards Heathrow to a pub called the Three Tuns, which they found hilarious, for obvious reasons. This time, they assured us, the meet would definitely be made.

It had to. Our bosses had had enough. 'If this doesn't work,' said SIO Ray, 'they can fuck their job.'

Commitments elsewhere meant I could not be at sea for the duration, so I dropped off the sailing crew. Instead I would hook up with the receiving team when our yacht returned and would motor out in a RHIB to fetch the gear from it, to take to the secluded landing site at King Harry Ferry. Then the cavalry would arrive. Hopefully.

For the fourth and final run, Beta used a different vessel. We had acquired a small, fifty-year-old harbour tug that had been lying out of commission in a Southampton shipyard, having previously been flooded. She had a wheelhouse and engine casing forward, a towing hook amidships and an open weatherdeck aft. Made seaworthy and provisioned over a matter of a few days, she was renamed *Adherence II* and set sail for the HORNY DEVIL coordinates west of the main Bay of Biscay shipping route, between the island of Ushant and Cape Finisterre. It was now October, late in the smuggling season, when the chance of bad weather was relatively high.

The crew was Eccles, Pigpen, Chameleon and Whitey. Once again they faced high winds and made slow progress. At one stage they had trouble with the engine fuel supply and an engineer with extra hydraulic oil had to be lowered from a helicopter sent from the Type 22 frigate HMS *Chatham* to sort it out.

In the meantime, we confirmed that David Huck had managed to collect four tonnes off the coast of Morocco in *Fata Morgana*, and was at last heading to meet the *Adherence* for the transfer. I was to await a call to collect and deliver the four tonnes to the receivers in several runs, fetching between 500 and 1,000 kilos a time in our RHIB. It sounded straightforward but I knew from experience that any venture at sea is fraught with unforeseen snags. I cadged a lift by RAF helicopter to Truro, booked into a small Cornish hotel and awaited instructions.

As I hung about the tiny lobby the next morning, my pager bleeped. It was a message from Ray. I was expecting an update but not the one I got.

'Boat sunk crew missing!!'

This was followed by: 'Get out of the hotel the targets are on their way into it now!'

I shot out of the back door as the targets came in the front. I was mortified.

As soon as I got somewhere safe, I called Ray. All he knew was that the *Adherence* had made the RV, carried out a dangerous handover in bad weather, and begun the long slog home. Then the tug had lost contact and vanished.

It looked bad for Pigpen, Eccles, Chameleon and Whitey.

The next few hours were the worst in many investigators' lives. Our ACIO running the operation from RNAS Culdrose, the Royal Navy airbase on the Lizard peninsula, was convinced they were goners. The wife of one of the crewmen was actually working for him coordinating intelligence and was not told her husband was lost – it was kept from her until they had valid confirmation. Each minute that passed felt like another nail in their coffin.

Then word came through. They were safe.

The story that later emerged was remarkable. Our crew had finally met the *Fata Morgana*, sailed by Huck and three henchmen, early on the morning of October 25, just north of the area known as the Abyssal Plain. The weather was poor, with a force-seven wind from the south-west and high seas.

They tried to transfer the drugs with a floating line but failed, so the tug crew launched an inflatable dinghy instead. Through a herculean effort they transferred and stashed 145 bales of hashish while simultaneously passing fuel and stores to the yacht, in itself a sterling effort of skill, courage and endurance. In the process they became soaked and exhausted.

The vessels parted and *Adherence* began its return, running before breaking waves in worsening weather. With the extra tonnage of the hash, the tug began to roll heavily and ship water. The lads turned to head directly into the seas, only for the bilge pump to fail.

Some twelve hours after the pick-up, they began to sink.

Instinct and training took over. The lads threw their inflatable Zodiac dinghy into the roiling sea and Eccles had the presence of mind to grab a VHF radio transmitter before clambering into it. But as they abandoned ship, Chameleon, a Royal Marines reservist, was hit by the mast and became tangled in part of the rigging. Whitey, risking his own life, cut him free and pulled him into the emergency dinghy just as the tug went down beneath the waves.

Tossed about like a cork, they managed to issue a mayday call via their handheld radio, although its range was less than twenty-five miles. Huddled in the dinghy, cold and wet, with little food, water or protective clothing, the four lads faced death through capsizing or exposure. A search by helicopter, supported by a Nimrod aircraft, failed to locate them.

They had been adrift for three-and-a-half hours when they were spotted by a large Norwegian container ship on its way to Guadeloupe. In a superb feat of seamanship, the captain brought his ship to a standstill very near the dinghy. The exhausted men then faced the daunting task of climbing a pilot ladder slung over the stern end. Amid massive waves, each one made the perilous climb, until the last was off and their dinghy bobbed away into the storm.

The ship's captain made sure they were fit and uninjured. He then questioned Pigpen, who tried valiantly to maintain a cover story that they had been prospecting salvage sites. His tale was undermined when the skipper revealed that HMS

Chatham, which had been searching the area, had been in touch. The lads finally had to explain how they came to be there, and after some time and another hairy crossing between the two ships, the UCs were safely on the *Chatham*.

Time was now against the job but the most important thing was that the lads were alive. Unfortunately their evidence was 15,000 feet down. After much deliberation, it was decided to push on. Huck's yacht had been shadowed by a Royal Navy warship with customs officers on board, and was now intercepted and boarded. Four men were arrested. In the meantime I contacted Norman and Ricky, who knew nothing about the dramas and readily accepted my excuse that bad weather would delay our arrival.

Our bedraggled crew was helicoptered back to Blighty and I was able to link up with a tired but still keen Eccles. There was no time for him to relate the gory details, as we still faced a seemingly insurmountable problem: the gear was deep six, along with the tug. We had to come up with something fast or the guys would have spent all those months on the Long Job – and risked their lives – for nothing.

Then some genius had an idea. None of the traffickers knew that our boat had gone down. What if we could obtain a replacement load and somehow deliver it to the shore crew? That immediately raised a host of other questions. Where would we find such a large amount of cannabis at short notice? How would we get it out to sea and then bring it in to the drop-off in a realistic manner? Would the shore crew smell a rat? Would our ruse stand up in court? Would it even be legal?

Protracted discussions ensued between our senior managers and legal branch, while the clock kept ticking. They said yes.

Officers from the Bristol ID office drove to the Queen's warehouse there and signed out a quantity of cannabis that had been seized in another job and was due for destruction. It would pass in the dark for the original load once it was similarly wrapped. No one was going to look too closely when hurriedly shifting it from the drop-off.

A call was put in to the shore party, as previously agreed, to say the cannabis was on its way. Officers then drove it to us at Queen Anne Battery on the south Cornish coast, where Chameleon, despite his ordeal, and I were waiting with a RHIB. We loaded it on, Chameleon got off and Eccles and Jock got on. Eccles, pretending to be still at sea, had already made contact with the bad guys and assured them that the load was on its way. Along with me and Jock, a fit, hard Scot, he would collect and drop off the cannabis in the RHIB, as originally planned. We were ready to go.

At the arranged time, in the pitch dark of an early morning, the three of us motored up the River Fal with hessian bales of cannabis. The landing team had to believe we had come from the boat – in fact we had set off from further around the shore – and that this was the first of several batches.

We beached on the opposite side to the ferry, just past three large ships laid up in the river. Standing in the bow, I could see a white van parked on the road leading down to the slip. I shouted a greeting and received an answer; it was the guy called Ray with several others, one of whom had a sack barrow.

'Shhh, keep it down,' he hissed.

Eccles and I threw the hessian parcels over onto the beach. Then we turned back down the river at speed, while the lad with the sack barrow wheeled off the first batch. We motored out of sight behind the stern of the furthest laid-up ship, and waited.

The weather was still poor, with fine, stinging rain.

For five minutes all went quiet – then hell broke loose. Our operational teams and armed officers frm Deven and Cornwall Police, having saturated the area and watched the delivery from a variety of hidden lookouts, converged from all directions. They quickly subdued our suspects.

Similar strikes, involving sixty customs and police officers in different locations, resulted in the arrest of all of the
land teams. At the same time, Huck's yacht was tracked and
boarded by a team from a naval destroyer.

The Long Job was finally over.

The main trial opened at Exeter Crown Court in July 1997.
Unusually, it involved charges of conspiracy to import but
with no actual drugs. Huck's team offered the defence that
they had been shipping the shrub henna, not cannabis, in a
scam to rip off the shore team. It was an unlikely story but of
course we had no drugs to contradict it.

There was heated argument about the dummy load we had
delivered and Chameleon and I endured long cross-examination about our role in taking the substitute drugs from the
Queen's warehouse. I was accused of setting things up by delivering drugs which had never been imported by the defendants.
The defendants were even less complimentary than their brief,
calling me 'fat bastard' from the dock under their breath.

The arguments lasted for days but the overwhelming evidence of the *Adherence* crew that this clearly was a conspiracy
to illegally import banned drugs, coupled with evidence from
the police, Eccles and myself about meetings and the instructions we were given, proved too much. The jury found against
all the defendants. Huck was jailed for fourteen years, at the
age of fifty-one. His house and land were auctioned off by
Ireland's Criminal Assets Bureau.

One matter never explained was that during the handover
at sea, Huck had insisted that our lads also take on board
two small fire extinguishers. We never discovered why, as they
sank with the boat, but have often wondered if all that was in
them was foam.

Some months later, the two Dutch suppliers were lifted on
a trip to the UK. They were tried and sent down too. The
operational team had made a clean sweep. Despite all the

disappointments and the loss of the vessel, the job was a great success, especially for Eccles.

It was not long before we found ourselves under scrutiny, however. Contrary to regulations, HMCE failed to report the sinking to the Marine Accident Investigation Branch, the body that investigates marine accidents involving British vessels. The MAIB only found out about it when the trial began, and subsequently launched an inquiry.

They found that, while the *Adherence* was seaworthy, her low freeboard made her unsuitable for the Bay of Biscay in late autumn. 'Any undercover operation involves taking risks, often substantial ones,' said the accident report. 'These have to be balanced against sensible precautions to ensure that those involved are not put to unnecessary risk. Had, for instance, one or more of the crew lost their lives when *Adherence* sank, searching questions would have been asked and the future of similar operations might have been placed in jeopardy.'

Every year since, on the anniversary of the sinking, the crew has reassembled to celebrate still being alive. I am privileged to be invited to this little get-together. In the re-telling, each participant now claims greater heroics than the next. Chameleon in particular has honed his version of events to a dramatic climax. It has enlarged into him selflessly throwing Pigpen and Eccles into the life-raft, then diving into the storm-tossed seas with a knife between his teeth, pirate-style, to swim back and rescue Whitey, literally carrying him from the stricken vessel. When asked about those terrible events, he will smile modestly, feign humility and say anyone would have done the same. As an afterthought, he might add that some believed he should receive a medal for rescue at sea, but he couldn't possibly comment.

Whitey was actually awarded the Military Medal for his extraordinary bravery.

14

COCAINE

Most of Guy Stanton's targets were heroin or cannabis smugglers, but by the late nineties the main currency of the drug world was cocaine. The Colombian cartels were targeting Europe in a concerted expansion of trade and consumption rose to US levels. The vast profits engendered were accompanied by a level of violence not seen before. Cocaine seemed to attract the most vicious, venal criminals, who would stop at nothing to further their own interests – and to avoid going to jail.

More and more British criminals were sucked into its destructive orbit. In 1997 Charlie Kray, older brother of the notorious Ronnie and Reggie, was targeted by no fewer than three police UCs posing as buyers. During several social meetings, Kray indicated that he could access large quantities of coke and introduced the officers to others who eventually supplied it. At his trial, Kray argued that he was a law-abiding elderly man of limited means who traded on his name to associate with wealthy people, and had simply pretended to be able to obtain drugs in order to cadge drinks and loans of money. He was jailed for twelve years for supplying cocaine. Disturbingly one witness, a nightclub hostess worker, claimed she slept with one of the police UCs after meeting him at a *party to celebrate Kray's seventieth birthday; the officer admitted going to bed with her in a hotel room but denied having sex.*

Customs had also started to deploy their UCs against the coke traffickers, and one early operation brought conspicuous success. Operation Begonia saw two investigators from the ID's Manchester office lure a Colombian sales team into a trap. They had been introduced by 'Jimmy', a larger-than-life former night-club bouncer and paid informant who was familiar with the narco scene in Colombia and Brazil. A senior investigator known as 'Robbo' posed as the corrupt company secretary of a British firm importing furniture from Holland, while another officer, Phil, was his runner and sidekick. Robbo had no UC training, while Phil's only previous role had involved a brief handover of illegal rhino horn. Phil had, however, learned Spanish as a child, which gave him an advantage with Colombians. Small and wiry, he also did not look like a policeman.

While Robbo dealt with two cartel representatives, Frank Lopera and Gerardo Baron, Phil used his apparent insignificance to win the confidence of one of them. When Lopera travelled back and forth to New York, he left Baron in Manchester alone. Desperate for company, he took Phil out for meals and drinks. Phil, playing the put-upon menial, started complaining about his treatment by Robbo. This immediately triggered Baron who, like all subordinates, had his own beefs with his superiors. 'I never even had to ask him a question,' recalled Phil. 'Once I mentioned being mis-treated, I couldn't shut him up.'

Baron was a sales rep, paid on commission. 'He said his job was to do three things: get out and make sales, make a profit, and keep finding more ways of doing it,' said Phil. 'It was like listening to a rep selling toothbrushes.'

The sting resulted in an importation of 243 kilos by air from Amsterdam in boxes of flowers, and Lopera and Baron were *both arrested. Further intelligence identified other shipments heading to Eastern Europe, and in all nearly 2.5 tonnes of cocaine was recovered. Described as 'the first members of the cartels to be brought before a British court', Baron was jailed for eleven years and Lopera for nine. The informant Jimmy was paid £100,000 as reward. Phil subsequently joined Beta Projects full-time and would go on to be a successful long-term UC.*

Jimmy's next job was equally promising: an introduction to someone who claimed to have access to tonnes of Bolivian coke. Beta was to run the infiltration and chose Stanton to lead it, even though he was immersed in the Long Job and several other cases. He was sent north and booked into the Copthorne Hotel, in Salford, to meet the informant.

Jimmy was good company but a danger to be with. He had a tendency to force the pace and appear too eager, which could arouse suspicion. He was also an adrenaline junkie who had swallowed the Hollywood view of undercover work and loved being in South America, a high-risk environment where they won't hesitate to put a bullet in you. Like every informant, you had to stay on your toes with him. You must always remember that they are criminal at heart, even if you like them, and will rarely turn down an opportunity to enrich themselves.

From the Copthorne we went to a nearby flat, where he introduced me to a South American called Francisco. In his early forties, of medium height and build, with black hair, a swarthy complexion and a strong accent, he had travelled a circuitous route from Sao Paulo, Brazil, via Brussels and Madrid, to get to Manchester.

'Jimmy tells me that we might be able to do business together,' I said.

Francisco said yes, he was looking to put together a deal. He had, he claimed, once been a pilot for Fabio Ochoa, a partner and ally of Pablo Escobar. He had left the game for several years at the insistence of his wife but in the past few months had moved back in, starting with small loads.

Francisco had both Bolivian and Brazilian passports and could travel easily. He had several ideas about how he was going to develop his smuggling, the main one being to use a deep-freeze container from the busy port of Belem in northern Brazil.

I told him I could get a reefer there, no problem. Running gear in reefers had a big advantage in that they were fast-cleared and rarely checked, as the contents would spoil if allowed to warm up. They also had disadvantages. Reefers need to be moved quickly and kept connected to electric power to keep cool. As time went on, the authorities noticed their popularity among smugglers and put them under closer scrutiny, but for a while they were almost foolproof.

Francisco suggested putting the cocaine inside a delivery of frozen juice and said he had contacts in that business. As with all the meetings Jimmy was involved in, there was a lot of bullshitting, but I felt there was something there.

As the evening wore on, we decided to take a cab back to the Copthorne to get dinner. Over our starters, Francisco asked about my trade. I said that, among other things, I was able to use my own ships, which got him very excited.

'It would be easy for me to transfer the goods at sea,' he gushed. 'That is something we must do.'

'Well, I need to tell you, I would only do that if the weight was worth it,' I said. 'Anything less than three tonnes would not be profitable enough for me. I'd have too many overheads.'

'I understand. But we only deal in one tonne this first time. So perhaps we stick to the container for this one?'

'Agreed. How long would it take you to get a tonne together?'

He mulled it over. 'About forty-five days.'

Francisco then told me about some friends of his based in

France who had been caught for a small amount but received long prison sentences. Anyone caught with a tonne in Europe would be looking at twenty years.

We discussed my transport price for powder and settled on between $4,000 and $4,500 a kilo, depending on how much my team would have to do. His tonne, if it materialised, would make me something north of $4 million. After agreeing in principle, we arranged to meet the following day to clinch the deal.

Next morning I was back in the Salford Quays flat, drinking my second coffee of the day and keen to hear more of Francisco's plans. His main concern was setting up the required export company in Belem without linking himself to it. I sympathised, telling him to be careful and not to discuss it with anyone he didn't trust. He was to buy the frozen juice from a cooperative he knew and I would place and pay for a legitimate order sufficient to hide our gear.

'But are you sure you can arrange a tonne?' I asked. 'I've dealt with people before who talk big loads but fail to deliver.'

'No problem, man,' he assured me. 'But it will take time to get it together. In my early days, I was in good with the cartel dealers. They loved me. But I never stored more than fifty kilos in one stash, so if anything goes wrong, you don't lose it all. Even now, the kitchen I use has to move every couple days. When I was well known, I ran a kitchen that could make six hundred kilos a day, top grade. But since the trouble with my wife, I just do smaller.'

'What do you mean by smaller?'

'Up to fifty keys a time.'

He asked if I would prefer to collect the gear in 'the zone', the remote area where it was produced. I said I would rather deal from Belem, the point of export. Heading into the jungle did not appeal to me.

His main concern was the setting up of the front company

that would load the juice into the container. I tempted him by repeating that loads in chilled containers were rarely checked and that if this went smoothly I would be looking for one a month, in which case I would be happy to take on some of his expenses in Belem. He was reassured.

We moved on to how I would pay for the pulp, to make the export look genuine. 'In principle, I have no problem paying on departure of the goods,' I said. 'But I will need to see the load personally before it goes in the reefer.'

'How would payment be made?' he asked.

'I would open an offshore account and make both me and you signatories. It will need both of us to sign at the bank in person for the release of the money.'

'Is cash not possible?'

'No. I never deal in cash.'

'I think it will cost me a lot to begin trading,' he mused.

'I can help you with that, but only if I'm happy with your set-up.'

'How will we talk? Can you get me a satellite phone? I will sometimes have to be in what we call the zone, and won't have access to a safe telephone. I know satellite phones are bulky to carry but it will be safer.'

'Yes, I can get you one. I've used them for my salvage business.'

'I am happy to pay for it. But can you bring it to Brazil to me, because if any of my rivals see me with it, it might cause trouble?'

'Sure.'

We exchanged numbers and Francisco said he was happiest communicating by fax as 'faxes can't be tapped'. This was untrue but I did not disabuse him.

He was a good talker and seemed to know his business down to small details, such as how his Bolivian coca pickers insisting on being paid in their local currency because there were so many fake US dollars around. Nevertheless, I told him that if anything went wrong or I even suspected he was going to let me down, he would never see me again. 'My phone numbers, business, everything, will vanish,' I said.

'No, no, man, I am the same. If things look bad, I don't threaten nobody, I don't use no violence, that doesn't work anyway these days. I just pull out.'

We confirmed my price of $4,500 a kilo and parted, with him planning to return to South America.

We next spoke three weeks later by cellphone. He said things were going well but wanted me to fly out and suggested Rio de Janeiro, as he had to travel there to collect a debt. I agreed and said I would bring his satphone.

We exchanged a few more calls over the next couple of weeks and I faxed through an order from my front company, Saber Investments, for a quantity of West Indian cherry pulp to be sent from Belem to either Valencia, Spain, or Leixoes, Portugal, which had weekly sailings onward to Liverpool. I arranged a day to arrive in Rio and he offered to collect me at the airport.

Then other commitments intervened. I was pulled away on the Long Job and had to stall Francisco, saying that a glitch had arisen with a delivery – which was actually true – and I needed to deal with it. I made out I was angry at the delay.

'Ah well, I hope you sort your problem out,' he said.

'It's other people who have the problem when I deal with them,' I replied.

He laughed.

Our last call came a couple of weeks later. We reassured each other that everything was on track and Francsico even suggested that on my visit I could speak to his 'backers' to confirm everything was good. He would await my call.

The next time I rang, his phone was dead. I never heard from him again.

So what happened? It could have been any number of things.

Perhaps he was never in a position to deliver what he promised. Perhaps he got a better offer from another transporter. Perhaps he fell out with his backers or suppliers. Perhaps suspicion got the better of him. Perhaps he was dead.

Our conversations had, however, been an invaluable primer for me on the cocaine world. The trade meant big money – and this could be a problem. Although the image I portrayed was one of power and wealth, my power was a façade and the wealth belonged to the government. Nick and Ray did their best to provide a budget for the necessary trappings but in the end we were a public department, accountable for every penny we spent.

I hit the limits of civil service cost-consciousness in a job conducted on behalf of Dutch law enforcement, with whom we often partnered. The target was a nasty piece of work called William. A Dutch Surinamese who had been in the trade for much of his thirty-five years, he was used to getting his own way and to hurting people when he didn't. The slightest slip-up with someone like that could result in a severe beating, or worse.

William needed a transport method to smuggle vast amounts of cocaine from Central America to Europe. I persuaded him and several goons to come to London to meet me, booking them connecting flights via Holland, which gave us a useful evidential trail. He was coming to get the measure of me, so it would likely be a heavy meet and I would have to be on my mettle. I hired the best suite at a Hilton hotel in the West End. My handler, Sheen, was stationed in the lobby, ready to summon the cavalry if needed.

All went smoothly. William and his team had got access to twenty tonnes of high-grade coke which they wanted to put out of Belem over several months in barrels of fruit pulp – the same means proposed by my earlier target, Franciso. The Colombians were going though a phase of using pulp, usually in fifty-gallon containers with lockdown lids.

We agreed on the amount and the price for me to ship from Belem to Holland. Then, to impress, I called room service and ordered two bottles of Dom Perignon champagne, 1983 vintage, at £250 a bottle. One would have done the job but I wanted to test William.

Our champagne duly arrived. The waiter opened a bottle with a practiced flourish, then discreetly retired as we toasted our forthcoming venture. I took a single sip and put down my glass. We continued to talk and I topped up William's glass but not my own.

After five minutes, I said, 'Right then, gents, shall we go and eat?'

William looked surprised. 'You're not going to leave that champagne are you?' he said.

I looked at the bottles, one half-empty, one unopened. My old mentor, Henri Exton, had taught me that it was always the little details they remember. The small things can kill you; conversely, the small things can make you.

'Bring 'em along if you need to, if you're that worried about the cost. It's only a bottle of champagne. Are you that cheap?' I said it in a playful way but with an edge that William was sure to notice.

His eyes narrowed. 'What do you mean?' he said, defensive for the first time.

'Well, you seem bothered about leaving a little drop of champers.'

His team were all looking at him, no doubt expecting an explosion.

'It doesn't bother me,' I continued, 'but if it upsets you so much, bring along the full bottle so we don't waste it. Have it as my gift.'

After a hesitation, William recovered his poise. 'No, it doesn't bother me. I just thought you might want it.'

'Well I don't,' I said. 'Cheapskate.'

He had got the message: I was a man who could sip expensive wine and then chuck the bottle without a second thought.

We went downstairs, but before we hit the street, I said, 'One moment, gentlemen, I have to make a call.' I went back to the foyer and rang Sheen's mobile. 'There are two bottles of very expensive champagne in that room,' I said quietly. 'One is unopened. Woe betide anyone who drinks it. Nick Baker will kill us over the expense. Give it back to the hotel.'

He laughed. 'All right, we'll get in the room and sort it.'

So much for Mr Big Spender. Even in UC mode, I was still a customs officer and aware of cost.

Every time we met from then on, I reminded William of the champagne or told others he was tight-fisted. It needled him to the extent that he never questioned my background.

It was while working on this job that I faced the most dangerous moment of my career. I had flown to Curaçao with a Dutch UC to meet William's team and was talking to them in a parking lot in broad daylight when we were spotted by a carload of armed lunatics, who attempted to jack us. From what details later emerged, it was an entirely random attack: the men were Colombian desperadoes who had busted out of the local prison and were driving around looking for victims, no doubt to steal enough money to buy their way off the island. We were simply in the wrong place at the wrong time.

I hid under the nearest car as bullets flew, then made off as local cops flooded the area. I later heard that at least one of the robbers died in the gunfight. After a quick conflab with my handler and the Dutch, we decided to leave the island immediately. I didn't even stay to make a witness statement, as I was there in secret and it had nothing to do with our job. My passage was cleared through the airport and before I knew it I was touching down in London, where Jo and Jessica were waiting to take me home. I wanted to keep working but my handler said, 'Just go home.' Maybe I had internalised the peril I had been in, but it was only that it started to sink in.

The operation continued, and with the information I was able to provide, local law enforcement and the Dutch took out William's shipment in Belem. They also rounded up him and seven of his team.

I had to give evidence at their trial. I flew to Holland and, in order to protect my identity from court observers, spent half a day being disguised for the hearing. They kitted me in a wavy wig, false teeth and make-up, and a badly-fitting suit, and took me under heavy escort to an underground court in The Hague known as 'the bunker'. There I sat in a glass box in the middle of the courtroom, beside a translator.

William and his team were handcuffed to a rail in the dock, behind a screen. The president of the court asked William if he saw undercover British officer in the court. 'No,' he replied. The president then indicated me and said, 'That's him there.'

'No it isn't, I'd recognise him,' said William indignantly. They must have done a good job with the make-up.

There was a priceless moment when the court adjourned for lunch. I had to stay in the room, while the gang were manacled to a bar in front of them. William banged on his screen and made the throat-slitting gesture at me. I responded by miming a man hanging from a noose. He went berserk and the guards had to quieten him. They all got long sentences.

The Belem gunfight was one of two occasions where I saw someone get shot. The other was in Colombia, at an exploratory meeting arranged through Keravnos, who had contacts everywhere. At short notice I went to a quiet café, where I sat talking business with two traffickers, one of them a garrulous ship owner called Nelson. I thought the meeting was going well, until the other man pulled a handgun from under the table and casually shot Nelson in the leg. He squealed and fell squirming to the floor.

'He was talking too much,' said the Colombian, without a flicker of emotion.

I made my excuses and left as soon as I was able, though it was a small gun and Nelson seemed more shocked than hurt. No-one else in the vicinity seemed remotely perturbed.

Witnessing such casual violence made me seriously wonder about working on the front line in South America. Then another opportunity would present itself that was too good to resist. If I had wanted a quite life, I reasoned, I could always have stayed in the Central Registry filing papers.

My best 'in' to the Colombians came via Keef, our financial expert. While working with the German police, he had found a way to access a major *cartelista*, a boss. The plot was put to management and after some thought they gave it the nod. I would be the point man.

My introduction to the target was to be made via a female Colombian informant called Imogen. Her husband, known as 'C', was serving a long spell in a German prison and there was talk of reciprocal aid for him if she helped the authorities. I was to meet her in Miami, where we would spend time getting our story straight. Her husband would meanwhile reference me to the cartel boss from his prison cell.

We met on a sultry Florida night in high summer. I answered a knock at my hotel-room door to see a lady of about forty years and no more than five feet tall, wearing the tightest, most revealing, most vivid tiger-print hot-pants and bra. Imogen was, to put it politely, well-proportioned, and a lot of her was not constrained by the tiger-print.

'Que pasa, caballero?' she purred. 'Am I hot or what?'

With that, she licked her finger, placed it on the outside of a well-rounded thigh and made a sizzling sound through blood-red lips.

'You're not,' I said sharply, doing my best not to laugh. 'Now go back and put on some decent clothes!'

Fifteen minutes later Imogen was back in jeans and a shirt. 'Spoilsport,' she pouted.

We hit the town. Imogen fizzed with Latin sass – and she was good. She introduced me to the main man in Florida, who would lead me, hopefully, to the next level, a genuine boss. She described our target, a man called Vittorio, as a main player, high up and trusted in the Medellin cartel. She warned that he was very sharp and would check out my background. I was confident that my legend would hold up.

Interestingly, Vittorio was said to be related to Pablo Escobar, the ultimate narco, who had been hunted by multiple agencies until his death in a rooftop gunfight on the outskirts of Medellin. It marked the passing of a crucial stage in the growth of the cocaine trade, which was now powered by massive financial interests and protected by corrupt state institutions. Even Pablo's legendary savagery could not fend off the forces he had helped to create.

Whether Vittorio really was his relative we did not know for sure; some people saw advantage in claiming to be linked to the infamous godfather, who was by then very dead and so unlikely to contradict them. But before we went, we ran it past senior management because of the implications for safety and cost. We would be unarmed. Customs officers never carried weapons; we were taught familiarity with them but only to be able to make a buy or to disarm one and make it safe. In Latin America you were actually better off not carrying a gun, as then you did not present an immediate threat if things went pear-shaped. Our deployment was approved.

Brazil was proposed as the location for our meet. Keef spoke to the Foreign Office and SIS about the do's and don'ts of operating there, as this would be the first major Beta Projects insertion in South America, and was explicitly told, 'Don't go to Rio, it's gun city. Kidnap and extreme violence are the norm.' We were advised to meet our man in the city of Sao Paulo which was, we were assured, bright, vibrant and, above all, safe.

We took a circuitous route from London to Paris, then Lisbon, across to Rio, and finally down to Sao Paulo. Keef and I booked into a city centre Crowne Plaza. He handled the official liaison, enabling me to concentrate on meeting Vittorio, which took a few more days to arrange. The idea was to win his trust and see where it led.

On the morning of our arranged meet, I sat drinking a strong coffee and trying to read the local paper in our hotel lobby. It was thronged with a mix of businessmen, sales reps and tourists, all mingling in the reception area. Keef, my only support, was at the bar pretending to scan a financial report.

From my seat I saw a blacked-out stretch limousine, complete with boomerang aerial, pull up outside. Two blacked-out Range Rovers fell in behind it. Four purposeful men jumped out – all carrying automatic weapons. Each wore black Kevlar body armour under a long black coat.

They strode into the foyer like extras from *The Matrix*, sending guests, staff and even the hotel security scurrying away. The Crowne Plaza wasn't exactly a fleapit, and seeing them walk in openly tooled-up was pretty impressive. This was going to be an interesting meet.

A small, bony guy, his eyes hidden by Ray-Ban aviators, emerged last from the limo. The only man not in Kevlar, he wore a beautiful suit and shoes sharp enough to cut glass. As I counted the heavies crowding into the foyer and scanning every corner, the skinny dude sauntered to my table and removed his shades.

'You must be Guy. I am Vittorio.'

I indicated a chair. 'Sit down, Vittorio. Fancy a coffee?'

He sat in silence, examining me, while his coffee was brought over by a trembling waiter. Then he zeroed in.

'So, how do you know "C" and Imogen? Where did you and "C" first meet? What trades have you done? Who else do you know?'

I sat and let his questions bounce off me. He fell silent.

'Vittorio,' I said finally. 'What's with your men's get-up?'

'Protection,' he said. 'When you are as important as me, you need men and guns to tell people to stay clear.'

I beckoned him to lean forward. 'Vittorio,' I whispered, 'if it all cracks off and there's a shootout, only two people are going to die – you and me. We are the only ones without body armour.'

He looked confused. I pointed at his gun-toting goons and repeated, 'We've got no armour.' I made a cutting motion with my finger across my throat. 'Kaput,' I said.

Vittorio sat back with a half-frown. Then he nodded slowly and recovered his poise.

With the obligatory amateur dramatics out of the way, we settled down to talk broadly about what I could offer. As ever, it was transport: he was desperate for shipping. He also offered a word of praise.

'You a very brave man.'

'Why?'

'No one comes to Sao Paulo, it's gun city. Very, very dangerous. I only came to save face. I said to myself, "If the gringo can come here with no fear, so can I."'

So much for the Foreign Office advice: the one place they claimed was safe, even the baddies were scared to visit.

'Where would you have chosen?' I asked.

'We'd go up to Rio or a holiday town. Have some fun. For us, this is a bad place. We have lost men here. Next time, we'll go up the river to Manaus. You'll like it.'

'Well, that's a long way.'

'Ah, but it's a good place. Very cultured. It has an opera house.'

Vittorio snapped his fingers. The Kevlar boys re-grouped around him.

'Nice to meet you, Guy. We will meet again at a café tomorrow. The location will be phoned through to you tonight.'

With that, he was gone.

The call duly came through, and the next day found me waiting in the sunshine outside the appointed café. A battered yellow Datsun pulled up. The door creaked open and out stepped Vittorio, wearing jeans and a sports jacket and not a gunman in sight.

'No bodyguards?' I said, grinning.

'No,' he said, a little sheepishly. 'You know how we are portrayed on television, like killers? We like to live up to that. It impresses people, and scares them. But it's nothing.'

Over the next few days we got to know one another. It turned out he really was a cousin of Escobar. He complained bitterly about how much it had cost to keep Pablo on the lam. 'He kept borrowing money off me. Every month, he needed half a million, a million, and he never paid it back.' He was still wondering how he would recoup it.

The fall of Pablo didn't slow Vittorio. He let me know that he was still a big mover in the coke trade, and I pondered how much money he and his associates really had. I was soon to find out.

A few days later, I was collected outside my hotel by Vittorio and an associate. 'I need your help,' he said. 'But first, please, you must put on this blindfold.'

I was concerned, but there was no edge to his manner and he kept on chatting in a non-threatening way. My gut told me it was safe, so I put on the blindfold and off we set.

I tried the usual trick of remembering twists and turns and listening out for sounds that might signal our location, but in truth I had no clue where we heading. We drove for some half an hour before stopping. Vittorio took off my blindfold and apologised.

'Sorry, but it is for security. You do not need to know where we are.'

We were outside a large, prefabricated warehouse on a small industrial estate on the city outskirts. It had white painted walls and a green corrugated roof. We went in through a small wicket door within a main door and Vittorio flicked on the lights.

For as far as I could see were pallets of shrink-wrapped paper. Closer inspection revealed the paper to be stacks of US dollars. The pallets filled the warehouse, except for narrow pathways down which a small forklift rattled. Through the wrapping I could see denominations of twenties, fifties and hundreds in used bills.

'How much is here?' I asked, struggling to keep the awe out of my voice.

'That is the problem, we don't know.'

'What do you want me to do?'

'Get it into the system for us,' said Vittorio. 'We have just got too much, it is a real security problem.'

I wandered down the middle aisle and noticed that a corner of the roof was damaged. Water had come in, probably during a storm, and seeped into a pile of unwrapped notes. They had turned into a greenish mulch, probably the world's most expensive papier-mâché. It was, I thought, criminal in more ways than one.

I promised to try to help and was driven away blindfolded. Again I memorised turns, timings and traffic light stops, but no matter how often I tried later, I could never relocate that warehouse. For all I know it is still there.

It all seemed so outlandish that I did wonder if some, or all, of the dollars were counterfeit. But a few years later a money stash inside a Bogotá apartment building was found to total $35 million in genuine currency. So I guess it was real.

I did not in the end do anything with Vittorio's money but

that meeting cemented our friendship, and I flew back to the UK promising to keep in touch. I did, and he turned out to be a likeable guy. It is a fallacy that all criminals are mindless thugs. Some are highly intelligent but have chosen to use their brains in unlawful ways. Vittorio was one. We soon felt we had known each other for years.

After several months, he even accepted my gift of a satellite phone so we could keep in touch. That phone became priceless. For months afterwards, he would call me on it and tell me what he was up to. Often he would be phoning from a coca-processing farm deep in the jungle. These random and impromptu buddy calls were an intelligence goldmine for HMCE and the DEA.

On one occasion he called me at 3 a.m. when I was in Dubai working.

'Ah, Guy, how are you?'

'Fine. Where are you?'

'I am up in the hills.'

I thought, *this is good, if they have locked onto this they have got him.*

He said, 'I need to see you, we need to start talking about a load.' He was getting prepared for a big one, a fruit pulp load that was going to Belem for onward shipment. Once again the Dutch police were leading the investigation into it and I fed my intel to their operation. It led them to make a sizeable seizure. Importantly it could not be traced to me, which kept my relationship with Vittorio intact.

I continued to speak with, and occasionally meet, Vittorio over the next couple of years, including in Europe, and all the time passed info back to the Dutch. His manner never changed but I noticed that he looked thinner and paler each time we met.

He was preparing with my help for another big shipment, which would again have been seized, when I heard he had been taken to hospital in great pain, suffering stomach cancer. Then one day, while I was working in the Middle East, I took a call from one of his team. Vittorio had died on the operating table. I admit I felt sad, and that night I sat alone in my hotel room and raised a glass to him. He had been an interesting man, and in other circumstances we might have been friends.

My bosses were less sentimental. I was later chastised at my annual appraisal for losing the satphone, which was never recovered.

My next South American trip took me to Venezuela, in the days before Hugo Chavez was elected president. It was a job the DEA and FBI had their hands in and again came through an informant. A Colombian group was looking for sea transport and I was recommended.

I flew to Caracas with Harvey as my handler. He was a cool, laidback guy and an experienced UC whose cover legend was taking photographs for holiday brochures. This gave him licence to visit exotic places and to scout hotels, beaches and other locations without arousing suspicion. Ours was a hush-hush mission and only our DLO and the ambassador knew we were there. We told the ambo we were in deep cover and would not be declaring ourselves to the Venezuelans unless things went badly wrong.

The problem was that Venezuela had a strange kind of intelligence police, with a questionable remit. They had informants everywhere, including the hotels, and our bedroom and any phone lines would probably not be safe for more than a short period. And if they decided we were iffy, anything could happen.

I met the Colombian group in a bar. Their leader had the unlikely name of Eric. He worked for a big team wanting to use shipping containers for regular runs. He had good English and quite a pleasant guy, but appeared to be under considerable stress and his team seemed distracted, even downcast.

Eventually he said, 'We have got problems here.'

'Problems with me?' I asked.

'No, no, we want to do business with you very much.'

'So what are you unhappy about?'

He leaned in closer and lowered his voice. 'Just before we came here, I had to arrange a drop by air for my bosses. It was four tonnes. We broke it into packages, put floats on them and threw them from the back of a C5 aeroplane. They were meant to land in the Rio Negro, which goes into the Amazon, and be picked up by a boat but instead they fell in the jungle. My boss is now saying to me, "I don't care about your excuses, go and find it all." We have to fly back to look for it.'

'Jesus,' I said in genuine sympathy. 'That sounds like a nightmare.'

'Yes. I think I know where it is, but it will be very hard to find.'

And off he went with his men.

I returned to the hotel and made some calls to the cartel that evening to keep things going. But Harvey, watching my back, was convinced something was wrong. Our room phone sounded crackly, as though people were listening, and strange guys seemed to be loitering around the general area of the hotel. Was it the cartel, suspicious of us? Was it corrupt local cops, hoping to shake us down? Or had something triggered genuine law enforcement, who thought we were drug dealers? On our own with no back-up, we were in a difficult position.

Eventually Harvey declared, 'We need to go. We are crossing the line of safety and starting to attract attention.' I reluctantly agreed. We packed up, I used the fax connected to my Psion Organiser to message the UK, and we booked the first flights out we could.

The following day we checked in separately at Caracas Airport and queued to go through security. Harvey breezed through but as I waited, a couple of burly officials in uniform appeared. One put a hand on my shoulder and dragged me out of the line. I was marched to an interview room and sat down.

Harvey boarded the flight, fearing the worst. The rule was to stick in legend and not break cover, no matter what, which we both did. I was quizzed for half an hour about who I was and what I was doing in Caracas, while the flight was kept waiting. Fortunately they could not find any holes in my story and eventually let me go. I was the last person to board and was mighty relieved to get out of there.

The world of the Latin American narcos was generally too dangerous to infiltrate directly. My attempts had mixed results. Where Beta did deploy successfully against them was on the money laundering side, much of which could be done from the UK, which was safer and more controllable.

As our team's banking specialist, Keef was often called in to jobs that needed someone to transfer or wash large sums and his services were in great demand, especially from Colombians. Like many people who are good with sums, Keef was a little OCD. He kept his London offices spotless and his desk immaculate: blotter in the exact middle, pens lined up, pencils arranged in height order. Sheen and I liked nothing better than visiting him and subtly move his pens about. It would drive him to distraction, until he felt compelled to throw us out.

We also teased Keef incessantly about how safe his role was. We would rib him about going out to fine dinners, travelling the world to high-level meetings in exotic spots, flying Concorde. While some of us had been held at gunpoint, I used to say, the worst that ever happened to him was that he reached for his pen to sign a cheque and there was no ink in it. Or the paper tore as he ripped it from his chequebook.

Of course none of this was fair. Keef dealt with the upper echelons of the Colombian and Mexican cartels, men renowned for ruthlessness, and handled it all with quiet calm.

He used to chide us, 'All you have to do is sail a bloody boat from one place to another. I'm sitting with the heads of the cartel, who want to know exactly when their money is coming and how I'm going to get it to them. The hard bit has been done, now their cash is with me, a bald-headed Cockney on the other side of the table who could piss off with it all. The first thing they think is that I'm going to rip them.'

Sometimes the Americans he worked with would ask Keef where he kept his gun. He would wave his pen at them and say, 'This is my gun. I've put more people away with this than anyone with a shooter. The pen is mightier than the sword.' He had a point.

While we would travel to meet drug barons in Colombia, we always tried to get them to the UK or near-Europe if possible, where we had more control. The bosses rarely came in person but would send representatives to inspect warehouses we had set up, vehicles we ran or boats we owned. They were entrusting us with their product and it was sensible to check us out. There was nothing worse for them than seeing off a ship or lorry with their valuable merchandise and wondering if they would ever get paid. In later years they took to providing their own men to babysit loads on sea voyages and guard their interests. It made our job harder but we devised methods to deter them.

On one occasion, a cartel wanted to inspect one of our vessels anchored offshore. That was fine but we did not want them hanging around too long, being nosey and getting in the way. So when the narcos arrived at the dockside, in their suits and crocodile-skin shoes, we arranged to collect them in a fast RHIB. They had barely jumped in when Eccles, looking as sun-browned and salt-blasted as the Ancient Mariner, set off at speed, making sure they got a good buffeting and a coating of sea spray. At the main vessel they then had to clamber over the side, which was filthy and covered in oil. Dirty chains lay around the deck, a generator belched fumes and spilt diesel oozed underfoot.

'Okay, okay,' said their boss, eyeing his previously spotless shoes and trouser cuffs. 'We've seen enough. We go back now.' They couldn't wait to get off.

In Scotland, Beta had a two-man team who could have been twins separated at birth. Tommy and Wullie, nicknamed 'the Krankies', were smart, savvy lads who used their strong local accents to advantage. It was hard enough for me to understand them, and when they got going they produced an outlandish growl like the 'Jimmy' parody by the comedian Russ Abbott.

One summer's evening, three Colombians touched down at Glasgow Airport from Amsterdam to negotiate a cocaine shipment, which was to be picked up off South America and required detailed negotiations. Wullie went into the terminal to collect them.

'Welcome tae Glasgae,' he greeted them. 'It's the greatest place oan God's earth.'

The Colombians stood mute, wondering what strange language the man was speaking.

'Let's gang tae th' motur,' said Wullie, indicating the exit. His bemused visitors followed. Outside, in a gun-metal BMW 7 Series, waited Tommy. One of the Krankies' trademarks was a love of the Rat Pack, whose songs they played often and loudly. Dean Martin's 'That's Amore' was belting from the car.

The Colombians slid into the back while Wullie jumped into the front passenger seat. Surveillance footage from a hidden camera captured the next few minutes of pure comedy. As they pulled away, one of the Colombians nudged his compatriot, spoke in Spanish and giggled at the music, which was now 'Everybody Loves Somebody'. Tommy suddenly anchored up in a screech of tyres and the Colombians lurched forward in their seats.

'De ye no like Deano?' he demanded, with a hint of menace. He turned to Wullie.

'I am just scunnered wae them. Oor relationship is nae working oot at all,' he said. 'They're geein' me the boak.'

'Aye,' said Wullie.

The Colombians sat motionless, trying to work out if this was some kind of test or if the driver was as mad as the man who had met them.

'Well?' said Tommy, turning to look directly at the Colombians with even more menace.

'Okay, ees good, jou like? Sí, sí, we like Sammy, Frank and Dean,' one of them stammered.

'That's better,' said Tommy, with a scowl. 'Now, aw tae-gether, "Everybody, loves somebody, sometime ..."'

The car sped out of the airport, Dean Martin crooning from the stereo and three terrified narcos singing in the back. These are the things they don't teach you in UC school.

15

ONCE UPON A TIME IN MEXICO

Seven years is a long time to pose as someone else. Perhaps too long. My peers were being promoted to more senior ranks and I needed to look to my future career. As a new millennium approached, I received some welcome news: I was being promoted. Our SIO, Ray, was moving to another team, having run himself into the ground making Beta Projects the success that it was, and falling ill in the process: he suffered a serious bout of pericarditis. Nick decided that it would take two SIOs to replace him and manage the team jointly, and wanted a former UC to be one of them. Ray would admit that you can be hoodwinked by UCs, who after all are trained to lie, whereas I could act as poacher-turned-gamekeeper. My fellow SIO, Tommy, was a non-UC but a highly experienced investigator and an oasis of calm, never flustered under pressure.

Being the boss changed my relationship with the team. They were no longer just my mates but my charges. Running any team brought pressures but this lot were in a different league, a bunch of super-egos all with demands, be it boats, cars, property or jewellery. At team meetings, I was now the person on the receiving end of all the moans and groans: 'Why has he got a Rolex when I've got a Timex?' and so on. Some thought they were being mistreated while others were being favoured and little divisions were inevitable. Fortunately I have never been afraid to tackle problems head-on. I also don't bear grudges. I can flare up but then forget about it.

Some of the originals had moved on. There would always come a time where a UC had been successful, done good jobs, but the opposition were talking about him and it was time to move. Some officers were with us for only a couple of years before their success meant they had to return to an operational team for their own health and safety.

I had a lot more paperwork to stay on top of – mundane tasks like the tax liabilities for our vehicles, which were basically classed as company cars – as well as handling all the intel and interfacing with the operational teams. Rightly or wrongly, however, I reserved the right to still deploy in the field if I felt my legend was the best one for the task. And within a matter of months an unusual opportunity arose that I could not turn down.

I took an urgent call at my desk from the boss of one of our investigation teams. He said a large cargo vessel was heading into a port somewhere in Mexico. The ship, crewed and controlled by a Colombian cartel, was either carrying or was due to pick up a huge quantity of cocaine to take to Europe. We had been tracking the ship but had lost it at sea.

The job, I was told, should be 'simple': fly to Mexico and find the ship. If possible, could I also get a job in the dock to help load her – and in the process, attempt to confirm where the cocaine was hidden on board?

Some might think it a doddle to trace and follow a ship; after all, they are big, slow-moving, and can only load and unload at a finite number of ports. This particular merchant vessel, the *Castor*, was 258 feet long, 37 feet wide and 50 feet tall, and weighed 1,415 tons. Designed as a carrier for timber, she now plied her trade taking bulk goods around the Caribbean.

But compared to the oceans, even the biggest tankers are microscopic and tracking them is an inexact science. Our sketchy intelligence suggested the *Castor* might be heading into Tampico, a tropical city of 300,000 souls on the Gulf of Mexico, to collect a cargo of sugar.

I would be double-handed with my old oppo Sheen, who would travel with me to help on the job and liaise with our embassy in Mexico City and our intelligence and operational teams back in London. Our deployment was so secret that only the British ambassador would know. It was not a standard UC job, as there was unlikely to be any infiltration as such, but we still needed full legends.

Partnering with Sheen would certainly make the journey eventful, and a laugh. Like me, he came from a working-class family, in his case from New Cross in south-east London. He was brainy enough to qualify for grammar school, reached international standard as a young swimmer and was even offered a scholarship by Millfield, a posh private school. But at sixteen he 'got sick of it and became a waster', in his own words, barely holding down a part-time job in one of London's first-ever McDonald's outlets. Many have said that he missed his true vocation as a burger flipper. He screwed up his 'A' levels, flunked out of college, became a punk rocker and bummed around Wardour Street. He was working as a pool lifeguard when his dad finally snapped and told him to get a proper job or leave home. So he left home.

After sleeping on a Greek beach for eight weeks, he had sunk low enough to apply for a clerical job with HMCE. Somehow he was accepted, and immediately hated it. But slowly he found his feet. In the mid-eighties he was accepted onto the ID and suddenly became focused. He worked against Nigerian smugglers, Scouse gangsters, Turkish heroin bosses and rogue ex-spooks for the Iranian intelligence service SAVAK. He went on a money laundering team, tracking millions of pounds in drug cash being changed into guilders at bureaux de change and sent to Holland, and supported the DEA on covert ops.

When I returned to London from Birmingham, I joined the same branch as Sheen's then-girlfriend. We met socially , shared a few beers and became part of an after-work clique. He was eventually approached by Nick Baker to apply to Beta Projects. Sheen completed an application and a CV and put them in a double-sealed envelope in the internal post, with the giveaway heading 'Application for Undercover Duties'. Unforgivably it was lost. After a lot of embarrassment and shuffling of feet, he was prevailed upon to apply again and was accepted.

Concerned about the security breach of his lost application, Sheen resolved to rely on no-one more than himself. He set his own standards and made a fetish of double-checking everything. When combined with his quirky sense of humour, this was not always appreciated. His first deployment was as a minder and gofer for our money man, Keef, in a long-running cocaine investigation, and when driving to meet the bad guys at a hotel, Sheen insisted they concoct a cover story to explain how they knew each other.

Keef had a distinctive aquiline nose. 'I know,' Sheen said as they arrived. 'Let's say that I used to work as a doorman at Aspinalls. You came up and started talking to me, and as a rich punter I was being nice to you. Then out of the blue you propositioned me and said that if I went home with you, you would pay several hundred pounds to give me a blowjob. I punched you in the face, knocked you down the stairs and that's how you got your broken nose. Then you later asked me to work for you.'

Keef considered this for all of two seconds before saying, 'No.'

Sheen found his true forte as a handler. He like to have control of a job whereas, he argued, the UC is just a pawn. His legend was as a travel industry specialist, looking to drum up tourism opportunities in the locations he visited. In Mexico, however, our cover was that we ran a business looking for freight opportunities and offshore reclamation, and were seeking ports from where we could salvage sunken or abandoned vessels. In some ways legitimate salvage work is like criminality, in that those who do it keep it tight, especially if it involves sunken treasure, as they don't want competitors to know. It's a nice cover.

Sheen and I flew to Mexico City, hired a four-by-four Landcruiser and set off. The Mexican capital lies in a bowl-like depression covered for much of the time in yellow smog. This smog, when combined with an insanely complex ring-road system, makes navigation tricky. It was like being in Hampton Court maze when you realise you are passing the same place for the fourth time. We took three hours just to clear the suburbs.

Things looked up, literally, as we passed through the Sierra Madre mountain belt to the east. I fulfilled a lifetime ambition when I spotted a big 'Desperate Dan' cactus, properly known as a *saguaro*. Having only ever seen them in Westerns and the pages of *The Dandy*, I leapt from the car and snapped a photo. I need not have been so keen: over the next two hours, we saw more than we ever wanted to see again.

We eventually reached the Best Western Tampico, one of the lowlight hotels of my career, and I have stayed in many – good, bad and weird. The receptionist, a small, anxious man, took me up to my room; Sheen was next door. He opened the window and pointed out the view of the town square, where scruffy figures dozed in the late afternoon sun. I protested that it was too hot to leave the window open, and asked him to turn on the air-conditioning. That was a mistake.

He took out a long thin rope and wound it round a spindle on top of a generator in the corner of my room. Then he whipped the rope off the spindle, like an old-fashioned petrol lawnmower, and it chugged into life. The room filled with thick, black smoke, the smell of burning diesel and a deafening din.

'Ees good, yes?' said my host. 'Very cool.'

'Very noisy,' I shouted

'Jes' a leetle,' he said and left.

I listened as the whole performance was repeated in Sheen's room.

That evening we wandered into the town, a mix of Blackpool seafront and Fawley oil refinery. Big and industrial, it has a beach, funfairs, seaside entertainments and loads of Mexican tourists. We found a local cantina and sat quietly, drinking beer and watching the unfriendly locals eye us up. They stared especially intently at my Rolex watch, which I was wearing in my legend as a wealthy salvage boss.

'Take it off,' said Sheen.

'Nah, sod that,' I said. 'We can't let them think we're push-over gringos. They won't take us on.'

'Listen, they'll chop your arm off here for a watch like that. At least put your jacket on.'

We faced them down but when we got back to the hotel I had to concede that Sheen had a point. This was the territory of the Gulf Cartel, a deadly criminal syndicate that recruited Special Forces soldiers as their enforcers. Maybe it was better to keep the Rolex out of sight.

Our team back in England told us that Tampico would be 'easy to navigate'. They had obviously never been there. After several drives around the docks and outlying installations, Sheen dropped me off and I headed into the estuary on foot, where I could see the larger vessels moored up. There was no sign of the *Castor*.

Tampico has a long sea-to-inland dock canal. From open water to the dock was well over two miles and provided numerous berths for vessels based on their size and load. Security was tight at the terminal but eased off as you went along the berths. We could observe arrivals inconspicuously.

I made several dry runs into the main dock while we waited, as we would need to be close when the vessel docked and was unloaded and reloaded. I was challenged by security staff but told them that I was planning salvage work in the area and was scouting a suitable berth for my boat. I was able to obtain a temporary dock pass and spoke with the authorities about berthing and victualling of my craft when it arrived.

For three days we swept the docks, the estuary and the feeder canals. I even joined up with various itinerant dock gangs, but to no avail. No ship matching our target came in.

Then London called. They said that while it did not look like the opposition were aware of law enforcement interest and were going ahead, they would be using a different port. Our ship was now believed to be heading to Veracruz, 'just a little way' down the coast.

'How far is a little way?' asked Sheen.

'I'm not sure,' said the desk officer, 'but on our map it's about a thumb width.'

Sheen and I could not shake off the feeling that we had been royally had over. It was more than 600 miles.

The following morning we wandered down for a hearty breakfast before our long drive. I had my normal bowl of cereal but Sheen was getting into the swing and decided to brave the local fare. He came back to the table with a large plate of black pork stew, refried beans and fresh Scotch bonnet chillies, a dangerous combination in anyone's book. I stopped, spoon halfway to my mouth.

'Do you think that's wise, mate?'

'When in Mexico, do as the Mexicans do,' said Sheen, and wolfed down a plateful.

We set off on a seven-hour drive to Veracruz. After about

150 miles, Sheen turned a remarkable shade of green and began to expel gas loudly and long. He then lay down in the back of the Landcruiser and began to retch.

'I don't feel good,' he groaned.

'Ah, but when in Mexico,' I reminded him.

He moaned even louder.

The next couple of hours were punctuated by a number of emergency stops to allow Sheen to stumble from the car and do what he needed to do. Whatever it was, it didn't sound good, and on his return our vehicle increasingly smelt like a public toilet.

In the wee hours, we stopped in darkness at a small town. We were dog-tired and Sheen was now about two stone lighter. He fell out of the car and, to the accompaniment of the baying of every dog in the village, limped over to a little rustic hotel set facing a square. The mutts began to whimper when they picked up his ripe scent. The funniest sight was watching Sheen miming 'room for the night' and 'bad diarrhoea' to a bemused young hotel receptionist.

We left early, certain in the knowledge that no one could ever use that room again.

The road to Veracruz was long and straight and the last stretch was breathtaking, with the sea to our left and mountains to our right. The weather was good, the road quiet, Sheen's body had ceased to rebel and we knew where our targets would be. What more could go wrong?

About twenty minutes in, we hit a militia roadblock. This was bad news. The loyalty of the troops in parts of Mexico was questionable and extortion, or worse, at checkpoints was a fact of life.

The captain in charge came towards our car wearing a large grin. I stepped out to talk to him. Stocky, unshaven and sweaty, he looked like Eli Wallach's 'Il Brutto' in *The Good, the Bad and the Ugly* and had more gold in his mouth than the Federal Reserve. His uniform, which may have been green at some stage, had not been washed for some time – and he was the cleanest and neatest of his six-man squad. The others fingered their weapons while the captain maintained his unnerving smile.

'Qué pasa?' I said, which was about the extent of my Spanish.

He began to speak but I stopped him. 'No español,' I admitted, hands spread.

He narrowed his eyes and looked at me with his sinister grin. The sunlight reflected from a mouth of gold.

'Do you have any goons?' he asked, in heavily-accented English.

'Goons?'

'Jou know, gringo, goons.' He made a gun gesture with his hand, one finger acting as the barrel and the thumb as the hammer, and pointed it at my head. 'Bang, bang. Jou dead.'

'Oh, guns,' I said, catching on. 'No mate, no guns. We are crew going to join our ship.'

'Oh.' He looked disappointed. 'No goons?'

He wandered to the back of the Landcruiser, inspected its newness and then looked long and hard at his own wreck of a police jeep, possibly considering a vehicle exchange. In the interests of cooperation, and cowardice, Sheen and I would have readily agreed. Instead his gaze turned wistful as he wandered back.

'Where jou goin'?'

'Veracruz.'

'Okay, gringo.' He smiled his best golden smile. 'Jou be careful there, ees a very bad place.'

'I will,' I said. The roadblock peeled back and my gold-toothed friend waved us through. He continued to watch until we were a long way down the road.

Eventually we pulled into Hermosa Veracruz, as the sign

said. If Tampico was a mix of Blackpool and Fawley, Veracruz was Tilbury Docks crossed with a Mexican Margate – but with a welcome dollop of culture thrown in.

We pulled up at another Best Western. This one had a drive-in lobby; you drove into reception and filled in your papers while seated in your car. Sheen and I childishly drove in and out a few times just for the hell of it. Then we got our rooms, dumped our gear and headed out into the wide docks.

Veracruz is actually a beautiful 16th century port, founded by Spanish settlers. The docks are overlooked by a small island, San Juan de Ulua, which was first a fortress, then a prison, then a museum. It turned out to be a prime observation post for Sheen.

He dropped me in the docks. Security was almost non-existent. I used my cover story again and filled in docking, re-fuelling and victualling requests for my imaginary salvage vessel. I also got access to the main dock area. Then Sheen and I moved hotels to another spot further up the coast, in case we had to make a speedy exit.

A couple of days later, we spotted the *Castor* docking in one of the inner centre berths. She had been repainted and her superstructure had changed – something the cartels often did in an attempt at disguise – but I was able to get alongside and confirm it was her. She was carrying a cargo of mainly timber, which dockers were offloading by hand.

Sheen and I maintained a watching brief, worried that we could lose the ship at any stage. I was able to drink at the dock bar-café and, in a sunburnt and filthy state, did not attract much attention while sitting there for hours. Sleep was snatched, especially on night watch, but during the afternoon siesta the docks came to a standstill anyway. The offloading by hand was very slow, and it was several days before the *Castor* was ready to take on new cargo.

Nothing came.

The ship lay in the full glare of the sun for days, as her new cargo was obviously not ready for loading. Whether this would include the cocaine, or whether it was already aboard, I did not know. I stayed close, helping around the docks and keeping an eye out for the expected arrival. The port authority in Veracruz had only been formed a few years earlier and was in its infancy, so it was easy to get in and out without being challenged.

About six days into our surveillance, things began to stir. Some cargo arrived, a mixed load of timber, machine parts and various odds and ends. Crewmen also began to pitch up and load some large hessian sacks delivered by flatbed lorry. I saw that the sacks, marked with a trade name, contained brown Cuban sugar.

Over the following days the sugar was craned and manhandled onboard. The weather remained savagely hot, my face burned almost beyond recognition and my hair turned platinum blond. Some of the unrefined sugar began to melt in its sacks. Soon the deck was covered in what looked like treacle toffee. It then re-crystallised and set as the evening air cooled, taking on the appearance of burnt caramel.

Always expect the unexpected.

The loaders fetched jackhammers and began stripping the treacle off the deck and sides and throwing it overboard. The torn sacks were stacked on the dock. Any company marks or adverts on them could give our intelligence teams clues as to the owners, but try as I might I could not get hold of one, and they were quickly cleared by the dock team.

Loading resumed and the pace picked up. Large sacks were craned into the hold, smaller sacks onto a deck holding area. I watched unimpeded from alongside the ship. What I could not do was take photographs. There were so many men around – and more seemed to be watching than loading – that producing a camera would have been suicidal, though I saw no weapons other than those carried by official dock guards. All that remained was to monitor her departure and decide when to intercept the shipment.

Sheen continually updated London. We had little respite but did manage to escape into town one evening for a meal at a local ranchero restaurant. Neither of us could understand the menu, so we ordered a bottle of rough red wine and asked the waiter for his suggestions. He recommended a big plate of *criadillas a la Mexicana*, which sounded delicious. 'Bring it on, my man,' I said. The waiter smiled and went off.

We wolfed down our first plateful with salsa, warm bread and fresh chillies and it was lovely, like high-quality hotdogs. 'This is the dog's bollocks,' said Sheen, smacking his lips. We were tucking into a second helping when we found out that the dish was, more accurately, the bull's bollocks, a well-known Mexican delicacy. We suddenly lost what remained of our appetites.

The next day, in the midst of the loading chaos around the ship, I saw a new batch of full hessian sacks being delivered, added to the main load and slowly carried aboard. I could not see what they contained, but I had my suspicions.

Eventually the work was done and the ship was set to go. And then – nothing. She just lay there, loaded up, crewed up and ready to sail. They were obviously waiting for something, but what? I spent hours sitting on a small, stone-walled jetty overlooking the harbour entrance to ensure she didn't cast off without us knowing, armed with a throwaway camera to take shots as she left. Sheen moved constantly between me on the jetty and the fortress island. We were exhausted and sun-frazzled but the adrenaline was running and we knew we were part of a very good job. Still, the days dragged.

Then late one afternoon, without warning, the *Castor* slipped her moorings and slowly manoeuvred into the dock basin. An hour later, she was sailing gently past me and out to sea. I could see two men distinctly on the flying bridge near the wheelhouse. I took out my camera, feeling now was the time to bash off some shots, but in the dim light the automatic flash went off. The men on the bridge seemed to look straight at me. Feeling idiotic, I lobbed the camera over my shoulder. A long few seconds passed before the men returned to their conversation.

Sheen met me at the dock gates and we shadowed *Castor* up the coast road by car. For half an hour she made her way along the coast, eventually arriving opposite the very hotel that Sheen had booked. There she slowly turned and headed out into the Gulf of Mexico. We cursed the fact that we could have sat on our balcony with our feet up, a jug of margaritas and a pair of binoculars, and watched her leave in comfort.

Our cocaine intel team were delighted when we reported the departure to London. They had their own sources but needed confirmation that the *Castor* was moving, presumably so that they could position a warship to track or interdict her. All that remained was to check out of the hotel and make the long drive back to Mexico City. We were keen to leave pronto, given that we were there at a top-secret level. Once we had boarded our flight, our ambassador could finally sleep easy. He apparently endured the worst period of his life, fearing we might be arrested, kidnapped or killed at any time, and kept ringing London to ask, 'Are they out yet?'

Sometime in the next forty-eight hours, possibly while Sheen and I were still in the air, the ship was taken out at sea near the small Caribbean island of Margarita by the British warship HMS *Marlborough*, with support from the DEA and the US Coast Guard. A search team boarded her and put the captain and crew under arrest. Buried beneath the bags of sugar I had seen at the docks, they recovered around four tonnes of cocaine, with a reported wholesale value of $68 million.

It was easily the largest seizure that Sheen and I had been involved in, in fact probably the largest coke seizure involving British law enforcement up to that time. 'DRUG-BUST JACKPOT!' was the headline in *Navy News* magazine.

Only later did I find out how big the operation was. That seizure was just one part of a vast, global investigation into a cartel that had acquired an entire fleet of merchant vessels. These motherships, as they were known, had been taking tonnes of coke to both Europe and the US for several years. My colleagues had penetrated the organisation, partly by cracking the supposedly secure satellite phones they used. It was a brilliant piece of investigative work and a superb example of numerous agencies pulling together internationally.

Sheen and I only found this out much later. As UCs, we were given limited information and a very specific brief. I agreed with this approach; some did not. I never wanted to know everything about a job. The UC is just another asset, albeit an important one as they can give real-time information, enabling operational and intelligence teams to execute their plans. The *Castor* job was a great example. I reported what I saw but was only ever told as much as I needed to know. It was a good system.

Likewise very few people knew of our deployment. This was brought home to me some years later when I visited the British DLO in Miami, a friend of mine. I recognised a photo of the *Castor* on his wall and told him I had been involved. Despite having worked on the same operation, he didn't even know I had been to Mexico.

As for the *Castor*, she was later taken out to sea and scuttled as part of a programme to create an artificial sunken reef off the coast of South Florida.

16

OUT OF AFRICA

A lot of my time as Beta SIO was devoted to training newbies. We devised our own course and incorporated a week abroad to test the candidates in a foreign environment. We would take them to Cyprus or the Netherlands and put them through meetings, set-ups and buys, with our foreign counterparts providing their own officers to help. I adapted some of Henri Exton's methods to our needs and made sure our course was as demanding as his.

We would send lads into the toilets of a public bar to make a buy and then steal their money. Another favourite was to arrange a meet in a nice restaurant, where I would pose as their target. As we sat talking, I would kick off on the staff, telling them the wine tasted like piss, or the service was crap, or they had overcharged us, and generally be as rude as possible. It was important to see how the recruit coped in awkward public situations with an aggressive, obnoxious counterparty.

Sometimes we improvised. One of the funniest examples involved a lad I was putting through his paces in Amsterdam. We arranged to meet near the Grasshopper, a famous pub and cannabis coffeeshop near Central Station. He knew me but I told him, 'You are in role as a buyer and I am going to be Guy

Stanton, drug dealer.' His task was to persuade me to supply him.

Halfway through our meet, a loud English drunk entered the pub, a brute of a bloke. He was actually a Mancunian cop called Danny, who had been loaned to us by Henri for the exercise, but the trainee did not know that. Lurching to the bar, Danny engaged him in loud conversation. The more the lad tried to brush him off, the more persistent he became.

I acted totally pissed off, and kept asking, 'Do you know this bloke?' The poor trainee did not know where to turn. In the end I said, 'Look, I'm going. I'll give you half an hour with your mate here, then I'm going to come back and we can have a chat. Get rid of him. I don't know who he is, but I don't like him.' I stormed out.

Danny, under instructions, left the trainee alone after finishing his drink. What he did next had a certain mad genius to it. He wandered down to the docks, found a party of Polish trawlermen drinking in another bar, and befriended them. Already in a mess, they responded heartily when he said, 'I know a great pub, fellas, do you want to come?' He promptly brought them back to the Grasshopper. The poor recruit and I had re-engaged and were deep in conversation when a knock came at the window and there was a grinning Danny with a gang of pissed-up Poles. They swamped the place, causing chaos. The poor trainee was in a terrible state. Later on we told him the real story and explained that the idea was to put him under pressure. I'm not sure he ever saw the funny side.

The advantage I had as SIO was that it was hard to pull the wool over my eyes. If a trainee, or indeed an experienced UC, told me something could not be done, I would know if they were right or not – because I had been there and done it myself. Only once did a trainee blurt out, 'What do you know about it?' The whole room stopped and I could see him thinking, *oh no, that just came out.* 'I was a UC before you even thought about it,' I replied, and left it at that.

Beta Projects also began to run training courses for police forces around the world. I went to Poland and Cyprus, and in Jordan met a chief of police who throughout our meeting played with a live cattle prod on his desk that he called his 'persuader'. I was invited to Lebanon by their government to advise on a long-term job they were considering, which was so sensitive that my deployment was to be kept hush-hush. To my horror, when my plane landed the chief steward made an announcement asking me to make myself known to the crew. I was then greeted by a party of unsmiling men in dark suits and escorted to a waiting fleet of police cars, all in the name of security. So much for low-key.

Keef and I went to Poland to give lectures on our covert techniques and on money laundering. The police training school, just outside Krakow, was a dismal place where even food was scarce. We were given tokens to pay for breakfast (a bit of toast and weak tea), lunch (an apple and hot chocolate) and evening meal (borscht and weak tea). But the Poles were keen and they were brave. We were assisted by Eddie, a Polish UC and martial arts expert, whose own 'lectures' mainly involved beating up unwilling colleagues in a demonstration of karate punches and judo throws. Before an admiring audience, he proceeded to tell me that he had infiltrated the Russian mafia as a lorry driver, smuggling caviar over the Polish border. I said this must have been very dangerous, because if I were the mafia I would simply shoot the driver after payment for the load and take it back over the border to be smuggled again. There was a long silence, interrupted by the occasional embarrassed cough, until Eddie admitted that that was exactly what had happened. He was lucky they had only shot him in the leg.

If I were to mark down my own scorecard as SIO, I was still doing some UC work myself when I should not have. That was my ego talking, I guess. But I had amassed so much experience, and was so comfortable in the role, that I sometimes found it impossible to resist using those skills and wiles I had honed for so long.

From the mid-nineties onwards, HM Customs made a conscious decision to move into what it called 'upstream disruption'. The aim was to capture traffickers, or at least take out their illicit drugs, before they could impact on the UK. This was a belated recognition that, as one of my fellow investigators put it, 'You don't defend the goal from the edge of the six-yard box.' With the agreement of various countries around the world, particularly in source areas, we targeted major organisations. We would work with the host authorities to elicit as much intelligence as possible on what the kingpins had for sale and their methods, systems and routes to market. This led to many successful ops.

We owed a lot to our DLOs abroad. They were experienced, talented investigators, selected from our domestic teams and sent to various British embassies and consulates. From there they carried out a multitude of tasks, not least grooming local informants to produce high-grade intel that could be used in the host nations, the UK, or other countries affected. If we did not have enough evidence to arrest the bosses, we could at worst interdict their shipments and take out their underlings, causing them major losses and sowing dissent in their ranks.

Having moved from fieldwork to running the team, I should have been at the end of my field career. Nearly ten years in harness was long enough by any reckoning. However when a job presented itself that was too big to pass up, I sent Guy Stanton out into the world for one last time.

In May 2000, Keravnos brought me an opportunity. He had befriended a group who operated out of Africa but came from Balochistan, an arid, mountainous region on the Iranian plateau. Named after the Balochi tribes who live there, it includes parts of south-eastern Iran, western Pakistan and south-western Afghanistan – all badlands for Western law enforcement. It is a wild area and the natives are hardy men, used to fighting other tribes, government forces and indeed anyone else who upsets them. They are also adept at trading the one commodity they have in abundance: heroin. This particular group had access to large quantities of brown, which they had managed to ship to Kenya for onward distribution. They were looking for European buyers.

May 20 was FA Cup final day and I had been looking forward to watching Chelsea play Aston Villa on television. Where I was brought up you were either Fulham or Chelsea and, since my grandad had sold programmes at Stamford Bridge from the club's birth in 1905, I was a staunch Blue.

Instead, duty called. I flew to Nairobi with Sheen, my handler, on a twofold mission. Firstly, I was to ingratiate myself with the targets Keravnos had given us and prep for a large-scale buy. Secondly, I would identify the members of the organisation to the Kenyan police. With this information, their links and movements in Kenya and more widely in Africa could be uncovered and disrupted. Sheen would interface between myself, our DLO in Nairobi – a colleague we both knew – and local law enforcement, leaving me to get on with the job.

In many areas of the world, the police are ill equipped, poorly paid and badly trained. Sometimes they have little loyalty even to their own government, which leads to rampant corruption. I do not condemn people in that situation. If you are paid a pittance, have little equipment and are routinely placed in danger with minimal support, I understand why you might accept bribes or off-record payments. It is easy to decry such acts from the safety of a secure, prosperous democracy.

Thankfully I came from a well-resourced organisation with minimal, if any, corruption, operating to the highest standards. But I was well aware that the rules overseas were often different. It was up to Sheen to protect me as much as possible from any internal betrayal, and I relied on his judgement.

Our plane touched down in Nairobi on a sultry afternoon. The sky was prematurely dark and thunder rumbled ominously. Outside the airport we were besieged by scores of locals offering food, trinkets, tour guides and a myriad of other services, none of which we needed.

'Hello, gentle Englishmen.'

The voice came from a very tall, heavily built African. He wore a canary-yellow kaftan with a matching yellow skullcap, and was standing by a dilapidated London black cab.

'I am Basil and I can be your guide. Look, I have my own vehicle.'

At this point a front wheel hub, the only one left on the car, fell off and rolled away with a clatter.

'Good car,' I said.

'English car,' countered Basil.

Sheen and I had learned over the years that the best form of security was a local who you paid well over normal rates to act as a guide. Once on your side, they could open doors, speak to people in their language, get things done that you would never be able to and, most importantly, provide some basic security – they were, after all, protecting their meal ticket. Whatever you paid was money well-spent and in its own way boosted the local economy.

From that point on, Basil was our man, even though it would mean travelling around Nairobi in the most conspicuous of cars. He turned out to be a mine of information and very discreet. He asked little about our business, happy that on $100 a day he was earning more than the local mayor. We based ourselves at the Hilton Nairobi on Mama Ngina Street, a cylindrical tower atop a large rectangular base, like a rocket ready for take-off. Basil handled our room booking and haggled a cut-down rate.

That night I took a phone call from the Balochi team leader. He was ready to trade and would come to my hotel the following morning. I worked into the small hours to perfect my cover. Keravnos had vouched for me but it always paid to have a convincing backstory.

Sheen and I decided to do things differently on this trip. We knew each other and our undercover roles so well that we felt confident enough to breach our usual demarcation lines, for good or ill. We reasoned that Kenya was a difficult place to work in. Not long before, suicide bombers driving a truck full of explosives had blown up the US embassy in Nairobi, killing more than two hundred people and injuring thousands. Given how little we knew about the place, and our distrust of the local cops, I suggested that Sheen act not just as my handler but as a UC, posing overtly as my right-hand man and watching my back in a more open way.

I thought it would seem suspicious to the criminals if I was over there alone, and much more plausible if I had a sidekick. It would mean, however, that Sheen was taking extra risk, as he would be in full-scale UC mode whilst also having to liaise covertly with London, our local DLO and the Kenyan police. Being the man he is, he readily agreed. With no other investigative resources, we both felt it was the only way we could pull off the job.

After an early breakfast, I waited in the lobby, wondering how the boss man and I would recognise each other. I need not have worried, for he arrived accompanied by Keravnos's wife. This lady, a member of the defunct Afghan royal family who I had known for many years, had led an adventurous life herself. Importantly for me, she was trusted by the Balochis.

The team boss was a small, dark-haired man, elegantly attired but with a badly pockmarked face. He introduced himself.

'Hello Mister Guy. My name is Wadhir.'

I doubted it was his real name, but I shook his hand, noting that he wore a permanent smile. I was much the bigger man but something in that smile put me on guard. I sensed he found nothing funny at all.

'You are alone?' he asked.

'No,' I said, 'my team is nearby and they can see us, so please don't do anything stupid. They won't be attending any of our meetings. They are just here to watch my back.'

'Of course, of course,' he said, as his eyes darted around the lobby. In reality all I had was Sheen, slouched nearby and dressed like a safari tourist, reading a guide to the Great Rift Valley.

'We need to go,' said Wadhir, moving towards the entrance. This was an unexpected concern. Would Sheen spot us leaving?

I needn't have worried. In his finest Allan Quatermain outfit, he was quickly up and outside ahead of me – tailing from the front is much harder but more effective than from behind – where he had a local surveillance team ready, accompanied by our DLO. Keravnos's wife stayed behind.

This is where absolute trust between me and Sheen was necessary. With no way for us to communicate, I had to hope that he was ready for any move. We had discussed this scenario, knowing they would take me away from the hotel at some stage, and the risk that he might lose me in the city's chaotic traffic. Just in case, I secretly dialled Sheen's mobile as we left the hotel and kept the line open. I hoped this would allow him to monitor our chatter in the car, and I could drop in odd hints about landmarks that we passed, to keep the surveillance team on the right track.

We crossed the road and climbed into a large four-by-four, me in the back and Wadhir in the front passenger seat. He said something to the driver, a huge Balochi who was easily six foot six, built like a bear and looked like he crushed people's skulls for fun. The Balochi grunted, threw the vehicle into gear and sped from the hotel compound.

After an hour's driving, and just as I was starting to feel stressed, we arrived at a small, white-painted house with a neatly kept garden on the outskirts of Nairobi, and drove into a parking compound in front. We were met by three heavily armed men, flanked by a pack of guard dogs. I later learned that the property was owned by a local warlord. Amazingly my open phone line to Sheen had held all the way, only to drop out as we entered the compound.

Wadhir visibly relaxed once he was on safe turf. I was shown to a downstairs living room and offered tea, while he disappeared upstairs with his huge driver. I was alone on their patch but, despite the usual nerves, did not feel threatened. As a precaution, Sheen made a safety call to my mobile to check I was okay.

After ten minutes they came back downstairs, struggling to carry three sports holdalls, which they dropped on the settee. Wadhir opened them and said that this was half of the load they had ready.

'A sample of our wares,' he said, smiling.

'How big is the sample?' I asked. In the UK, an ounce, or about thirty-two grams, would have been considered an out-sized sample. Few dealers would let that much out of their sight to be tested.

'Enough,' said Wadhir. 'Sixty kilos.'

I tried to look cool. 'Sixty kilos?' I repeated, sounding a little hoarse.

'It's half the load,' said Wadhir.

This meant they were holding 120 kilos of brown heroin. This was way more than we had prepared for, and I knew we were not ready to call it on for that amount. It was a mark of their faith in me that they let me see that much.

Wadhir invited me to take samples to test, as was normal practice. The heroin was packed in one-kilo blocks, and I said that I would take a little from several different blocks, to confirm they were of consistent quality. His men lifted the holdalls off the sofa and dropped them onto the stone floor. A thin cloud of dust rose from the bags. Our eyes began to water and everyone started sneezing. I tried to stay unruffled.

'I'll take a sample from that bag, one from that one, one from there and one from there,' I said.

Wadhir and his men moved from bag to bag, wheezing and coughing while taking the samples and putting them into one plastic bag. In larger loads, one or two samples, or 'twists', are usually taken from various parts of the shipment. Such samples are typically very small, but on this occasion I took just under an ounce and no-one raised a word of complaint.

Five minutes later, I was back outside in the courtyard with four or five coughing guards and their sneezing dogs. Had I wanted to rip them off, I could have done it there and then while they were all high on heroin dust.

With nothing more to be negotiated for now, I told Wadhir I would phone one of my men to collect me, and called up Sheen. I made my own way out of the villa and was picked up a little way down the road. I immediately told him that a minimum of sixty kilos was on site. I also gave him the envelope with the heroin sample, which he put in his top pocket. Within ten minutes, he was complaining of nausea and moved it to the glove compartment.

Once we were back in Nairobi, Sheen met with the local police and our DLO and handed over the sample to be checked for purity. They told him the warlord's house was now under constant surveillance. It had been a good, if stressful, day.

The following day we had down for a spot of R&R, as the opposition said they would be away planning the delivery and we had said we would be out of town meeting our transport team. Basil showed up in his cab late that morning.

'Today we go on safari,' he announced.

'Surely not in that?' said Sheen

'This best vehicle for the bush,' smiled Basil. The black cab had its for-hire sign illuminated as we climbed in. Basil turned it off and the meter started.

'We will go to Nairobi Park. Big park,' said Basil.

The park was alongside the city and was, indeed, big. For us it was an unmissable opportunity, the first undercover safari, albeit a trifle unorthodox. Secure in the back of our cab, we watched exotic fauna flee each and every way at the sight and sound of our taxi as it rattled around the dusty tracks. The largest animal I spotted was a startled giraffe, which had been quietly minding its own business when along came our black cab, belching diesel. The giraffe stopped chewing, assumed a look of abject fear and bolted into the bush. That was the last mammal we saw for a while.

All day in stifling heat we bounced around the park. Basil was genuinely shocked that we were not seeing many animals. The crash we had near the dried-out waterhole probably scared off the leopards, he mused. Scared off, I thought, it's a wonder they didn't attack us. The hippos at least were more visible, even if they were about half a mile away. Not one lion, elephant or rhino came near us.

On our return, Sheen again met the police and got the test results. The heroin was between eighty-five and ninety per cent pure. At the cutting rates in the UK, each kilo would have produced five or six on the street. It was a very valuable load.

Wadhir picked me up the next day and we drove to the White House to finalise our plans, arriving in the early afternoon. The heavy gates clanged shut behind us and we were once more met by the unsmiling guards and their raving dogs. Such tight security made me wonder if the two sixty-kilo loads had been linked up at this site, but I saw no more drugs.

Wadhir said they wanted to air-freight the powder into Europe hidden in spices. I knocked this back immediately. 'It's far too risky running cargo like foodstuffs,' I said. 'It's bound to be examined by customs. We'll need good cover and you will need to provide a company that checks out as legitimate.'

I managed to convince him that, for a load this size, a ship was safer and cheaper, and said I could have one ready and waiting in Kilindini port, Mombasa, within twenty-four hours. I had already researched the port, the biggest on the East African coast.

Wadhir liked this idea. 'I have men at the docks who can help with the loading. In fact,' he confided, 'that is the entry point for some of our product.' The problem would be moving the load to the port. It was nearly 500 kilometres away and would take eight to ten hours to get to by road, depending on which route was taken.

I would remain with Wadhir throughout. He would provide two four-by-four vehicles and one or two men from each of our teams would travel with the gear. A separate four-by-four with armed guards would accompany them. Payment in full would be made in Dubai when the gear was loaded onto our vessel. Beta already had a UC there working on another case, and he was tasked to pose as our money man on this job. He would not have to meet any of the criminals so did not need a fresh legend.

We went over the route and the plan again and again. I asked about military roadblocks, of which there were many, often extorting money by way of small fines. Wadhir had no qualms, saying that they had a method of dealing with any stops. He did want details of my vessel to check.

We had no intention of actually shipping the load but wanted to draw things out long enough to confirm that the two sixty-kilo loads had been brought together in one place. At that point the Nairobi drug unit would be able to seize all of the heroin and arrest any team members there. If Wadhir was still in the country, he would be taken out too.

Our discussions dragged on. There were no raised voices or

shouting, just a long, repetitive and occasionally uncomfortable back-and-forth, sometimes with the armed guards and dogs wandering around the room. We discussed the pick-up and carriage of the load and verified that the main transshipment would be on the coast. The immediate difficulty was safe delivery to a place some eights hours' drive away.

Eventually we agreed that collection of the load for transport to Mombasa would be in three days' time, from the new stash-house. The load would be guarded by a mixture of both teams' men but, in a slight change of plan, the three SUVs would move the load that night to an undisclosed destination. That way I could not rip them off and, as no money had yet changed hands, things were even.

This was to be just the first leg of the journey. It was then proposed that the main load be driven from Mombasa up the coast road. I was asked if my vessel could also move up the coast, away from the main port and its docks, to avoid attention. I said I would need time to plan it out. We agreed to use LAHORE CITY as a ten-letter code for the coordinates at sea, just as we had used HORNY DEVIL in the Long Job years before.

In a late twist, Wadhir said he also wanted four of his team to accompany the load on our ship. I stalled him on that.

'Do you want to stay the night?' asked Wadhir, with his constant, sinister smile. 'Eat, have a few drinks. And protect your investment.'

I declined, saying I had a meeting with my team that night and had a lot of arranging to do. In truth I didn't fancy an evening with him and his men. Instead I had Sheen collect me and we drove back to the hotel.

That snap decision probably saved my life.

The Kenyan police team were waiting on a parallel street, ready to raid the house once I was off the plot. Inexplicably they held back. Long minutes ticked by. When the order to go in finally came from their boss, Wadhir was no longer there and neither was any heroin. All they found, apparently, were five kilos of cannabis.

Something had gone terribly wrong. Our targets and the narcotics had vanished. If they had been tipped off, it could only have been someone high up in the local drugs unit. And it likely meant that they knew I was undercover too.

Sheen and I absorbed this news back at the hotel and urgently discussed our options. None of them sounded good.

Then my phone rang.

It was Wadhir. He was friendly, his manner unchanged. He made no reference to any raid or arrests. All of the heroin was together at the new stash, he said, and we should meet there that very night. It would mean a trip out into the bush, to a secret location. I said I would call him back.

'What do you think?' I asked Sheen, after putting down the phone. 'He sounded normal. Maybe he still doesn't suspect us. Shall we chance it?'

'Not in a million years,' said Sheen.

'What? Why not?'

I had eyes on the prize: a huge amount of smack and an entire international gang. We had taken calculated risks before. Why not now?

Perhaps I had been doing the job too long. Perhaps my judgement was deserting me. Sheen brought me back to earth.

'It's on top. We can't trust them. You know that.'

He was right.

Instead Sheen implemented an extraction plan. Before I knew it, we were at Nairobi Airport, waiting for that night's outbound flight to London. We basically hid in the British Airways club-class lounge toilets until take-off, figuring that if senior police here were corrupt, they could pull off anything.

I made one last call to Wadhir. He still gave no indication that anything was amiss. He was either a brilliant actor or

genuinely didn't suspect us. He said his crew were nearly ready
and he was eager to get underway. If we couldn't meet at the
stash that night, could we meet tomorrow? I agreed. He gave
nothing away, but all I kept seeing was his mirthless smile.

We finally boarded our plane but neither of us relaxed until
we had left Kenyan air space. We had been so close to one of
the largest, purest loads of heroin that we would ever see. But
at least we were alive.

We found out later that one of the top drug cops was in
the pay of a Kenyan called Barry, who was Wadhir's right-
hand man. When Sheen reported to the surveillance team that
'Barry and Wadhir' were at the house, this chief overheard.
We believe that he deliberately delayed the raid until Wadhir,
Barry and the gear had left the house.

I sometimes wonder what would have happened if they
had learned who I was while I was at that last meeting.
Remembering Wadhir's sinister smile, I have little doubt they
would have tortured and killed me.

*Getting 'blown out' was becoming more and more of a risk
for the undercover officers. High-profile operations like
Green Ice had alerted drug cartels to the threat of infiltration,
and the smartest of them had become more careful as a result.*

*In the late nineties, the DEA and the FBI launched a
wide-ranging probe into a Mexican cartel active in southern
California. The National Drug Intelligence Center produced
an 800-page strategic analysis, including organisational
charts and graphs, identifying the main targets, and in 1998
the White Tiger Project, named after a failed attempt by one
of the main narcos to smuggle an endangered white tiger pup
across the US border, was approved for action. The cartel and
its associates were found to be operating not only in the USA
but in Colombia, Peru, Costa Rica and probably Europe, and
became the target of almost sixty separate investigations.*

Beta Projects officer Keef was asked to help out as a British financial adviser who could launder their money. He and a handler, Sheen, flew to the States and rented a house in Coronado Cays, an upmarket seafront area of San Diego near the Mexican border, where the DEA put them together with two informants to work out a plausible cover story. Keef was to attend a private party where one of the informants would introduce him to the Mexicans. He and Sheen fretted, however, at the Americans' lackadaisical approach to security, with government cars coming and going to their supposedly secure house.

They were right to worry. The Mexican drug barons were uniquely merciless. A decade earlier they had tortured to death a DEA agent, Kiki Camerena, something even the Colombians would have baulked at. In this case, one of the informants went rogue and told the Mexicans they were being set up. At the same time, details of White Tiger leaked to a magazine, which reported how law enforcement was going to insert agents into a Mexican cartel. Keef and Sheen flew home before anything more could go wrong.

Harvey, one of Beta's longest serving officers, had an even closer escape. He was sent to Curaçao on behalf of the Dutch police to trap a gang believed to be supplying automatic weapons. It was a so-called cold infiltration and he had to earn their trust from scratch. He first bought a small amount of cocaine from them, then asked if they could get him a couple of handguns. His plan was to buy them, win the gang's confidence, then see what other weaponry they could supply.

One evening, he drove in a hire car to a remote area of the island to make the buy. He was sitting in the car with one of the gang, checking that the two weapons, a Colt pistol and a revolver, were safe, when men in masks appeared and put a gun to his head. After recovering from the initial surprise, Harvey responded in character, telling them they were fools to mess up a much bigger deal, and was backed up by his target, who tried *to talk the robbers down in local patois. Nevertheless they took Harvey's legend jewellery and $3,000 in buy money. He was able to get the car started and raced back to his handlers, then broke down with the shock and adrenaline rush.*

This period also marked the end of Guy Stanton.

Everything has a shelf life. By the turn of the century, I was fairly certain our methods were getting known. We had run so many successful jobs, and had had to declare so much in court, that the more intelligent criminals, and their lawyers, were catching on. It was getting harder to introduce a boat team to an organised crime group without them wanting to turn the boat, and the crew, inside out. The days of walking into a bar and falling into conversation with a bunch of crims were over. One of our boat crews started to spend a lot more time in the Caribbean, where they could still operate under the radar.

Stanton had also become too notorious. In fact he had been so successful that in the end the only way we could deal with closing him off was to kill him, as someone like him could never 'retire' to a quiet life. There was too much about him, too much around him; he had become trackable. Any curious law enforcement agency could see his spending patterns, see where he had travelled and who he had met. His legend had been *too* successful, and became a liability.

He died of natural causes. We thought about putting an obituary, a small 'Sorry to see you have gone' notice, in the *Evening Standard*, but decided it was unnecessary. Instead we just put the word about.

I didn't feel anything emotionally. I had kept a broad wall between me and him. Undercover work for me was acting and I always thought about Stanton in the third person: he was another bloke, as were all of my legends. They existed in the world for a short period, then they were gone.

17

BETRAYED

Having flown back from my deployment in Kenya to resume managing Beta Projects, I was called to give evidence in a difficult trial. One of our boat crews had picked up cannabis off the coast of Morocco to bring to the UK. The gang behind it had been arrested, but my team subsequently faced complaints that they had coopered the load in Moroccan territorial waters without seeking official permission. Despite the fact that boats literally queued up there to collect hash, we as law enforcement needed legal authorisation from the Moroccans. Our evidence could be tainted without following the rules.

As the Beta SIO, I had been part of a ship-to-shore call with the captain, Big Pete. He said they would have to go in closer than anticipated to make the pickup, and wanted my consent. This meant moving into Moroccan waters without time to get formal permission. I was faced with a dilemma: do I tell him to go ahead or order him to stand down? The latter course might well blow the cover of both our crew and their boat, as the villains would query why they had bottled out. I told him to collect the gear and move out with a minimum of fuss. This he did, quickly and cleanly.

In hindsight, my decision was flawed. Even though it was only the pickup, with no arrests made, and we secured the drugs, I should not have agreed to it. Nick Baker and I later received a tongue-lashing from our boss, Terry Byrne. Terry could be quite fearsome.

'How close to the shore did you think they were?' he demanded.

'I don't know, Terry,' I said. 'I was told there were other boats around though.'

'They could see people on the quay fishing!'

They had obviously gone all the way into the harbour. There was no blagging my way out of that one.

In court, counsel for the defendants tried to use our actions to stay the proceedings. I was given a hard time in the witness box, facing cross-examination about the distinction between international and national waters and fielding sarcastic questions about whether I knew the rules of the sea. These arguments failed to sway the court but I couldn't blame them for trying. One of the lads later gave me a framed admiralty chart, showing Cape Spartel in Morocco and inscribed with the words: 'If you look carefully you can just see the boundary between international waters and Guy's career!' It adorns the wall of my office at home.

The witness box was not the worst of it though. During the trial I began to feel unwell. I couldn't put my finger on it but felt tired and rundown. That was not unusual; my hours were long and the pressure intense. But this felt different.

I made a request to be recused from the trial but one defence barrister would not agree, as he thought he could influence the jury by quizzing me. He was within his rights and doing his job as he saw fit, and I don't hold any grudges. I gritted my teeth and stuck it out to finish my evidence.

Afterwards I was exhausted, and went to the doctor. My GP, a lovely chap who had been our family physician from the time we moved into the area, gave me a thorough check-up and could find nothing wrong, but decided to take a sample of blood.

When the tests came back, he came to our house, sat me and my wife down, and said he had bad news.

I had leukaemia.

After the initial shock, I began to research my illness. The diagnosis was chronic lymphocytic leukaemia, or CLL, a slow-acting disease – I was not going to die right away. In fact predicted life expectancy was another twenty or twenty-five years, possibly more. My GP arranged a swift appointment with an oncologist, who, after a consultation, confirmed that the disease was indolent, which I learned means slow.

I completed a course of chemotherapy medication and then met with my bosses. As I felt okay, I was to continue in Beta for the short term but was to prepare for re-entry into mainstream investigation.

By late 2000, I felt fit enough to take over as SIO of the Strategic Customs team. Our remit was to investigate breaches of EU and international (mainly American) sanctions, embargoes and export controls, as well as arms smuggling and the proliferation of unlicensed chemical, biological and nuclear agents and weapons. It was fascinating, sensitive work and the officers were a committed bunch. I resumed a normal working life. I had survived a long period undercover without going mad and had kept my feet on the floor.

HMCE did miss a trick, however, by moving me so abruptly from Beta Projects. One day I was in charge of it, the next I was gone. There was no attempt to debrief me or utilise my long experience of the covert side. My bosses could, I felt, have parachuted me into my new job but allowed me a couple of days a week to share my hard-won knowledge with those who followed. But they didn't.

My arrival on the new team coincided with a sharp increase in weapons smuggling from the Continent. Despite legislation banning handguns after the school massacre at Dunblane in Scotland, street gangs were still somehow acquiring handguns and even heavier weaponry like machine pistols, which they referred to as 'artillery'. We went after the suppliers.

We soon found that a number of gunrunners followed the same few steps. They would pay an out-of-work or down-and-out couple to drive to the France-Belgium border, often near the city of Courtrai. There they would go to a hotel, where their car would be collected from them, taken away overnight, and returned the next day. The couple would then drive back on a ferry or through the Channel Tunnel and leave the car at a designated point, locked and with the keys left on top of a front wheel. The recipients would pick up the car with the smuggled weapons hidden inside.

This system worked well for them until we got our first hit, an old BMW with a couple in it returning from 'a shopping trip in Calais'. Suspicious border control staff contacted us and we told them to look deeper. In the fuel tank they found a batch of handguns, greased and wrapped in plastic sheeting, with spare magazines and a large quantity of 9mm subsonic ammunition.

This led to further interceptions and enabled us to give the police great intel for their own operations against armed gangs. Yet despite our success, the seizures were not big enough to raise public alarm, and the belief prevailed that this was a series of isolated incidents rather than a major threat to our streets. I never felt our work received the priority it deserved, given its deadly implications.

Nevertheless, things jogged along nicely back in the 'real' world. I enjoyed running the team, my leukaemia was being held in check and I settled into a less stressful existence.

Then in June 2001, during a period of quite hard work, I began to feel tired again. I also developed lower-back pain. I mentioned this to my oncologist, who did not like the sound of it and admitted me to hospital for a colonoscopy.

For my next consultation, the nurse asked for my wife

to attend too. We were taken to a small office, where my soon-to-be surgeon informed me that I had a bad colorectal tumour. He described it as Dukes' C carcinoma – the second most severe on the Dukes' staging system for bowel cancer – in the lower rectal passage. It would, he said, need immediate, radical surgery.

Within a week I was in hospital being prepped for an operation. In all my years undercover I had never felt so scared.

At my pre-op, the doctor said he needed to know what I did for a living. I felt I had to tell him, so I admitted I had been an undercover officer. I then went through what my job had entailed.

'How long did you do that?' he asked.

'About ten years.'

He looked aghast. 'That's far too long,' he said. 'The stress on you must have been formidable.'

He sent me downstairs to prep for surgery. As I lay there, waiting to go, I watched a bloke scrub up nearby. He was handsome in a broken-nosed way, with a vivid scar across his face. I saw the words 'Blood Group O' tattooed on his arm. Special Forces.

'Where are you from?' I asked from my gurney. 'Hereford or Poole?'

He looked at me curiously. 'Hereford. How do you know that?'

'Blood group on your arm.'

He laughed. 'Showing off when we were kids, we all had it done when we joined the Mill. Have you worked with us then?'

'Yeah, I've worked with Hereford and Poole.'

He told me that, as well as the SAS, he had worked on battlefield trauma for six months. We joshed a bit and as a wind-up, I said, 'You know, I always found Poole to be far more professional.'

Still scrubbing his hands, he replied, 'What a stupid thing to say to your anaesthetist just as he's about to put you under.'

'Just joking!'

They operated to remove the tumour and a portion of my bowel. The SAS lad was waiting at the end of the bed when I came round; he had stayed behind to check on me.

'How are you feeling?'

'Like death.'

'You will do, for a while. But you'll do alright.'

It was good to feel a bit of the old camaraderie at such a grim time.

I was hospitalised for several weeks and left with an ileostomy, where a part of the small intestine is diverted to an exit in the stomach, the waste being collected in an ileostomy bag. I had this for over a year and the adventures I had with it could fill a book. I also had two long, punishing spells of chemotherapy.

I returned to work in the spring of 2002. I then used a holiday period to go into hospital and have my ileostomy reversed. Afterwards I continued to work, albeit at a much slower pace, as the combination of cancer and chemo had taken its toll.

Then in late 2003, during a routine scan at the Royal Marsden, came more bad news. I was diagnosed with liver cancer. One tumour had lodged beside the main blood supply. This time I thought my luck had run out, and that those years of burying stress had caught up with me.

In the biography *M: Maxwell Knight, MI5's Greatest Spymaster*, author Henry Hemming writes: 'The pressure of lying to people you know, not once or twice, but hundreds, possibly thousands of times requires some form of release. For some people it is enough to talk it out; others may turn to drink, become depressed or experience panic attacks – perhaps the only constant is that the pressure of this work requires an outlet and that usually the spymaster is a vital part of this process.' I had been able to talk out most of my tiredness, fears and anxieties before I hit breaking point. Here good handlers and Ray and Nick were of tremendous help. Only when I became ill did I realise that my body had its own way of dealing with the strain. Mentally, I coped well. Physically, my body eventually gave up.

A further six-month course of punishing chemotherapy, on a drug called oxaliplatin, reduced the tumour enough to operate on. I put on a brave face, joking with friends that I was collecting as many cancers as I could, but to say I was poorly was an understatement. The side effects were severe and I have numbness in my fingers and toes to this day. The strangest effect was cold burns: any cold weather, water or even drinks would cause instantaneous blistering.

The treatment I received from the surgeons, doctors, nurses and all support staff at the various hospitals was nothing short of miraculous. I had thought that my job was cutting edge, but the manner in which the NHS staff dealt with my disasters put my career in the shade. All I had done meant little when faced with a real killer.

I finally underwent further surgery and was released home to prepare for another six months of chemo.

Two days later, as I lay on my living room sofa, ill and weak, the phone rang. It was my then-boss. Sounding unusually hesitant, he eventually blurted out that the police were searching my office. They were, he said, investigating accusations that I had accepted bribes and perverted the course of justice while a customs officer.

I was devastated.

All of my working life I had been a loyal, honest servant. I had enjoyed my career and embraced the culture of an admirable organisation. Now it all seemed to have been wasted. I was also utterly bemused. I had never taken a bribe or even considered acting corruptly in my life.

The initial details were sketchy and I never heard much from my boss again. I did eventually learn that the police had begun an operation called Fallen Angel, a name someone evidently found funny. Police management didn't see the joke and renamed it Operation Virtue.

I was not the only one under suspicion. Nick Baker, to a large extent the architect of the hugely successful Black Box project, recipient of the OBE and by then deputy chief of the entire National Investigation Service, was also dragged into it, as were several other old colleagues.

The allegations, it transpired, stemmed from my long relationship with Keravnos who, despite getting on in years, had lost none of his devilment. One way Keravnos had of wooing criminals was to say he could help them. He would claim to have close relationships with customs and police officers and, if villains told him what they knew about drugs, implied they would not only get reward payments but might also get some protection from prosecution in other areas of crime. All the while, of course, he was informing on them.

On this particular occasion, he had been approached by a middleman on behalf of a defendant charged with a multi-million-pound VAT fraud. This guy asked Keravnos if he could help to get the trial postponed. Keravnos apparently replied that, for a fee of £50,000, he could get his most senior contact, Nick Baker, to delay proceedings. The guy paid the money and Keravnos simply kept it. There was a later insinuation that I had accepted a similar bribe of £25,000.

Neither Nick nor I knew anything about it, or the people concerned. However, when the defendant was subsequently jailed for four years without any of the promised intervention, he complained furiously, alleging serious corruption. The complaint went to the Metropolitan Police, who I believe found nothing concrete in it. For some reason it was then passed to Thames Valley Police, perhaps because they were already investigating some alleged Customs and Excise malpractice in an entirely unrelated matter. They decided to run with it and quickly concluded that Keravnos had been corruptly setting people up, or extracting money from them with false claims. As his chief contact, I fell squarely in the frame with him.

Two terrible years of investigation followed. Detectives went through my office at work, then arrived to search my home, all while I was seriously ill. They took my notebooks, diaries and personal papers, never to be seen again. I was interviewed several times while undergoing a long period of powerful chemo, for which no allowances were made. Yet I voluntarily answered all questions put to me, honestly and truthfully.

On one occasion they taped an interview with me in a room with a video camera. I knew they would have had people watching in another room, so I said, 'Who have you got watching? They are looking for my tell, aren't they? I bet they are UCs. Do I know them?' The cop in charge grudgingly conceded that I had actually trained them. But they never spotted my tell (and I'm not going to reveal it now).

Jo was brilliant. When they searched the house and garden, there was a moment where she accosted them and said, 'I'm taking my daughter to Brownies. I know you'll have a surveillance warrant for Guy, and probably for me, but you won't have one for my daughter, so don't you dare follow us.' They didn't.

For my part, I was too ill to cope and the slow grind of the investigation took a further toll. The chief inspector in charge was particularly aggressive. At one formal interview, during a period in which I was undergoing therapy for my liver cancer, I asked for an adjournment so that I could attend a chemo session. He refused, saying I would be charged if I left the interview room.

I was so tired and unwell that I told my solicitor that they could proceed but I would answer no further questions; the best they would get would be 'no comment'. After some discussion with my solicitor, the chief inspector reconsidered and came in with a diary to rearrange the interview. What a theatrical waste of time. All of the other officers, I must say, behaved impeccably.

The police seemed hellbent on securing convictions, yet the further they delved, the more it should have been clear that no crime had occurred. They asked a lot about money. Fortunately I could show them all of my accounts, receipts, ticket stubs and travel records. Not a penny I had ever been advanced was unaccounted for.

When they reached a dead end in one line of inquiry, they started another. I was even accused of plotting to smuggle the 120 kg of heroin in the Kenyan job. They suggested that Keravnos had paid for the load, I had gained control of it, and somehow we had got it back to the UK and sold it – all, presumably, under the noses of my handler, the Kenyan police, our operational team and my bosses. It was so preposterous that at first I thought they were bluffing to rattle me. But they were adamant and insisted I had hidden the money offshore.

My home and work phones were tapped. The police also sent officers to Armley Prison in Yorkshire to interview a cannabis smuggler who had given information to me in the past. They asked him to dish the dirt on me and dangled the carrot of early release if he said that I was a corrupt officer. To their chagrin, he told them I was totally straight, even though he had nothing to gain by it and much to lose. Fair play to him.

The police had also apparently intercepted a call between two men discussing paying a bribe to 'Guy', and had assumed this meant me. It later transpired that the speaker actually said 'a guy', which could have been anyone. From such small mistakes are careers ruined. In a final twist, it transpired that the main source for the accusation against me was a petty criminal with a conviction for perjury, of all things. Hardly a reliable witness, I thought ruefully.

During this time I was not allowed to return to work and I regret to say that the firm, apart from a small number of friends, turned its back on me. Some colleagues were heard to suggest there was 'no smoke without fire'. I even learned that our chief investigation officer had sanctioned monthly payments to Thames Valley Police to conduct the operation. He said he was determined to root out corruption; his mistake was that it did not exist.

Thankfully my closest friends knew I was innocent. Sheen rang in the middle of it all and asked if we wanted to go down to Cornwall with him and his wife. We used to holiday there as families.

'Are you sure, mate, with what has been going on?' I asked.

'Yeah, yeah. Don't be daft. By the way, what did you do with the twenty-five thousand pounds?'

Given the likelihood that my phone was being tapped, I enunciated clearly, 'For the benefit of the tape, Mr Sheen is joking.'

'No, I'm not. I want to know what you did with it.'

'Go away, you idiot!'

Sometimes his sense of humour could be misdirected.

Ultimately not one of us was charged. But when the police finally wrote to say that no further action would be taken against me, they added that they reserved the right to reopen the investigation if new evidence came to light.

This was the proverbial straw that broke the camel's back. The long inquiry, coupled with the bowel cancer, leukaemia, then liver cancer, pushed me to the lowest point in my life. I fell into depression. I am very good at putting things in a box, but that doesn't help when you go through prolonged ill health. I had some kind of nervous breakdown.

Normally if I am low or down, I retain my sense of humour. Even with all of my cancer, I always found some sort of level plane. But this time I could not get out of my funk. Over a two-week period it got worse and worse. Morose and unmotivated, I even stopped talking to my family.

It was Jo who pulled me back. She left for work one day, decided she was unhappy about my state of mind, and returned home. She came in to find me unshaven in my dressing gown, sitting at the table doing a jigsaw puzzle.

'Come on, up,' she said. 'Get shaved and get dressed.' Then she rang the doctor and without waiting to be allotted an appointment, said, 'I'm bringing him in now.'

We went to my GP's surgery and it was the best thing I have ever done. The doctor was a great source of sympathy and support, and helped pull me out of the slough of despond. She has remained a great help ever since.

Sadly HMCE tried to blame my depression on my cancer. Several oncologists and surgeons wrote to them on my behalf to point out that, in their professional opinion, it was the department's shoddy treatment that had pulled me down. They also pointed out that I had continued to work through my illness and never succumbed to the temptation to give up.

Nick Baker had retired early in 2004. I had assumed that I would reach retirement age with the firm, but I guess my many scrapes with the grim reaper caught up with me. In December 2005, I left HMCE after thirty years due to ill health. I had finally lost and accepted that my time was over.

The loyal friends I had made in the military held a 'top table' for me, a special dinner thrown for a departing comrade where they eat, drink and tell stories about you. Yet I had no leaving 'do' with my own firm. Some of the lads did give me the ensign from our old trawler as a keepsake. Otherwise, nothing.

To cap it all, the chemotherapy somehow aggravated a gene in my body for ankylosing spondylitis. This causes slow bone fusion, particularly in the base of the spine. It left me in constant pain. Most of the time it is manageable but occasionally it flares up and is excruciating, and I now walk with a stick.

Operation Virtue was a monumental waste of time, effort and money, and a horrible slur on the reputations of some honourable people. Some speculated that it was fuelled by petty jealousies, or was a personalised witch-hunt to settle old scores against Keravnos, or was politically motivated to destroy the ID. In truth, I don't know what was behind it. I just know it was nonsense.

It was no secret that the police and the ID hadn't always seen eye to eye at the higher levels. Yet my personal dealings with cops had always been good. Some customs officers forgot that the police have to deal with the worst of life, with cases of murder, sexual and physical abuse and other vile crimes. For their part, some cops thought our investigators were ama-teurs. But the best results came when the two joined forces and threw their resources at a common foe.

The drug world unfortunately became, at times, a battle-ground for the enforcement agencies, a contest over who seized the most, who got the headlines, who was the best. I still see the same headline-grabbing comments today after a drug bust: 'Largest seizure in history' and the like. *Plus ça change, plus c'est la même chose*, as the French say.

I do know that inter-agency arm-wrestling was expen-sive, time-consuming and fruitless. It hastened the demise of HMCE Investigation and the shift of much of its personnel to a newly-created organisation, the Serious Organised Crime Agency (SOCA), later itself rebadged as the National Crime Agency. HMCE, reconstituted as Her Majesty's Revenue and Customs (HMRC), retained an investigative arm but its undercover capability all but died with the birth of SOCA.

Beta Projects went out with a bang. The year 2005 saw one of its greatest successes, the dramatic conclusion of a long-running investigation into a huge cocaine conspiracy. It began on the Costa del Sol when Spanish anti-drug police observed contacts between British gangsters and one of the main crime clans of Galicia, an area of remote coves and inlets notorious for cigarette and drug smuggling. The Brits made regular trips to Portugal for meetings, adopting strict security measures to avoid being tracked. The Spanish police contacted their British and Portuguese counterparts and they began to gather intelligence together. They soon discovered that an unholy international alliance of traffickers was preparing to import up to thirty tonnes of coke over a six-month period.

The first run, of four tonnes, would be sent from Colombia to Venezuela by river, sailed out into the ocean and coopered to another vessel to cross the Atlantic. Somewhere off the coast of northern Spain or Portugal, the Galicians would run out in speedboats to collect it and bring it ashore. From there it would be dispersed to customers across Europe, with a tonne going to the UK. 'It was the only case I recall where we had the whole supply chain,' recalls a British customs officer who worked on the case. 'We knew the suppliers in Colombia, the transport people, the Galicians, and the people sending vans from Ireland and Liverpool to pick up this tonne.'

A Beta Projects boat team, including several of Guy Stanton's ex-colleagues, managed over many months to penetrate the conspiracy and were recruited by the traffickers to smuggle the cocaine in a fishing trawler, the Atlantic Warner. Matters were complicated when the narcos insisted on having their own men aboard the vessel, but the team agreed and eventually collected 157 bales of white powder off Isla Margarita, Venezuela, before heading north.

At a location off the Cape Verde islands, the ship was boarded from a Spanish navy patrol boat with Portuguese naval support and all four tonnes were seized. Simultaneously, agents arrested three Brits resident in the province of Malaga and eight Galicians, including Daniel Baulo, considered the most important trafficker in Spain. The Beta UCs retained

*their anonymity, reportedly even scuffling with the boarding
party to maintain their cover, so that their boat might be used
again in other operations.*

*In their enthusiasm to publicise the bust, however, someone
in Spain revealed the role of HMCE to the newspaper* El Pais,
*describing the UCs as resembling extras from an advert for
Fisherman's Friend lozenges, and blew their cover. Even
worse, they photographed and identified the undercover boat.
The Spanish media portrayed it as 'one of the most brilliant
sting operations in the history of British Customs', which
it was, but they had not wanted anyone to know. Still, the
targets went down for long jail terms.*

*By then about eighty per cent of Beta's work was drug-
related. So when SOCA took over the major drug investigation
role from HMRC in 2006, it was inevitable that the covert
unit would go with it. Most of the UCs and handlers moved
over, leaving only a skeleton team behind in HMRC. SOCA
UCs were still supposed to service the needs of HMRC's own
investigations, providing a lorry driver or a money mover if
required, but once SOCA found its feet they concentrated
more on what had traditionally been police operations, targeting distributors more than border smuggling. HMRC even
drifted towards getting its own UC capability back up, but
by then the millions of pounds of assets had gone to SOCA.*

*In any case, the crime world was evolving and new methods
of intelligence gathering, reflecting fast-moving communications technology and social media, came to the fore. 'SOCA
took the bulk of Beta but it wasn't the same by that stage,'
said one ex-officer. 'The old way, a big bloke walks into a
pub, was changing. The newer intake were different. I don't
think they had the character or the robustness of the old lot,
but they had different skills, more IT-based. More ethnic, less
white, middle-aged man.'*

The golden era of Beta Projects was over.

EPILOGUE

My various brushes with death taught me that life is too short for grudges. You have to get on or get out. I chose to get on.

An old colleague, Chris, got in touch and asked me to meet for coffee. He had left HMCE to take the money in the private sector, retraining at one of the big five accountancy firms to great success. Chris told a tale. About a year before, he had been asked to track down an allegedly bent ex-customs officer. If he could find and discredit this person, it would undermine a fraud prosecution against his client. 'I went to everyone I could,' said Chris, 'even convicts in prison who had been put there by this bloke. I told them we were sure this man was corrupt but we needed their help to prove it. And all of them said the same thing: "You've got the wrong man. He's definitely not bent. You're barking up the wrong tree."'

The officer in question was me.

Failing dismally to get what he needed, but with a sharp eye for business, Chris instead asked me to work with him in the private sector. I had no prospects, no job and a bleak outlook, but I still had a great deal of determination. My new career began.

We took jobs around the world, mainly corporate fraud investigations. Most of them came through word of mouth.

I never advertised. A quiet period might be followed by the arrival of four jobs in a week.

So it was that in April 2006 I stood in a small village at the head of the Panjshir Valley, 150 kilometres north-west of Kabul. The Hindu Kush mountains towered in the distance. The day was bright, clear and bitterly cold. I had come to inspect an emerald mine that both we and some clients were looking to invest in.

Once again, it came about through Keravnos. At his request we had met an Afghan gem dealer called Mohammad Ashraf. His company, based in Dubai, owned emerald mines in northern Afghanistan. Ashraf turned out to be a good man, as pro-British as he was anti-American. He offered two things: a chance to buy emeralds at source, the main business opportunity for me and Chris, and the chance to travel in-country with the protection of his men.

I flew into Afghanistan and was collected at Kabul Airport by Ashraf's men and my bodyguard, 'The Bear', a huge, silent Afghan. After a night in the capital, we set off for the Panjshir Valley. The drive took us through Bazarak, where we visited the tomb of Ahmad Shah Massoud, the 'Lion of Panjshir'. They revered this man and wanted me to see his resting place.

Massoud, a politician and a brilliant guerrilla commander, led his forces against the Soviet occupation between 1979 and 1989 and then against militias that attacked Kabul, the Taliban, al-Qaeda, and various other would-be despots. When assassinated by al-Qaeda suicide bombers just two days day before the 9/11 attacks, he had secured his place in history. He was undoubtedly charismatic – one witness described him as looking 'like Bob Marley with a bazooka' – and his people worshipped him. The Western intelligence agencies held a more nuanced view but everyone agreed he could fight like hell.

All of his men were fighters, used to hard living. Ashraf himself had fought for Massoud's militia against rival warlord Gulbuddin Heckmatyar. I told him that in my early days of travelling with Keravnos, I had met a man in Dubai who could have been a potentially powerful ally in the fight against heroin from Afghanistan. That man was Heckmatyar. A warlord known to his many enemies as the 'Butcher of Kabul', he was renowned for both brutality and cunning, which he possessed in equal measure. It was a casual meeting and nothing came of it. Had I known his importance, I could have gained much more, but I was a relatively new UC and knew little about him.

Massoud's tomb was half-completed in a desolate area but with views of the rugged terrain. A burnt Russian troop carrier lay near it. We later passed fields of burned-out Russian tanks and it struck me that a good scrap merchant could make a fortune here. The houses had shell cases hammered down to support the gutters and tank tracks as stair risers. The Afghans are ingenious at recycling.

Eventually we came to a small village alongside the Panjshir River. Ashraf told me the valley was nearly a hundred kilometres long and led into the Hindu Kush by two main passes: the Khawak, which went to the Northern Plains, and the Anjoman, which crossed into Badakhshan. Both exceed twelve thousand feet above sea level. The Anjoman had been used by Alexander the Great, he said with some pride. I asked how big the Soviet army was that invaded. He fell quiet, then said simply, 'Big.' The Panjshir operations saw nine major campaigns from 1980 to 1985, with some of the bitterest battles of the whole Soviet invasion.

He took me to a small stone hut by the river. Inside was a table and chair. The river was in flood and roared by. Here, he said, was where a despairing Soviet commander cut his own throat. I noticed he was looking at me carefully.

'You should know, English,' he said. 'You have tried to invade us three times and each time you have lost.'

From my love of military history, I knew that we had indeed invaded in the 1830s, the 1870s and around 1919, each time with limited success.

'You will never understand us,' he went on. 'When we are left alone, we fight one another, and then when someone invades, we fight them. Finally, when we beat them, we go back to fighting one another. We like to fight.' He showed a broad grin.

After a night in the village, we moved up the valley by donkey and foot towards the Hindu Kush and the emerald mines. There I spent a few days watching as they used RPGs to blast out the mountainside. At one point Ashraf gave me a satellite phone and I managed to ring home, only to be interrupted by a thunderous explosion as an RPG slammed into the hillside nearby. They also showed me disused missile storage sites, custom-built deep excavations always on flat land and covered in the scree that was everywhere.

It was cold and desolate but had a haunting natural beauty. Chris and I traded emeralds from Ashraf for over a year but it became too dangerous to go up country and slowly we lost contact. I still have a few gems from my time there.

We also ventured into Sierra Leone, where the government's telecommunications division wanted to open dialogue with the big providers to modernise the country's infrastructure. Another friend of mine had a company that specialised in high-level security for government personnel in dangerous environments, and asked if there might be an opportunity in Sierra Leone for him too. If you don't ask, you don't get.

On our arrival at Lungi International Airport, it became apparent that chaos was the norm. The airport was packed and hot and tempers were frayed. In my UC days I always found a local to act as my ears and eyes when anywhere new. I quickly sorted out an official, and with a $100 bill in his pocket he set to work on our behalf.

The airport lies across an estuary from Freetown. By car it takes hours on bad roads; by water the sea coach will do the seventeen-mile journey in half an hour for a few dollars. Chris and I trumped this. Our new-found interpreter, guard and general factotum located a helicopter; not a nice modern one but an ex-Soviet Army Mil Mi-8, crewed by two Russians who looked like villains from central casting. It had no glass in the windows and you sat on the floor or on a large palletised cargo. It was exhilarating.

We travelled to Man of War Bay and the delights of the Bintumani Hotel, which barely had electricity. My worst moment was when I found a fridge full of much-needed Carlsberg lager, only to discover it could not be plugged in and the lager was warm. The hotel did, however, offer a magnificent coastal view.

We met various government intermediaries, some wanting 'introduction fees', some wanting to be made part of our company, all wanting something. It was a pity that nobody could make a decision. Sierra Leone is a beautiful country but had been ravaged by five years of civil war and was struggling to get to its feet. Telecoms is vital to any modern state but, try as we might, we could not get the right people involved. This had less to do with corruption than with the inertia and disarray of various departments of state. Another complication was the fallout from the blood diamonds trade that had fuelled the civil war. I had no interest in that side of things but met a lot of adventurers who did.

Things have greatly improved since. Sierra Leone is now a tourist destination, having survived the ravages of war and Ebola. A bit like me, it keeps on going. My lasting memory is of drinking cold beer in Alex's Bar with the military and NGO personnel from the Mammy Yoko United Nations Mission. The bar opened just after the Second World War and has a picture of its founder, a grizzled seaman, on the wall.

A few weeks later, the helicopter that we had flown in crashed on landing at Lungi Airport, killing twenty-two Togolese football fans who had chartered it. The only survivor was the Russian co-pilot.

Chris specialised in helping people with tax and financial problems while I handled work for private clients and businesses suffering internal frauds, counterfeiting and internal theft. I had a few strange encounters, none more so than my investigation of an arrest warrant believed to have been illegally issued for a Rwandan national, a successful businessman. The international warrant did not look right and I was asked to check it out. As I delved, it began to look as if his business competitors had arranged for the warrant's issue on trumped-up charges.

Chris and I flew to South Africa, where we were introduced to Kevin Trytsman, a self-described private investigator who said he could find out who was behind it. A fascinating character, he had a lot of contacts. He claimed to have testified before the country's Truth and Reconciliation Commission and received amnesty after admitting having access to a secret arms cache. He also claimed to have had links with the Civil Cooperation Bureau, purported to be an apartheid-era death squad working under the defunct security agency BOSS.

Trytsman was the kind of shady oddball that inhabited this twilight world. The more I saw of him, the stranger he became. Needless to say he did very little to help us, and we went on to use more legitimate means to find out about the warrant. Our client went on to become a famous philanthropist, helping the needy and setting up a foundation for impoverished children.

I never had contact with Trytsman again, but one morning Chris rang and told me to look at a newspaper article. There was a photo of Trytsman's body on a stretcher, being carried from the offices of his attorney. It appears that the two had argued earlier at a café, as Trytsman was unhappy at the way he was being represented. What happened next is unclear but it is believed Trytsman demanded his papers and files back. Things got heated and Trytsman was shot twice in the chest, dying instantly. The solicitor later fled South Africa, reportedly with millions in trust fund money.

I learned two things from that: stay away from shady characters and never mess with your solicitor.

The work took me around the world: Romania, France, Norway, Bulgaria, the UAE, Cyprus, Hong Kong and China. One suspected fraud required surveillance in Poland, for which I employed some of the lads from my old firm; the trail ended in the British Virgin Islands, where we ran up against their banking and company secrecy laws and had to pull away. I worked for three years for the government of Mauritius, investigating the smuggling of gold and rosewood, a protected timber. Mauritius was being used as a transit point to move the timber illegally into China. Rosewood was valued at about £1 million a container-load and they were doing five to ten containers a month. Our investigation, while making no arrests, stopped the smuggling. We suspected that highly placed figures in Madagascar were behind it.

In Egypt, my evidence identified several targets in a fraud case. Having driven from Cairo to Alexandria to collect evidence, I noticed on my return journey that there were more and more army checkpoints. Cairo is always chaotic, like a super-Bombay, but when I arrived back in the early hours it was ghostly quiet. Even the airport was dead and I flew out on the scheduled BA flight with just a few other passengers. It turned out to be the start of the unrest that led to a successful coup against President Morsi. It was a frisson of the old life, and I can't deny I enjoyed the buzz of it.

I stay in touch with old colleagues and we meet up semi-regularly to talk a little treason. Keravnos is now in his nineties, has prostate cancer and can barely walk, but is as cantankerous and indestructible as ever. For a secondary school lad who was going to do nothing in the world I have had quite an adventure. I still have leukaemia and maintain a regime of six-monthly check-ups but as they say in the Middle East, 'Inshallah' – it is God's will. New adventures still beckon and I hope I have a few more left in me.

ACKNOWLEDGEMENTS

The Betrayer concentrates mainly on my tenure as an undercover officer, but across my whole working life I met many great characters. Some are now ghosts but my memories of them remain. I look back with fondness and pride at my time in HMCE in so many roles, in particular in the Investigation Division and its later incarnations.

These are the names of those I recall, from my time as an administrative officer (AO), executive officer (EO), higher executive officer (HEO) and senior investigation officer (SIO). Where I cannot remember a name fully, I have used initials or first names. Those I have forgotten, please forgive me – and also excuse my spellings of surnames! For the undercover group, I have used first names only and surname initials. You know who you are.

AO, Kings Beam House, 1975: Mr Thorn, Mr Dass, Geoff Brickell, Graham Puckey, Jack Kiriakou, Julian 'Morning in America'.

AO, London ID CRU, 1976–77: Tom Petitpierre, Richard Staniseveski, the lad from the Sealed Knot, Doug Allen, Graham Gere, Steve Fuller, Neil Flory, Keith Field, Kevin Field, Rod Stone, Bob Shellswell, Richard Merritt, Tim Wooley, Anne B, Clorinda G, Christine, Rose Wooley and the girls from the typing pool.

AO, London ID Customs Intelligence and Customs Targets (Delta Yankees), 1977–1979: Alan 'Chiefy' Baker, Ron Hand, Don Green, Tony Buckingham, Carl Poulter, Dave Holliday, Kenny Cartmel, Frank Wong, Tony Corless, Neil Bailey, Brian Matin, Dave Parr, Les Beaumont, Len Caley, Don Dewar, Wayland Braithwaite, Brian Wilson, Neil Hubbard, Roger Hiatt, Charlie Baroudi, Paul Morgan.

AO, Birmingham Airport Preventive and Long Room, 1979–82: Alan Blackett, Ken Marlow, Terry Powell, Linda Edgecumbe and Denise, Alan Jones, Frank Thorn, Digger Gardener, Harry Suddaby, Garth Powell, Joe Martin, Vernon, Shama and Dave Milton, Diane Haddock, Merv Adams, Bob the Scotsman, Jill Casson, Pauline, Cathy, Helen, Joe Kelly, Mo Bashir, Dave Smith, Dick Evans, Neil Dorman, Brian Matthews, Mike Lucas, John Grice, Fred Heap, Debbie Rimington, Micky Ballard, Geoff Pullen, Mickey Bannister, Jack Smith, Tony Hole and Tony Tikka.

EO, Birmingham VAT South, 1982–83: Mike Purser, Arthur Miller, Iestyn Davies, Richard Young.

EO, Birmingham CIU, 1983–88: George Coulson, Terry Howe, Keith Wilson, Tony Walker, Stuart Shelley, Bob Lynne, Debbie Rimington, Jo Clarke, John Couch, Bob Williams, Ross White, Ian Cruxton, Leighton 'Buzz' Jones, John Romagnoli, Tommy Carrol, Pete Kozian, Mike Pugh, Kim Wedgebury, Vince Curly, Norman Brand, Mike Williams (and Annie), Dave Stone, Gareth Jones, Dick Kitchen, Mark Hampton.

HEO, London ID VAT, 1988–91: Pat Cadogan, Dave Parker, Reg Lowe, Brian Turner, Dave Thomas, Ken Head, Martin Crago, Kelvin Clamp, Nick Cole, Paul Cook, Sarah Osborne, Theresa Denahey, Barbara Rook, Pat Dunn, Roy Afleck, Bill Boyd, Christine Richie, JonJo O'Neil, Helen Chard, Ashley Worcester, Ged McCann, Mike Bigus, John Dickinson.

HEO/SIO, London ID Beta Projects, 1991–2001: Ray P, Nick B, Tommy C, Sheen, Big Fella, Elvis, Chameleon,

Mungo, Charlton, Pigpen, Big Pete, Steff, Frankie, Little Tony, Harvey, Badger, Anne, Keef, Little Arab, Big Arab, Chelsea, Eccles, Quiff, Sonia, Little Scouse.

SIO, London ID Customs A, 2001–05: Dave West, Peter York, Kevan Moyle, Jason Hulme, Phil Davies, Mike Surry, Bernie Crossey, Simon Terrell, Andy Sturgeon.

I particularly wish to thank those who set my undercover career in motion and put me on the path to a great adventure. Again, apologies for anyone missed out. At the Met, they include Dick H, Graham C, Larry C, Chris W, John 'Monkey' M, Rocky R, Frankie F, Pete B and Jason S. And from Greater Manchester Police, Degsy, Danny, Macca, Scouse, Julio and Pete G.

I owe a special debt to the two UCs who had the greatest influence on how I operated and who were both giants in the field: from the Met, Peter H, and from Manchester, Henri Exton, better known as 'The Raven'.

Throughout my life I have had few very close friends, but Len Caley, Sheen, Big Fella, Badger, Elvis, Bill Browning, Matt Evans, Paul Cook, Aadel Kardooni, Dai Griffiths, Roger Bolton, Steve Letchford and Vince Quigley all helped me through very difficult times, when my health failed and the job that I loved was destroyed by false allegations.

Since I left the department in 2005, two groups have been of great support to me and have provided the occasional chance to 'swing the lamp' and 'talk treason'. They are the OTC & Drinks group (battlefield tours in particular) and the 'Gobdads'. They know who they are. My physical and mental health suffered a great deal at the end of my career and these two groups have helped me more than they will ever know.

Leaving the department was a traumatic experience but one person helped me to find new work and purpose in life: my thanks to Chris C and his family. My deepest thanks also go to all the NHS and Royal Marsden staff who helped me through my battle with various cancers, in particular Professor D. Cunningham, Royal Marsden, Sutton; Doctor L Jones, Epsom Hospital; Mr P. Toomey, surgeon, Epsom Hospital; Professor N. Karanjia, surgeon, Guildford Hospital.

Above all, I owe everything to my family: my wife of thirty years, Jo, our daughter, Jess, and latterly her fiancé Ben. They put up with over ten years of intense, interrupted life while I was deployed abroad for long periods. Jo coped quietly and calmly and got on with life. Jess was born while I was deep into my undercover career (I even took calls at the hospital during her birth, as Sheen will testify) but Jo held everything together, never complaining and giving me total support. They have been my greatest comfort in some very dark times. I owe them everything.